Scarecrow Studies in Young Adult Literature
Series Editor: Patty Campbell

Scarecrow Studies in Young Adult Literature is intended to continue the body of critical writing established in Twayne's Young Adult Authors Series and to expand it beyond single-author studies to explorations of genres, multicultural writing, and controversial issues in YA reading. Many of the contributing authors of the series are among the leading scholars and critics of adolescent literature, and some are YA novelists themselves.

The series is shaped by its editor, Patty Campbell, who is a renowned authority in the field, with a thirty-year background as critic, lecturer, librarian, and teacher of Young Adult literature. Patty Campbell was the 2001 winner of the ALAN Award, given by the Assembly on Adolescent Literature of the National Council of Teachers of English for distinguished contribution to Young Adult literature. In 1989 she was the winner of the American Library Association's Grolier Award for distinguished service to young adults and reading.

1. *What's So Scary about R. L. Stine?* by Patrick Jones, 1998.
2. *Ann Rinaldi: Historian and Storyteller,* by Jeanne M. McGlinn, 2000.
3. *Norma Fox Mazer: A Writer's World,* by Arthea J. S. Reed, 2000.
4. *Exploding the Myths: The Truth about Teens and Reading,* by Marc Aronson, 2001.
5. *The Agony and the Eggplant: Daniel Pinkwater's Heroic Struggles in the Name of YA Literature,* by Walter Hogan, 2001.
6. *Caroline Cooney: Faith and Fiction,* by Pamela Sissi Carroll, 2001.
7. *Declarations of Independence: Empowered Girls in Young Adult Literature, 1990–2001,* by Joanne Brown and Nancy St. Clair, 2002.
8. *Lost Masterworks of Young Adult Literature,* by Connie S. Zitlow, 2002.
9. *Beyond the Pale: New Essays for a New Era,* by Marc Aronson, 2003.
10. *Orson Scott Card: Writer of the Terrible Choice,* by Edith S. Tyson, 2003.

11. *Jacqueline Woodson: "The Real Thing,"* by Lois Thomas Stover, 2003.
12. *Virginia Euwer Wolff: Capturing the Music of Young Voices*, by Suzanne Elizabeth Reid, 2003.
13. *More Than a Game: Sports Literature for Young Adults*, Chris Crowe, 2004.

More Than a Game

Sports Literature for Young Adults

Chris Crowe

Scarecrow Studies in Young Adult Literature, No. 13

NORMAL PUBLIC LIBRARY
NORMAL, ILLINOIS 61761

The Scarecrow Press, Inc.
Lanham, Maryland, and Oxford
2004

SCARECROW PRESS, INC.

Published in the United States of America
by Scarecrow Press, Inc.
A wholly owned subsidiary of
The Rowman & Littlefield Publishing Group, Inc.
4501 Forbes Boulevard, Suite 200, Lanham, Maryland 20706
www.scarecrowpress.com

PO Box 317
Oxford
OX2 9RU, UK

Copyright © 2004 by Chris Crowe

All rights reserved. No part of this publication may be reproduced, stored in a retrieval system, or transmitted in any form or by any means, electronic, mechanical, photocopying, recording, or otherwise, without the prior permission of the publisher.

British Cataloging in Publication Information Available

Library of Congress Cataloging-in-Publication Data

Crowe, Chris
  More than a game : sports literature for young adults / Chris Crowe.
    p. cm.—(Scarecrow studies in young adult literature ; no. 13)
  Includes bibliographical references and index.
  ISBN 0-8108-4900-3 (alk. paper)
  1. Young adult literature, American—History and criticism. 2. Sports in literature. 3. Sports stories, American—History and criticism. I. Title. II. Series.
PS169.S62 C76 2004
810.9'355—dc21
                                                            2003013561

Printed in the United States of America

∞™ The paper used in this publication meets the minimum requirements of American National Standard for Information Sciences—Permanence of Paper for Printed Library Materials, ANSI/NISO Z39.48-1992.
Manufactured in the United States of America.

For Elizabeth, who has seen me through many games and many books. I couldn't ask for a better eternal teammate.

"What's your novel about?" I said and glanced at the yellow sheets on the desk. A small pile of typed sheets were in the case for his typewriter. A big photograph of Lawrence, smashing one away, was under the jelly glass full of sharpened pencils. "It wouldn't be about a tennis player?" I said.

He wiped his face with the towel again. "Old man, a book can have Chicago in it, and not be about Chicago. It can have a tennis player in it without being about a tennis player."

I didn't get it. I probably looked it, for he went on,

"Take this book here, old man—" and held up one of the books he had swiped from some library. Along with the numbers I could see Hemingway's name on the spine. "There's a prizefighter in it, old man, but it's not about a prizefighter."

—Wright Morris, *The Huge Season* (179)

Contents

Foreword *Chris Crutcher*	xi
Acknowledgments	xiii
Introduction	xv
1 Is There a Place for Sports Literature?	1
2 From the Schoolroom to the Playing Field: A History of Young Adult Sports Literature	11
3 Young Adult Sports Fiction: More Than Just Game Stories	25
4 Young Adult Sports Nonfiction and Poetry	47
5 Sports Literature for Young Women	59
6 Coaches in Young Adult Sports Fiction	79
Resources on Sports and Sports Literature: An Introduction to the Appendixes	95
Appendix A For Further Reading	97
Appendix B Thousands of Young Adult Sports Books Classified by Gender, Sport, and Other Categories	99

Appendix C	Chris Crowe's Top 100 Young Adult Sports Books of All Time	155
Appendix D	Sports Literature and Related Topics on the Internet	159
Index		165
About the Author		171

Foreword

I was flattered when Dr. Crowe asked me to write a foreword for this book. I have respected Chris both professionally and personally since my early days as a writer, and have known his work to be highly informative and infinitely readable. (I also suspected there was a pretty good chance my work would be mentioned somewhere in the text.) Those things turned out to be true, but what I didn't predict was that I would find my work and the work of my peers put into such an enlightening historical context.

I am accurately quoted in these pages as being resistant to having my books classified as "just sports literature" because I intended for athletics to be a backdrop to the coming-of-age issues I address. But that stance clearly diminishes the importance of youth sports literature in the American experience.

In the 1950s and 1960s I spent my schoolboy years in a small lumber town, a town where the (eight man) football and basketball schedules determined the social calendar in the autumn and winter of every year. Parents' status in town was known to rise and fall in correlation with the athletic skill of their high school offspring. As a grade schooler my heroes were Dick Earl and Jerry Ready and Jack Hull and Georgie Hirai—guys who blocked and tackled and carried the ball on Friday afternoons and hung out at my father's service station telling tales of athletic glory while they lubed and washed their cars on the weekends. Like boys all over America, I couldn't wait for my time in the spotlight, and I spent hours throwing a football high into the air, then running under it to catch the game-winning touchdown, awash in the cheering of the crowd and the pounding of my team's fists on my shoulder pads. I pitched full nine-inning games against the side of our wooden garage (lacking the "heat" to even damage the siding) as Chris Crutcher or Whitey Ford or (when I was throwing *really* out of control) Ryan Duran, scorching the Dodger line-up one after another. I discovered and devoured the Chip Hilton series, sports' answer to The Hardy Boys and Nancy Drew, in which we followed young superhero Chip Hilton through four years of high school and four years of college as a three-sport letterman.

I read about their rich history in Dr. Crowe's book, then looked back at the integral part sports and sports stories played in the development of my young life, and I'm a little ashamed that I ever backed away from being called a writer of sports fiction. I am now proud to call myself an author of *sportlerroman*, a term I have come to know from reading the first chapters of *More than a Game*.

Chris Crowe has written a fully engaging book that articulates what sports and sports fiction means to this culture and to American literature in general. I'm proud to be a small part of that.

Chris Crutcher

Acknowledgments

This book could not have been completed without the thorough and thoughtful work of my magnificent research assistant, Kristana Miskin, whose wages were provided by a research grant from the College of Humanities at Brigham Young University. I am indebted to Kristana and to the College for their contributions to this project. The Harold B. Lee Library at Brigham Young University provided me with a fine collection of sports literature and critical sources and with a quiet place to read and write. Chris Crutcher very generously agreed to write a foreword, and I'm thankful for his kind words that preface this book. Finally, I am grateful to my editor, Patricia J. Campbell, and to my wife, Elizabeth, for their encouragement, suggestions, and patience as I worked on this book.

Introduction

What is sport?

Sometimes that's an easy call to make: badminton, baseball, and basketball would be sports in anyone's book. But what about ballet, bowling, or ballroom dancing—are they sports too? Do racquetball, rodeo, and rowing qualify? Millions of people enjoy Scrabble, skateboarding, and surfing. Are those activities sports?

Sports can be many things to many people, but in order to set a manageable limit for this book, I have used a contemporary, interscholastic definition of "sport." Generally, I considered books to be sports literature if they included athletic activities that involved face-to-face competition (i.e., an athletic game or contest) between athletes and if the success of that competition depended primarily on the competitors' athletic and physical skills. Because my focus is on young adult books, I favored books that featured sports that are typically sponsored by secondary schools or by clubs and municipal recreation programs. I realize that many athletic activities may be considered sport, and some that I've excluded from my review may generally fit the above definition, but I tended toward the mainstream traditional sports that have, as their literature has, grown out of school-sponsored activities.

For this book, I generally excluded stories about hunting, fishing, mountain climbing, auto racing, horseback riding, ballroom dance, cheerleading, skateboarding, "extreme sports," chess or other board or video games, mountain biking, motocross, or similar activities. Other sports may not be mentioned in this book, not because my definition excluded them but because I was unable to find them represented in young adult literature.

I have confined my review of sports literature to fiction and nonfiction prose works in book form. In order to distinguish young adult sports literature from adult or children's sports literature, I considered young adults to be readers in secondary school, in general aged twelve to eighteen. Often, the publishers recommended an intended audience; in the case of some novels, I relied on the age of the protagonist to help me determine the intended audience. In nonfiction, the distinctions are less clear, especially between young adult and middle grade. For nonfiction, I excluded books that, based on their content, writing style, or format, seemed exclusively suited for adults or for children younger than twelve.

Thousands of sports books for teenagers have been published in the last fifty years, and though I wish I could have reviewed all of them, it would have been an impossible task. I'm sure that for every book I've mentioned or included on a list, two or three others exist that I never heard about or couldn't find. Though I've tried to be comprehensive and fair in my review of young adult sports literature, I soon realized that I also had to be practical. It's inevitable that I've overlooked some important or favorite young adult sports books. I apologize for missing those books, and I encourage you, dear reader, to work on creating your own lists of worthwhile young adult sports literature that you can share with students and readers.

Chapter 1

Is There a Place for Sports Literature?

In the late twentieth century, after nearly one hundred years of dwelling in the cellar of subliterature, sports books finally began to move into the literary mainstream. The foundation for respectability and the serious study of sports literature was laid in the 1970s and 1980s with the work of a few pioneering literary scholars, including Christian Messenger's *Sport in American Literature, 1830–1930* (1974); Wiley Lee Umphlett's *The Sporting Myth and the American Experience* (1975); Robert J. Higgs's *Laurel and Thorn: The Athlete in American Literature* (1981); Messenger's *Sport and the Spirit of Play in American Fiction: Hawthorne to Faulkner* (1981); Michael Oriard's *Dreaming of Heroes: American Sports Fiction, 1868–1980* (1982); Michael Vanlandingham's *Winning is Everything: Myths and Realities in Selected Contemporary Novels of Sport* (1983); and David Vanderwerken and Spencer K. Wertz's *Sport Inside Out: Readings in Literature and Philosophy* (1985).

In 1983, aided by the momentum generated by the above-mentioned works, Lyle I. Olsen, a professor of physical education at San Diego State University, spearheaded the creation of the Sports Literature Association and its journal, *Arete* (later renamed *Aethlon),* which helped legitimize sports literature as a genre worthy of serious literary study. Since then, sports literature and the study of it have increased in volume and quality: many universities—and even some high schools—now offer courses in sports literature, and sports books themselves continue to increase in number, quality, and popularity.

Though it has not made gains in respectability comparable to adult sports literature, young adult literature has, in the last three decades, begun to move away from its subliterary dime novel roots. The field still has its detractors, but many teachers and literary scholars now recognize the value of young adult literature. Young adult *sports* literature, doubly damned by its juvenile and sports roots, has only recently begun to receive its due from critics, librarians, and teachers. Of course a number of lightweight young adult sports books continue to be published, but a good number of serious works—fiction and nonfiction—have appeared in recent years, and they have helped raise the quality, and consequently the reputation, of young adult sports literature.

It is therefore ironic that despite these recent gains in respectability, young adult sports literature remains virtually ignored by the Sports Literature Association; its journal does not review young adult titles, and its list of the fifty most influential works of sports literature in the twentieth century does not include a single young adult book (Dewey 161–162). The academics in the Sports Literature Association are not alone in their ignorance of young adult sports books; sports journalists suffer from the same literary shortsightedness. *Sports Illustrated*'s December 2002 article, "The Top 100 Sports Books of All Time," did not name any young adult titles among its top one hundred. The magazine did, however, include three nonfiction books that, while not marketed to young adults, are about high school sports: #4, H. G. Bissinger's *Friday Night Lights*; #65, Madeleine Blais's *In These Girls, Hope Is a Muscle*; and #70, Darcy Frey's *The Last Shot: City Streets, Basketball Dreams*. In a condescending and uninformed acknowledgment of young adult sports literature, the article included a small sidebar titled "Kid Stuff" that listed three sports series that were published in the 1940s and 1950s and two novels: John R. Tunis's *The Kid from Tomkinsville* (1940) and Roch Carrier's *The Hockey Sweater* (1979).

The field of young adult literature is accustomed to slights like the ones young adult sports books received from the Sports Literature Association and *Sports Illustrated*. Books for teenagers have long been overlooked or even condemned by "mainstream," "adult," or "literary" critics, so it's no surprise that sports literature for young adults suffers the same neglect, condescension, and criticism that its broader field endures. This mistreatment, however, has done little to stem the growth and popularity of adolescent sports stories. Thanks to the efforts of knowledgeable teachers, librarians, writers, and publishers, sports literature for teenagers thrives despite its lack of respect from some literary critics and popular journalists.

The growth of modern young adult sports literature reflects the pervasiveness of sports in America today. Because of Title IX and the nearly universal school requirement for physical education, more American youth than ever have at least some personal experience with competitive athletics. In addition to their personal involvement in athletic activities, teenagers now live in a culture inundated by sports. News about games and athletes dominate our print and electronic media, and professional athletes are treated like Hollywood stars. Sports products—athletic shoes, apparel, and equipment; sports drinks and food supplements; trading cards and team memorabilia—are a multibillion-dollar industry. Even our language has been affected: sports expressions and slang have become standard in the daily speech of teenagers and adults. At no other time in U.S. history have sports so thoroughly infiltrated American culture. Young adult sports literature, fiction and nonfiction, is a natural outgrowth of the widespread influence of sports in society and of the subsequent demand for books about sports and athletes.

No sports book has ever won the coveted Newbery Medal, but Bruce Brooks's basketball novel, *The Moves Make the Man* (1984), received Newbery Honor status in 1985, and various honor lists show that sports literature for teenagers has a long history. In his review of the best young adult novels written in the past 125 years, Ken Donelson includes ten sports novels in his honor list of nearly 120 novels published from 1868 to 1995. The first sports story on Donelson's list is Ralph Henry Barbour's *The Crimson Sweater* (1908); also included are John R. Tunis's *All-American* (1942), *Yea! Wildcats!* (1944), and *Go, Team, Go!* (1954); Robert Lipsyte's *The Contender* (1967), Richard Blessing's *A Passing Season* (1982), Chris Crutcher's *Running Loose* (1983), Brooks's *The Moves Make the Man* (1984), Tessa Duder's *In Lane Three, Alex Archer* (1989), and James Bennett's *The Squared Circle* (1995).

Sports books also figure prominently in the American Library Association's "Top One Hundred Countdown: Best of the Best Books for Young Adults, " an honor list of young adult books from 1967 to 1994. It includes eight sports novels: Brooks's *The Moves Make the Man*, Crutcher's *Athletic Shorts* (1991) and *Stotan!* (1986), Terry Davis' *Vision Quest* (1979), Carl Deuker's *On the Devil's Court* (1989), David Klass's *Wrestling with Honor* (1989), R. R. Knudson and May Swenson's *American Sports Poems* (1988), and Robert Lipsyte's *The Contender*. A similar but more recent inventory of young adult books published from 1966 to 2000, the American Library Association's "100 Best Books for Teens," mentions thirteen sports books, including Crutcher's *Chinese Handcuffs* (1990), Sharon Draper's *Tears of a Tiger* (1996), Davida Wills Hurwin's *A Time for Dancing* (1996), and Cynthia Voigt's *The Runner* (1985).

Sports books also regularly appear on other recommended lists. The American Library Association's "Popular Paperbacks for Young Adults 1999," cited twenty-three sports books, many of those already mentioned above as well as the following: H. G. Bissinger's *Friday Night Lights* (1990), Madeleine Blais's *In These Girls, Hope is a Muscle* (1996), Edward Bloor's *Tangerine* (1997), Sara Corbett's *Venus to the Hoop: A Gold Medal Year in Women's Basketball* (1998), Crutcher's *Staying Fat for Sarah Byrnes* (1993) and *Ironman* (1995), Thomas Dygard's *Halfback Tough* (1989), Donald R. Gallo's *Ultimate Sports* (1995), Dan Gutman's *Honus and Me* (1997), Kevin Hillstrom's *The Handy Sports Answer Book* (1999), Dayton O. Hyde's *The Major, The Poacher and the Wonderful One-Trout River* (1998), W. P. Kinsella's *Shoeless Joe* (1982), Gordon Korman's *The Toilet Paper Tigers* (1995), Sue Macy's *A Whole New Ballgame* (1995), and *Winning Ways* (1996), Claire Murphy's *To the Summit* (1992), Walter Dean Myers's *Hoops* (1981) and *Slam!* (1996), and Rich Wallace's *Wrestling Sturbridge* (1996).

At the beginning of the twenty-first century, sports literature continues to be well represented in the young adult market. The 2000, 2001, 2002, and 2003 ALA Best Books for Young Adults lists recommend a total of nineteen sports books: Russell Freedman's *Babe Didrickson Zaharias: The Making of a Champion* (1999), Lorri Hewett's *Dancer* (1999), Scott Johnson's *Safe at Second* (1999), S. L. Rottman's *Head above Water* (1999), Carl Deuker's *Night Hoops* (2000), Adrian Fogelin's *Crossing Jordan* (2000), Kathleen Karr's *The Boxer* (2000), Chris Lynch's *Gold Dust* (2000), Rich Wallace's *Playing without the Ball* (2000), Lance Armstrong and Sally Jenkins's *It's Not about the Bike: My Journey Back to Life* (2000), Susan D. Bachrach's *The Nazi Olympics: Berlin 1936* (2000), Larry Colton's *Counting Coup: The True Story of Basketball and Honor on the Little Big Horn* (2000), Chris Crutcher's *Whale Talk* (2001), A. M. Jenkins's *Damage* (2001), Markus Zusak's *Fighting Ruben Wolfe* (2001), Walter Dean Myers's *The Greatest: Muhammad Ali* (2001), Laurie Halse Anderson's *Catalyst* (2002), Randy Powell's *Three Clams and an Oyster* (2002), and Jacqueline Woodson's *Hush* (2002). The number and variety of sports titles mentioned above suggest that young adult sports literature is gaining a reputation that parallels the generally positive reputation of adult sports literature. The popularity of sports literature for teenagers is likely to continue for as long as sports remain such a prominent part of American society and culture.

It's difficult to deny the popularity and prominence of sports today, but do sports—or does sports literature—really matter?

In an essay arguing against the cancellation of sporting events immediately after the terrorist attacks on the United States on September 11, 2001, Frank Deford explains how very much sports matter to Americans, especially in the traumatic days after our country had been attacked:

> Sports, you see, really do matter. No, not the games themselves, not even the players—but the harmonizing effect of sports upon our society. Former baseball commissioner Bart Giamatti (who was Bud Selig's great friend) wrote, "Because no single formal religion can embrace a people who hold so many faiths, including no particular formal faith at all, sports and politics are the civil surrogates . . . for [an American] ever in quest for a covenant." A stadium is crucial for a democratic society because it's where all classes and all types of people come together to mix and share in a common public space. Calling off the games denied us the opportunity for that precious and comforting assembly. (63)

Does sports literature, especially sports literature for teenagers, matter as much as sport itself?

Yes, it does.

As precious and comforting as assembling in a stadium with fellow sports fans may be, the benefits of being among the crowd at a particular sporting event is only temporary and cannot be easily replicated. The memory of the game fades and real life intrudes to wash away the lingering pleasure or comfort that attending a game may have provided. A good sports novel, poem, or biography can have a beneficial effect on a teenage reader that's equal to or greater than the benefits of attending a sporting event. A sports book might not provide the same sense of democracy and unity that watching a football or baseball game might, but the work of literature may bring a vicarious recollection of that experience coupled with a thoughtful, comforting opportunity for the reader to reflect on sport, society, family, human nature, love, life, death—all the things that matter most to us as human beings.

Reading has always provided, among other things, a temporary refuge from some of the ugliness of reality and a helpful insight into the people and world around us. Reading about sports and athletes provides those same benefits while simultaneously connecting readers to sport, one of the most dominant elements of modern American society. In these troubled post- 9/11 times, teenagers need refuge and insight, of course, but they also need to feel part of the society around them, a society they will soon be responsible for maintaining and protecting. Good sports literature can help.

The popularity of young adult sports literature has increased in recent years, and it now appeals to a wide range of young adults: males and females, experienced readers and reluctant readers. A recent reading interest survey of high school students reveals that sports ranked as the third most popular genre for pleasure reading for males and females combined, and as the number one favorite genre for boys (Hale and Crowe 55–57). Publishers are, of course, well aware of the appeal of sports, and in recent years they have produced a wide variety of young adult books to accommodate teens' interest in sports literature. Teenagers who are avid readers or who prefer sophisticated, challenging stories can find pleasurable reading among the sports novels of authors like Bruce Brooks, Chris Crutcher, Tessa Duder, Chris Lynch, Walter Dean Myers, or Nina Revoyr. At the other end of the reading spectrum, many teachers and librarians testify that sports books are often the best way to reach students who normally avoid reading.

Because sports are so popular in America and because sports books usually include some fast-paced scenes featuring athletes and athletics, sports literature appeals to many reluctant readers. In "Cool Books for Tough Guys," Lawrence Baines says that the most popular young adult novels among his reluctant readers include the sports novels *Running Loose, Vision Quest,* and *The Contender* (43–44). Sam D. Gill's article, "Young Adult Literature for Young Adult Males," also recommends *The Contender* along with *Ironman, Striking Out,* and *Hoops* as books that will interest students who don't like reading (61). Working with reluctant readers in an alternative school convinced Lindy Purdy Carter of the power of sports novels in overcoming the reluctance to read and in helping students reflect on important personal issues:

> I have found that sports literature provides an effective means for combating negative attitudes toward reading. Furthermore, the study of

sports writing and fiction provides an excellent opportunity for a teacher to engage informally in bibliotherapy, as students are encouraged to re-evaluate their attitudes and ambitions in light of their reading experiences. (309)

Teachers like Baines, Gill, and Purdy Carter aren't the only professionals who appreciate the potential of young adult sports literature. The American Library Association also recognizes the value of using sports books with reluctant teen readers; from 2000 to 2003, sports books made up 11 percent of all the titles appearing on its Quick Picks for Reluctant Readers lists.

Authors of young adult sports novels share similar beliefs about the potential benefits of their books for teenagers. In discussing the popularity of his novels among reluctant readers, Robert Lipsyte suggests that boys tend to be reluctant readers for the following reasons:

> I think that boys don't read as much as we'd like them to because (1) current books tend not to deal with the real problems and fears of boys, and (2) there is a tendency to treat boys as a group . . . which is where males are at their absolute worst . . . instead of as individuals who have to be led into reading secretly and one at a time. (259)

Sports novels like Lipsyte's are especially helpful with these kinds of readers for at least two reasons. First, because these books deal with realistic problems of adolescent boys and girls; readers feel connected to the characters and their problems. Second, because sports and sports stories are inherently interesting to many teenagers, young adult sports literature has a built-in appeal. These two qualities of sports literature combine to pull reluctant students into books "secretly and one at a time."

It would be a mistake, however, to assume that young adult sports literature is somehow different from "regular" literature and that it can be used only with reluctant readers. Of course there are many sports books that rely on heavy doses of game action and suspense, the sort of stuff that holds the attention of reluctant readers, but there are also many excellent sports novels that embody the very best qualities of literature. The sport content of these stories will interest some readers, but in the best sports books, the beauty of the writing, the personalities of the characters, and the power of the story are what really attract readers.

Of course, young adult sports novelists understand the basic appeal of sports stories, but they also understand the power of those stories to reach all kinds of readers. Walter Dean Myers has published a number of successful young adult sports novels, and he hopes that his books reveal some of the complexity of sport and also reach his readers in meaningful ways:

> Sports books can be more than just a game or series of games, just as sport is most often more than just a ball bouncing off a backboard or a set of statistics. I want to bring an understanding to sports that I've developed in the streets of Harlem and on basketball courts across the country. . . . I have an absolute need to bring meaning to the acts which attract so many young boys and, in increasing numbers, young girls. (21)

Myers's attention to sporting detail engages reluctant readers in his novels, but in addition to the appeal of game action, sports stories like Myers's can accomplish what was attempted by juvenile sports novels more than a century ago: teach important lessons about life. Carter reports that after reading aloud a passage from Myers's *Slam!* her students joined in a lively discussion that "confirmed my belief that sports literature provides invaluable life lessons for adolescents" (309).

Those life lessons that Myers and other young adult writers hope to provide for their readers aren't necessarily sport specific, and that's why some authors of young adult sports novels don't consider themselves sports writers. From the writers' points of view, their stories are about people, not sports. For example, although many reviewers and readers consider Chris Lynch's novel *Iceman* a hockey story, he doesn't. "I may be writing about hockey, [but] it feels to me like I am writing about a teenager in turmoil who cannot properly express emotions" ("Reluctant" 23). Sports novelists like Lynch take their work seriously, and they want others to see their books as something more than just sports stories. "While I am grateful for the boys and sports fans who may be drawn to my books," says Lynch, "I can't help hoping that the work is more universal than that" ("If You Show" 8). The good news is that the best young adult sports novels are "more universal than that" because they present issues and themes that extend beyond the playing field, and because they explore ideas that appeal to readers who enjoy sports and readers who don't.

Many young adult sports novelists write about sports not simply because the subject appeals to teenagers, but because sports add depth and complexity to their stories. When John H. Ritter started writing coming-of-age stories, baseball seemed like the perfect subject. "Aside from my love of the game," he says, "it also lends itself so easily to literary metaphor. Our whole lexicon is filled with examples. 'Three strikes and you're out.' 'Life threw me a curve.' 'You sure hit a homer with that idea.' 'He really went to bat for us.' and so on" (quoted in Crowe 6). Sport as a metaphor for life is sometimes considered a cliché, but in the hands of a talented writer, sport can become a device that illuminates the complexities of life.

Like many other authors of sports novels, Walter Dean Myers sees sports and life as inextricably connected. He writes, "Athletes often discover parallels between the competition known as sport and the life experience," (21) and in Myers's sports stories, characters make discoveries that help them understand themselves and their lives better. Lynch also appreciates the connections between sport and human nature, and he believes that sports stories can provide a healthy outlet for adults and teenagers. "We all feel the rage and frustration at some point where we just want to raise a hand and SWAT our troubles flat. Or run them into the ground. Or exhaust them. In the sports story, we can watch the character do it literally for us" (26). Whether they're helping adolescent readers vicariously release rage and frustration, or understand themselves and their world better, or learn valuable life lessons, good sports stories provide much more than entertainment. The best young adult sports novels offer the same benefits, challenges, and intellectual stimulation as any other well-written novel.

This book recognizes the strong presence of young adult sports literature in contemporary publishing and reading, and its goal is to help teenagers, teachers, and librarians understand the literature, its history, and its importance in contemporary society. As Deford says, in America today "sports do matter," (63) and so does young adult sports literature. Because of its popularity and quality, it deserves a place in libraries and in secondary English classes.

WORKS CITED

Baines, Lawrence. "Cool Books for Tough Guys." *The ALAN Review* 22.1 (Fall 1994): 43–46.
Carter, Linda Purdy. "Addressing the Needs of Reluctant Readers through Sports Literature." *The Clearing House* 71.5 (May/June 1998): 309–311.

Crowe, Chris. "An Interview with John H. Ritter." *The ALAN Review* 27.3 (Spring/Summer 2000): 5–9.

Deford, Frank. "Delay of Games." *Sports Illustrated* 95.12 (September 24, 2001): 62–63.

Dewey, Joseph. "*Aethlon*'s Fifty Most Influential Works Survey." *Aethlon* 16.2 (Spring 1999): 161–62.

Donelson, Ken. "Honoring the Best YA Books of the Year: 1964–1995." *English Journal* 86.3 (March 1997): 41–47.

Gill, Sam D. "Young Adult Literature for Young Adult Males." *The ALAN Review* 26.2 (Winter 1999): 61–63.

Hale, Lisa A., and Chris Crowe. "'I Hate Reading If I Don't Have To': Results from a Longitudinal Study of High School Students' Reading Interest." *The ALAN Review* 28.3 (Spring/Summer 2001): 49–57.

Lipsyte, Robert. "Robert Lipsyte on Books for Boys" in *Literature for Today's Young Adults*, Eds. Ken Donelson and Alleen Pace Nilsen. New York: Longman, 1997: 259.

Lynch, Chris. "If You Show Me Yours, I'll Show You Mine." *The ALAN Review* 24.1 (Fall 1996): 7–9.

———. "The Reluctant Sportswriter." *SIGNAL Journal* 21.1 (Fall 1996): 23–26.

McEntegart, Pete, et al. "The Top 100 Sports Books of All Time." *Sports Illustrated* 97.24 (December 16, 2002): 128–148.

Myers, Walter Dean. "Of Games and Men." *SIGNAL Journal.* 21.1 (Fall 1996): 19–22.

Chapter 2

From the Schoolroom to the Playing Field: A History of Young Adult Sports Literature

Sports literature and young adult literature have a common ancestry: both evolved from the boys' school story. In the late nineteenth century, Thomas Hughes' *Tom Brown's School Days* (1857) and *Tom Brown at Oxford* (1861) were popular in England and the United States and helped to establish a market niche for books and stories for boys. It wasn't long before many books and periodicals filled this niche, and in the United States by the turn of the twentieth century, writers like Horatio Alger, Oliver Optic, Gilbert Patten, and Edward Stratemeyer; magazines like *St. Nicholas* and *Tip Top Weekly*; and publishers like Beadle and Adams and Street & Smith were enjoying unprecedented success. Of course, not all of the stories produced by these writers and publishers were sports stories, but they were written specifically for young readers. In time, as sports became a more essential strand in the American fabric, elements of sports began to play more prominent roles in boys' stories.

Tom Brown's School Days, called the "fountainhead of boys' sports fiction" (105) by Walter Evans, included scenes from school but also from school-sponsored sports, soccer and cricket, and his involvement in these sports plays a major role in the development of Tom Brown. Christian Messenger describes the novel as "the classic fictional portrayal of youth's initiation into traditions of school life in which athletic skill defined and singled out the leadership boys more than any other activity" (*Sport in American Literature* 159). He goes on to say that "by making school sport the basis of so much of the narrative action, formation of character, and social setting, Hughes practically insured the place of sport in the school story genre when it became a staple of popular literature in America" (159). The story pattern established by Thomas Hughes' novel was successfully followed by many writers in the nineteenth and twentieth centuries and is still apparent in today's young adult sports fiction. Wiley Lee Umphlett cites the success of these early school sports stories as the foundation for all sports literature—for young adults and for adults:

> It also started the tradition in American literature of the novel inspired by organized sports—a literary form that may be categorized as a subgenre but one whose cultural impact was dominant enough to influence the youthful reading habits of countless American business/political leaders as well as some notable fiction writers and their later attitudes toward certain aspects of American experience. This early influence itself should be reason enough to assess the juvenile sports novel's place in the mainstream of American fiction, but the continuing output of this tradition's serious adult fiction inspired by contemporary sports is even more reason. (26)

Before the advent of sports stories, though, dime novels and serial magazines provided the bulk of the popular reading for boys. The stories in these publications tended to be high on thrills and adventure but low on literary quality. Teachers and librarians lamented the popularity of these books and the corruptive influences they had on boys, but young readers gobbled up dime novels and serial magazines and the steady diet of mystery, suspense, and adventure.

The emergence of the boys' sports novel was directly related to the decline of the dime novel. Michael Oriard says that in the 1870s and 1880s the stories became more improbable and the violence more frequent until adult reaction against the dime novels forced most young readers to read them surreptitiously.

> What parents objected to in the dime novels was not their morality, but the emphasis on sensationalism, violence, and overwrought emotionalism. On the other hand, the child reader did not want the priggish books typical of the pre-dime novel juvenile literature. The reading public was ripe for a fiction that could satisfy the child's desire for stirring adventure and the parent's insistence on propriety; the juvenile sports novel filled this need. (45)

In his autobiography, America's most prolific author of juvenile sports novels, Gilbert Patten, who wrote under the pen name of Burt

L. Standish, is quite open about how he intended to use sports stories as a vehicle for preaching to his readers:

> Believing the old-fashioned dime novel was on its way out, I decided to set a new style with my stories and make them different and more in step with the times. As the first issues were to be stories of American school life, I saw in them an opportunity to feature all kinds of athletic sports, with baseball, about which I was best informed, predominating.
> Such stories would give me an opportunity to preach—by example—the doctrine of a clean mind in a clean and healthy body. And also, unlike the old dime novel writers, I would attempt to present even minor characters in such a manner that the readers could visualize them clearly. With me, plot would be secondary to character depiction as far as I could make it and still write a story of interesting action and suspense. (178–79)

Oriard explains that the success of the juvenile sports novels of Gilbert Patten and others grew out of the traditions that preceded it, a combination of the dime novel action with the morality of the Horatio Alger novels. "It is important to note that a single strain runs consistently through all three literary types—the concept of the self-made man" (47). Messenger adds that the dime novels began to incorporate sports into their plots because sport lent itself to formula fiction and because of the increasingly high profile of sports, especially professional baseball, in American society. "In 1890," he says, "the ultimate meaning of sport for modern America and its writers depended upon the continued growth of organized sport and the popular philosophy that would take shape around the role of the player" (34).

Umphlett also notes how the new novel form complemented American attitudes of the time. Authors of books for young readers in the 1890s–1920s made good use of American school and college settings because they provided the ideal arena for showing how athletics influenced character development (29). The move to "pure" sports novels was the logical next step. Umphlett explained that

> Writers of juvenile sports novels were quick to expand upon the implications of this intimate relationship between school, sports, and loyal son, especially when that son was an athlete. It is through this interrelationship that most of these writers expressed their understanding of a standard of quality performance, a striving for excellence that is best captured in the Greek concept *arete* but that supposedly predicted success in life

according to the American way. They felt, too, that this formulaic standard of behavior was most symbolically expressed in the dedicated athletic performance that occurred on the playing field. (27)

Although the protagonists' conflicts in these stories might be resolved through athletic performance, the characters themselves were more concerned with fitting into the school culture than they were with winning. In his article, "The All-American Boys: A Study of Boys' Sports Fiction," Walter Evans explains that the school sports story typically concerned itself with a boy's integration into school life. The integration usually comes about because of the boy's use of athletic skill to overcome some personal flaw that has heretofore hindered his success. The main character's potential is finally realized when he wins a key athletic contest and is recognized by his schoolmates as a school hero (107).

American publishers recognized the market potential of sports stories, and in 1868, literature and sports began their long relationship with the publication of the first novel known to use baseball action, *Changing Base* by William Everett. Football showed up a little later as a chapter in Mark Severance's novel *Hammersmith: His Harvard Days* (1878). These and later stories contained sports but used the game story as a way of presenting moral lessons to young male readers. In 1882, while a junior at Brown University, Charles Munroe Sheldon published "The Captain of the Orient Nine," a baseball short story about a player who knows that his team won an important game because of a missed call by an umpire. "There wasn't too much sport in the story," says Robert Cantwell, "but Sheldon worked on [the player's] moral dilemma until he looked like a character in *Pilgrim's Progress*, chasing a fly ball into the Slough of Despond" (69). Sheldon's story staked out new territory for publishers: fiction primarily about sports, fiction that unabashedly preached the American dream and middle-class morality to its readers. Initially, sports stories appeared in many of the magazines of the day like *St. Nicholas, All-Sports Library, The Young Athlete's Weekly,* and *Wide Awake*; two early baseball serials were Noah Brooks's "The Fairport Nine" (1880) and Robert Hughes's "The Lakerim Athletic Club" (1897–1898). The first novel to deal exclusively with a sport, baseball, was Brooks's *Our Baseball Club and How It Won the Championship* published in 1884 by E. P. Dutton.

Brooks's book and another baseball novel, Edward Wheeler's *High Hat Harry, the Baseball Detective; or The Sunken Treasure* (1885), appeared fairly early in the pulp fiction era when many books, mostly westerns and adventure stories, were being published primarily for male "juvenile" readers. The initial reception of *High Hat Harry* disappointed its author and his publisher, Beadle and Adams, but it did well enough to help establish sports fiction as an important market for the teenage audience (Cantwell 70). After that, baseball in print continued to find success. In 1888, the most famous sports poem ever written, Ernest Lawrence Thayer's "Casey at the Bat," appeared in the *San Francisco Examiner*. The poem was popular immediately, and later that year was picked up and performed by DeWolf Hopper, a young actor who would make a career out of Thayer's poem, reciting it more than 40,000 times before his death many years later.

By the beginning of the twentieth century, many writers were producing sports novels for teenagers, mostly baseball and football stories (basketball, which wasn't invented until 1891, took a few more years to find its way into juvenile literature). An army of writers turned to sports stories, including Gilbert Patten, Edward Stratemeyer, H. Irving Hancock, Lester Chadwick, Owen Johnson, George Jenks, Ralph Henry Barbour, William Heyliger, and Harold Sherman, and the market flourished. Patten's Frank Merriwell stories enjoyed the greatest commercial success, but many literary historians cite Ralph Henry Barbour and William Heyliger, each of whom published more than 150 novels in the early part of the twentieth century, as some of the best writers of early juvenile sports books.

Despite the large number of writers producing sports fiction, the popularity of Gilbert Patten was so great that he is generally given credit both for permanently establishing sports novels as a legitimate commercial genre and for creating the formula for sports stories that would last into the twenty-first century. Oriard calls Patten, "the real father of American sports fiction," who helped "establish the traditions of American sports fiction within which and against which serious authors wrote" (9).

Some of the earliest juvenile sports stories featured athlete/heroes who were also detectives engaged in solving a sports-related crime. Later stories were formulaic tales about white male athletes in high school or college. The protagonist was usually a prep school student who was wholesome, modest, honest, and handsome, and who excelled in several sports, especially football and baseball. In 1896, Patten's Frank Merriwell became the epitome of this schoolboy athletic hero. Frank's adventures spanned sixteen years, covering his education, adventures, and athletic accomplishments around the world while he was a student at Fardale Academy and Yale College. He succeeded at every sport he played—from baseball to billiards—and always, through his wit, athletic skill, and quite often through dramatic and incredible last-second heroics, managed to overcome whatever obstacles a story's villains threw his way. The Merriwell hero remained a staple of nearly all juvenile sports fiction well into the middle of the twentieth century.

Adults are minor characters in these stories, in part because the emphasis of the sports stories had to be amateur sports played by youths who remained untainted by professionalism, and also because excluding adults from important roles allowed the morality tales to feature characters the targeted audience could relate to and learn from. Coaches are among the most frequent adult characters, and they are portrayed as kindly and benign mentors who dispense wise advice at key moments. The plots typically involved some subterfuge in the locker room or on the playing field that threatened the reputation or well-being of the athlete/hero or the school. Naturally the novel's hero played an essential role in resolving the conflict through his courage, honesty, and superior athletic skill. These kinds of young adult sports novels have virtually disappeared, and readers like Cantwell miss them:

> A handful of good writers of boys' books still write about baseball, but their product is of a different sort. For one thing, there is only a handful where there were once a hundred or more. For another, they write relatively few books, where the giants in the field produced hundreds. At best the new breed resembles careful handicraft operators, trying—but failing—to keep alive a vanished art form that everybody once appreciated. Millions of future Little Leaguers are going to play ball without a deep source of solace and inspiration; the romance of the diamond, in which the young star walloped a bully, was disgraced by a false accusation, usually of theft (something was planted in his locker), but was cleared in time to play in the big game and often wound up saving the town from destruction by fire or flood as well. (68)

The Merriwell-esque sports stories that Cantwell loved are no longer being written, but the field of sports literature for teenagers has continued to expand since the 1930s, providing a variety of good books that appeal to all kinds of teenage readers. Ralph Henry Barbour's sports books, Lester Chadwick's Baseball Joe series and Matthew M.

Colton's tales of the all-American boy, Jack Armstrong, benefited from the momentum created by the success of Patten's Merriwell stories and carried on the tradition of sports literature for boys.

By the 1940s a legion of writers began to produce the next generation of sports stories for teenagers. Successful college basketball coach Clair Bee published his first of more than twenty sports novels for teenagers in his Chip Hilton series in 1948. In the same year, Wilfred McCormick's first book in his Bronc Burnett series appeared, and C. Paul Jackson published his second sports novel in a career that would eventually produce more than fifty sports novels for teenagers. Matt Christopher carried on the tradition in the 1950s, publishing more than 120 series and single title sports novels from 1954 to 1997. The main characters in these books generally resemble the clean-cut Frank Merriwell model, but instead of preaching morals and American ideals, these stories are more concerned with play-by-play game action. Of course, these books don't completely abandon the idea that readers need to see a character making ethical decisions, being a good friend, or overcoming obstacles, but with the action taking place primarily on the fields of play, these stories lack the heavy-handedness that characterized so many of the earlier sports books. Part of the appeal of these books is the unadulterated game action that provides readers with the vicarious experience of attempting the last-second free throw, making the game-saving tackle, or winding up for the crucial 3–2 pitch with two outs in the ninth inning. Some readers today still enjoy sports books that focus on game action, and in response to that demand, many of Clair Bee's Chip Hilton sports novels have recently been reissued, and several of Matt Christopher's books have been published posthumously.

As young adult sports literature matured, authors and readers were prepared for more sophisticated stories, tales that went beyond the playing fields and locker rooms, narratives that would develop characters more fully and allow them to wrestle with challenges on and off the field. Rebecca J. Lukens's characterization of sports fiction shows both how sports novels were once regarded by critics and how the genre has improved:

> Once a kind of formula fiction, sports stories have become increasingly individualized, with well-developed characters struggling with personal issues and discovering the forces and choices they must confront. . . . Once a genre of undistinguished stories, sports fiction is much improved. (17–18)

John R. Tunis was the pivotal figure in this improvement. After working as a freelance sports writer for several years, he wrote his first novel, *Iron Duke*, in 1938. Initially outraged that it would be published as a "juvenile" novel, a publishing category he knew almost nothing about, he continued to write quality sports novels for teenagers at the rate of almost one per year for the next twenty years. Nearly all his books earned praise from readers and critics, and Tunis's quality stories did more than the work of any other young adult writer to elevate sports fiction from its pulp fiction beginnings.

Though he still wrote sports stories for boys, in many ways Tunis departed from the established tradition of juvenile sports literature. Instead of stories about sports heroes pulling out a victory in the last seconds—and on the last page—Tunis's books were about more than winning the big game. Recognizing the new direction Tunis gave to juvenile sports literature, Margaret A. Edwards wrote that Tunis's *The Iron Duke* "was the forerunner of the modern sports stories where the emphasis has been on character rather than merely winning a contest" (88). His characters possess many heroic and athletic qualities, but their encounters with life are much more realistic, and the outcomes of many of those encounters are distinctly un-Merriwellian. Tunis's heroes did not have to be victorious in order to be winners. In an interview shortly before his death, he said, "My heroes are the losers. All my books have been in that vein" (Holtzman 261). Tunis loved sports, especially tennis, but he also knew that athletics were not completely pure and noble. "As a result," he wrote, "my writing became not so much about sport, as about the values, good or bad, of our leisure-time activities in the United States" (4).

Because of his more realistic view of sports, Tunis's stories blend athletics with important social issues, issues that were usually glossed over by his predecessors and contemporaries. For example, in *All-American* (1942, 1989), talented football player Ronald Perry chooses to leave his snobbish prep school to attend a local public school. While at his new school, he helps his teammates and the community at large learn a valuable lesson about racial discrimination. *All-American* contains plenty of game action, but Tunis expands the scope of the novel by integrating issues he considered important for young readers.

In his introduction to the 1989 reissue of *All-American*, Bruce Brooks praised the strengths of the novel:

As in Tunis's other novels, the athletic theme of the novel represents only one part—and a fairly superficial one—of the characters' lives. And as in his earlier books, Tunis darts back and forth from sports to tougher issues. In All-American, we find some of the old enemies of decent living (racism, capitalistic conservatism) and some new (snobbery, reverse snobbery, academic laziness), but as usual the challenge is met by defiant self-reliance, whereby young people take responsibility for the decency of a community by taking responsibility for themselves. (vii)

G. Robert Carlsen, an early leader in young adult literature, also admired Tunis's work. In writing about Go, Team, Go! (1954), Carlsen pointed out the qualities of Tunis's work that separate him from writers of sports series:

> [Go, Team, Go!] not only presents the actual excitement of the physical contest, but shows the distortion of values that can occur in an American community as the result of this adulation of young high school players. It is a critical book but not a didactic one. Each incident arises out of the characters of the people involved and the nature of the social values under which they live. It leaves the reader to make his own decisions of right and wrong for himself. More and more stories like Go, Team, Go! explore the fundamental problems of human relationships and goals. These are, therefore, quite different from the series books centering on sports that many of us read in junior high school, books in which the main concern was the contest itself and the struggle to win the game. (50–51)

Tunis refused to condescend to his young readers, and unlike the sports novelists who preceded him, Tunis believed that his readers would be able to learn important lessons about life and sports without being preached to. His attitude would have seemed heretical to Patten and other earlier writers of juvenile fiction:

> We do not have to indoctrinate our young people, or claim that our system is perfect. We need only to show the system with its drawbacks and defects, and hope our young people of today will do something later to change it. Do they understand a book that says these things? Do they get the point? Yes, because they are not yet corrupted. (260)

Tunis's more realistic presentation of sports and athletes and his refusal to preach to his readers aren't the only characteristics that distinguish him from all the juvenile writers who preceded him. In addition to his attention to details beyond the game action, Tunis also paid great attention to the art of writing. He knew that his writing had to be superior to the work of the hack dime novel writers he read as a boy:

> A book written for my audience doesn't have to be merely as good as a book for adults; it must be—or should be—better. Not only does youth deserve the best, but also no youths read a book because it is on the best-seller list. Nor do they read it because it has a huge advertising budget, or is well reviewed; they read it for one reason alone, they want to. They find it says something to them in an area they know and understand. These readers are important, perhaps the most important audience in the country today. (259)

Tunis's respect for his audience raised the standards for all sports novelists who followed him and cleared the way for authors to incorporate important adolescent themes with sports, the most pervasive social influence of the last few decades.

Thomas J. Dygard, another sports journalist turned young adult sports novelist, followed the literary path established by Tunis. Play-by-play action is an important feature in all of his novels, but, like Tunis, the protagonists in his books confront—and grow from—important issues outside of the locker room. In *Outside Shooter* (1979), a high school basketball player must learn to cope with personality problems that affect him and his teammates. *Infield Hit* (1995), is the story of the son of a well-known major league baseball player. In addition to being saddled with the baggage that comes with being the son of a famous athlete, he must also deal with his parents' divorce and fitting into a new school. Dygard published more than fifteen sports novels for teenagers from 1977 until his death in 1996, and all of them combine character issues and sports in the manner established by Tunis.

In recent years, young adult sports literature has changed in some important ways. First, since the establishment of Title IX, publishers and their authors have expanded the boundaries of sports literature to include female athletes. Second, since the 1970s, sports books have featured sports besides football, basketball, and baseball, and it is no longer impossible to find young adult sports books about soccer, tennis, swimming, track, and other so-called minor sports. A third change is the target audience. While they were once aimed at teenage readers, more and more sports novels are being written for and marketed to preteens. Dean Hughes's multiple-sport *Angel Park* series and his later *Scrappers* baseball series are good examples of this trend. Hughes's *Scrappers* series also suggests a final departure from the earlier game novels. In most sports novels prior to the 1970s, the major characters were white males. The *Scrappers* books and most other recent sports stories feature male and female athletes from a variety of ethnic groups.

The most recent development in young adult sports literature began in the 1980s, when a handful of writers took sports novels a step beyond the work of Tunis and Dygard. These young adult sports books are a kind of novel I call a *sportlerroman*, a form of the traditional *bildungsroman* apprenticeship novel, where the protagonist is an athlete struggling to maturity. Like the *künstlerroman* where the protagonist is an artist, the *sportlerroman* is a coming-of-age story of an athlete. Sports figure prominently in his or her story, but the central conflicts of the *sportlerroman* lie beyond athletics. As Brooks points out, the *sportlerroman* differs from traditional sports novels in that play-by-play game action is not central to the story. "Back then," he writes, "a book wouldn't qualify [as a sports book] if it contained more than a smidgen of 'real life' blurring the focus on pure sports; now, a book is wedged into the classification if it has an athlete as a character or a little sports action to cut the 'real life' themes" ("Playing Fields" 20).

The *sportlerroman* combines modern America's preoccupation with sports with its fascination with youth, and this combination allows authors to create conflicts that integrate the agonies of adolescence with the potential agonies of athletic competition. In some *sportlerroman*, conflict begins in a sporting event and eventually works its way into other aspects of a character's life. In others, sports provides an outlet—and often a mentor—to help a protagonist deal with off-the-field troubles. Still other *sportlerroman* provide the central character with problems in and out of sport that are in some way related. In any case, by including sports in the narrative, authors are able to expand a character's conflict and create more opportunities to confront that conflict in different and interesting ways. Bruce Brooks, Chris Crutcher, Chris Lynch, John H. Ritter, and Rich Wallace are among the most notable authors of *sportlerroman*.

Young adult sports literature has come a long way in the last 100 years, and now, thanks to the efforts of serious writers and publishers, it can take its place alongside adult sports literature which has earned the respect of critics, teachers, and most importantly, readers. Though it is indebted to its preachy pulp novel heritage, today's best young adult sports literature can truly be called *literature*. Given America's growing preoccupation with sports, it is certain that sports will continue to play a part in many young adult novels, not because teenagers like sports but because sports help authors reveal the best and worst of society and human nature, and those revelations are what make stories worth reading.

WORKS CITED

Brooks, Bruce. Introduction to *All-American* by Tunis, John R. San Diego: Harcourt Brace Jovanovich, 1942, 1989.
———. "Playing Fields of Fiction." *New York Times Book Review*. 6 April 1986: 20.
Cantwell, Robert. "A Sneering Laugh with the Bases Loaded." *Sports Illustrated* 23 April 1962: 67–76.
Carlsen, G. Robert. *Books and the Teenage Reader*. New York: Bantam, 1967.
Donelson, Ken. "Attitudes Towards Sports: Six Representative Writers of Boys Novels, 1900–1960." *Arizona English Bulletin* 18 (April 1976): 122–32.
Edwards, Margaret A. "The Rise of Teen-Age Reading." *The Saturday Review* 37 (November 13, 1954): 88–89, 95.
Evans, Walter. "The *All-American* Boys: A Study of Boys' Sports Fiction." *Journal of Popular Culture* 6.1 (Summer 1972): 104–21.
Holtzman, Jerome, ed. *No Cheering in the Press Box*. New York: Holt, Rinehart and Winston, 1973.
Lukens, Rebecca J. *A Critical Handbook of Children's Literature*, 4th ed. Glenview, IL: Scott Foresman/Little, Brown, 1990.
Messenger, Christian K. *Sport in American Literature (1830–1930)*. Diss. Evanston, IL: Northwestern University, 1974.
———. "Sport in the Dime Novel." *Journal of American Culture* 3 (Fall 1978): 494–505.
———. *Sport and the Spirit of Play in American Fiction: Hawthorne to Faulkner*. New York: Columbia University Press, 1981.
Oriard, Michael. *Dreaming of Heroes: American Sports Fiction, 1868–1980*. Chicago: Nelson-Hall, 1982.
Patten, Gilbert. *Frank Merriwell's Father: An Autobiography of Gilbert Patten ("Burt L. Standish")*. Norman: University of Oklahoma Press, 1964.
Saul, E. Wendy, and R. Gordon Kelly. "Christians, Brahmins, and Other Sporting Fellows: An Analysis of School Sports." *Children's Literature in Education* 15.4 (Winter 1984):234–45.
Shereikis, Richard. "How You Play the Game: The Novels of John R. Tunis." *The Horn Book Magazine* 53.6 (December 1977): 642–48.

Smith, Leverett T., Jr. "John R. Tunis's American Epic; or, Bridging the Gap between Juvenile and Adult Sports Fiction." In *The Achievement of American Sports Literature: A Critical Appraisal*, edited by Wiley Lee Umphlett, 46-61. Rutherford: Farleigh Dickinson University Press, 1991.

Tunis, John R. *A Measure of Independence*. New York: Atheneum, 1964.

Umphlett, Wiley Lee. "Formulaic Sources of the American Sports-Fiction Tradition: The Code of Quality Performance in Juvenile Sports Fiction." In *The Achievement of American Sports Literature: A Critical Appraisal*, 25–45. Rutherford: Farleigh Dickinson University Press, 1991.

Chapter 3

Young Adult Sports Fiction: More Than Just Game Stories

Despite the long tradition of young adult sports fiction and the widespread popularity of sports in America, sports novels were absent from the *School Library Journal*'s "One Hundred Books That Shaped the Century," a list of significant children's and young adult books published in the twentieth century. The exclusion of young adult sports books from the *School Library Journal*'s list parallels the Modern Library's rankings of the most important adult books from the last century: no sports book appeared on their list either. The literary snub triggered an editorial from *Coach and Athletic Director*:

> How come in a country that boasts of its glorious sports tradition and great sports heroes, not a trace of either appears in our great literature? . . . We have in front of us a list of the '100 Best Novels' of this century, compiled by the editorial board of the Modern Library, and not one of these novels contains as much as a sub-plot on anything having to do with sports. (Masin 10)

The answer to the editorialist's question is offered by well-known sports literature scholar Michael Oriard, who himself has observed the irony. "We have long been aware of a basic anomaly, that the literature about the most popular form of American mass culture has itself never been popular" (Oriard, "Sports History" 188). The popularity of sports and the growing quality of sports literature obviously haven't convinced some critics that sports literature is *literature,* and in his review of the state of sports literature in 1983, Oriard makes this clear:

> the sports novelist has not yet achieved total acceptance. His position in the literary world remains at least slightly ambiguous. Read any review or critical essay on major sports novels like *The Natural, The Universal Baseball Association,* or *End Zone* and the implicit message is clear: these are great novels because they are about much *more* than *just* baseball or football. ("On the Current" 8)

Fortunately, young adult sports fiction has made significant gains since Oriard's review of the state of sports literature in 1983. Tom Hulburt's 1992 review of young adult contemporary sports fiction for *School Library Journal* points out that sports fiction has overcome the formulaic writing of its past and that successful sports novels "look at sports in the context of larger social issues" (30). Sports fiction for young adults has continued to improve since then, and now young adult sports novels regularly appear on national and state recommended reading lists, and many publishers are actively looking for more sports fiction (Haverstock 1).

But the books have changed; the days of sports stories that focused exclusively on game action are gone. Now publishers insist on books that are more than just stories about a sport; they want stories that are also quality fiction, books that can stand on their own without being propped up by game action. To be successful in today's market, a sports novel must contain an interesting story with interesting characters and be able to be judged by the same standards of quality as other books. One of the most successful writers of contemporary young adult sports fiction, Chris Crutcher, knows this better than anyone. His books always contain vivid sports action, but the action is not the heart of the story. According to Crutcher, in his novels, "The main characters not only want to play the game but also have a personal problem that, in most cases, affects their playing" (Haverstock 3). His protagonists are athletes who care about their sports, but unlike the traditional formula for sports fiction, the central conflicts of his stories do not hinge on victory in the big game. The conflicts in Crutcher's novels are more personal and, while game action may play a part in their resolution, the real work of resolving the conflicts comes from the protagonists' personal decisions and actions. Crutcher's approach to his stories typifies the best young adult sports literature being written today.

So, in the twenty-first century, what can legitimately be considered sports fiction? When sports fiction became a subject of serious literary study in the 1970s, the field needed a definition and boundaries to help scholars determine what qualified as sports literature. At the time, publishers' categories were not helpful because classifications were arbitrary or inconsistent and because, in most cases, any book that contained sports action was classified as a sports novel if the publisher determined that such a label would help marketing. Conversely, some books that could be considered sports novels might not be classified that way because the publisher feared that the sports label would hurt sales.

To guide scholars—and his own study of sports literature—Oriard, one of the field's most articulate and prominent authorities, offered a definition for the adult sports novel:

> A definition of the sports novel, then, as one in which no substitutes for sport would be possible without radically changing the book, also embodies the most basic criterion for judging its quality. Contrary to the reviewer's inevitable claim, a good sports novel is not "about more than baseball" (or football or basketball), but is deeply about the sport itself. (Oriard, "On the Current" 14)
>
> I define the sports novel simply as one in which sport plays a dominant role or in which the sport milieu is the dominant setting. . . . A sports novel is not a novel that happens to be about an athlete; rather, it is a novel that finds its vision of the individual and his condition in the basic meaning of the sport he plays, formerly played, or watches. (Oriard, *Dreaming* 6)

Oriard's definitions do not apply perfectly to young adult sports novels, but they do provide an excellent foundation for considering the field. Young adult novels with sports settings certainly should be considered sports fiction, even if the novels are not "deeply about the sport itself." Because the young adult world lacks the depth and breadth of adult experience, even superficial influences on teenage characters' lives are important, so young adult novels with athletic settings, even if the settings remain in the background, ought to be considered sports fiction.

A definition of young adult sports novels must vary from Oriard's definition at one essential point. Oriard says that a book cannot be considered a sports novel if it merely "happens to be about an athlete." His qualification should not be used to exclude this type of young adult book from the category of sports fiction. Because most serious young adult novels concern themselves with a character's coming of age, the social or school label of a character—jock, preppie, doper, whatever—affects the character's development. In the case of jocks, their adolescent identities and their connections to sport are an essential part of their nature and will influence their actions, decisions, and what they learn from their actions and decisions. So, a young adult novel like Bruce Brooks's *The Moves Make the Man* (1984), must be considered sports literature even though the protagonist and narrator, Jerome Foxworthy, does not play on organized sports teams, and even though sports action makes up only a few scenes in the entire book. It must be classified a young adult sports novel, a unique kind of sports novel that I call a *sportlerroman* (which I will define in detail later in this chapter), because Jerome is a basketball player and views his world from the perspective of an athlete. His interest in and understanding of his unusual friend Bix come precisely because of Jerome's athletic background. If Jerome had not been an athlete, he would not have befriended Bix and the novel's complications would have never materialized.

Other than that, the best definition for the young adult sports novel differs little from Oriard's definition. Simply stated, a young adult sports novel is a novel in which sport plays an integral role, whether in setting, plot, or character.

This definition applies to all books in this category despite the dramatic changes in the young adult sports fiction in the last few decades. In his 1976 review of six important boys' sports books from 1900 to 1960, a period when most young adult sports writers were still heavily influenced by the Frank Merriwell tradition, Donelson made six generalizations about the moral stance of young adult sports fiction of that time:

1. Fair play is the only way to play. Being a good sport, in winning or losing, is essential for the athlete.
2. School spirit is important and separates life's winners from life's losers. That assumes, of course, that the school has the proper spirit.
3. The individual counts for less than the team, and the team counts for less than the school. That assumes, of course, that the school counts for what is worthwhile.
4. Sports can (not *will*, but can) make a man out of a boy.

5. Sports can teach a boy how to choose and make important moral commitments and how to face life's problems.
6. Sports establishes the validity of the protestant ethic. Hard work and team effort are good in and of themselves, assuming, of course, that the hard work and the team are aimed at something morally sound. (132)

Donelson concluded his review of these sports books by stating that there are no truly great young adult sports novels that can compare with some of the classic adult sports novels, and that there will never be any.

> Writers for adults can be as angry or tragic or coldly detached or mythic or sardonic or profane as they wish, using sports only as a framework to say something about man and his present state. Those approaches are nearly barred to the writer of boys' books. The writer of boys' sports books owes his readers an exciting and believable and honest picture of athletics and athletes, and in the process he may sometimes be able to say something about life despite the narrow focus and limited approach he can employ. (132)

Donelson's observations held true until the early 1980s when the realistic trends that had influenced young adult literature in general also began to affect young adult sports fiction as well. Jack Forman, writing in *Horn Book Magazine* in 1987 about the recent young adult sports novels *Juggling* (1982) by Robert Lehrman; *Football Dreams* (1980) by David Guy; and Brooks's *The Moves Make the Man*, notes the change:

> In a very real way the young adult sports metaphor novel exemplifies the major changes the young adult novel in general has undergone in the past two decades. Plot development has been subordinated to character growth, and homilies have been dispensed with. Sports action, however, is still an intrinsic part of the story, but its function has changed from subject to motif. Using sports as a microcosm of teenage experience, the sports metaphor novel sets its character-players loose from the confines of the game to play for real. In making the mundane meaningful, it typifies the achievements of the best young adult realistic fiction. (502)

Forman did not claim that formulaic sports novels no longer exist but that a new form, one with richer literary possibilities, was now available. In this new kind of young adult sports fiction, as in most modern fiction, almost anything goes.

Many kinds of sports books exist, and to help distinguish among the variety available to teenagers today, I divide young adult sports fiction into four general categories: short stories, game novels, more-than-a-game novels, and *sportlerroman*.

SHORT STORIES

American sports fiction had its start in boys' magazines of the nineteenth century and continued to appear regularly in magazines for teenagers until the last few decades of the twentieth century. Fiction in general and sports stories in particular are much rarer these days in young adult magazines, but readers can occasionally find short fiction about sports in magazines ranging from *Boys' Life* to *Cicada*. It is interesting to note that short sports fiction has lagged significantly behind adult and young adult sports novels in its development away from the preachy pulp fiction roots of the nineteenth century.

Thanks to Donald R. Gallo, the leading collector of young adult short stories, publishers in the last twenty years have produced more young adult short story collections than ever before. Anthologies of sports fiction, however, are rare, especially in recent years, and young adult sports novels outnumber short story collections about sport by a huge margin.

In the 1940s and 1950s, a number of collections of short fiction about sports were available; some featured stories on a single sport and some covered a variety of sports. *Teenage Sports Stories* (1947) is typical of the short sports fiction of the middle of the twentieth century, much of which was still influenced by Frank Merriwell and American society's notion that fiction for teenagers, especially sports fiction, should teach young people important lessons about life. In the introduction to this collection, editor Frank Owen writes, "All of the stories meet with the rigid standards of the Teen-Age Library: they are clean and wholesome; they are interesting; and they mirror some phase of the lives and problems of teenagers. It is to be hoped that they will in great measure be of aid in the process of good character building" (vii).

Owens's book contained stories on the big three sports—baseball, football, and basketball— but it also included minor sports that usually didn't appear in sports novels of the time: sailing, rowing, lacrosse, and rodeo. Perhaps the most notable story in the collection, because of its ground-breaking subject matter, is Thelma Knoles's "Double Play," a story of a girls' high school softball team. Stories about girls' sports or sports stories by female authors were—and continue to be—rare.

The Boys' Life Book of Sports Stories (1965), a representative example of books of sports stories from the 1960s, contains stories from the main source of sports short fiction of the time, *Boys' Life*. These stories continue the tradition of sports fiction of the 1940s and 1950s, featuring wholesome stories about white male athletes overcoming adversity and learning important lessons while competing in school-sponsored sports. In addition to featuring stories on the big three sports, it also had stories about hockey, swimming, boxing, tennis, and other sports. Bill Gutman's *My Father, the Coach: And Other Sports Stories* (1976) suggests that young adult sports short fiction of the 1970s was unaffected by the realism that shaped young adult novels in that decade. Nearly all of Gutman's stories previously appeared in *Boys' Life* and were written in the style reminiscent of previous decades. One story in the collection, "Smitty," stands out as a type of sports story that began to appear shortly after Title IX passed in 1972: a female athlete trying to play on a boys' team.

Winners and Losers: An Anthology of Great Sports Fiction (1968), edited by L. M. Schulman, was distinctly different from most sports short story collections of its time. Schulman points out that "These tales do not belong in the Frank Merriwell category" (vi), and instead of a set of stories by juvenile sports writers whose work most often appeared in *Boys' Life*, this anthology contains twelve short stories written by established adult authors, including Ring Lardner, Jack London, Ernest Hemingway, and William Faulkner, that might appeal to teenage readers. At the time, serious short stories about sports were not being written for teenagers or by young adult authors, so young readers with an interest in literary sports fiction had only adult work to turn to.

Chris Crutcher's set of six stories, *Athletic Shorts* (1989), is a good example of contemporary sports stories that break from the Frank Merriwell/*Boys' Life* tradition. Crutcher's stories deal with complex social issues like racism, homophobia, isolation, and death. Unlike sports stories from earlier in the twentieth century, the stories in *Athletic Shorts* do not focus on an athlete dealing with an athletic challenge. Crutcher's characters are athletes confronting social or emotional challenges; his stories feature some game action, but their main conflicts lie outside the field of play. Gary Soto's *Baseball in April and Other Stories* (1990) is often mentioned as a sports stories collection even though not all of its stories feature a sport. Like Crutcher's short stories, Soto's tales put sport in the background and feature characters who encounter problems not directly related to athletics.

The Random House Book of Sports Stories (1990) is an anthology of quality short fiction. With stories from literary heavyweights like James Thurber, Ernest Hemingway, Ring Lardner, and John Updike and from talented young adult authors like Bruce Brooks, Toni Cade Bambara, and Jay McInerney, this anthology raised the standard for short stories about sports. The stories feature a variety of athletes—male and female, black and white—in a variety of sports, including karate, pool, skiing, horse racing, and hunting. The anthology's introduction makes clear that these stories, though they are certain to appeal to teenagers, are not of the juvenile sports fiction tradition. The book contains stories that feature "games of youth and games of age, games of love and games of hate, games of discovery, and games of disillusion. They are games in which games of every kind play a vital part, but their victories and defeats go far beyond numbers on a scoreboard" (Schulman viii). None of the stories in this collection panders to a reader's desire for mere game action; instead they use sports as a stage for stories about more important issues.

One of the most significant collection of young adult sports stories is Gallo's *Ultimate Sports: Short Stories by Outstanding Writers for Young Adults* (1995). Gallo's book is similar to earlier collections of sports stories in that it contains a variety of stories by a variety of authors, but it is distinguished from most other sports anthologies because its authors are not necessarily known for writing about sports. The book features stories by well-known writers of sports fiction like Crutcher, Robert Lipsyte, Thomas J. Dygard, Carl Deuker, and Chris Lynch alongside stories by noted young adult novelists like Norma Fox Mazer, Graham Salisbury, Virginia Euwer Wolff, and Todd Strasser. In his challenge to the book's authors, Gallo said he wanted stories "that were more about the teenagers involved in sports activities than about the conduct of the sports themselves. I wanted stories about believable teenagers involved in challenging activities that reveal their motivations and show their emotional as well as their physical conflicts as they prepare for and participate in a variety of athletic activities" (vii). He accepted sixteen stories about mainstream sports but also one-of-a-kind stories about boxing, triathlon, outrigger canoeing, racquetball, and scuba diving, and although all the stories contain scenes of sports action, none of the stories bear much resemblance to sports stories of the past. These tales feature young people dealing with contemporary conflicts that would likely surprise and maybe even offend sports authors of an earlier generation. Old-time writers of sports fiction would also be surprised, and perhaps displeased, by the absence of baseball, the most common subject in sports literature, in Gallo's book.

One of the most recent anthologies of sports fiction is Sue Macy's *Girls Got Game* (2001), the first contemporary collection of young adult sports fiction solely about girls. In addition to a handful of sports poetry, the book features stories by a few popular young adult authors, Linnea Due, Virginia Euwer Wolff, and Jacqueline Woodson and six other writers. In her introduction, Macy explains that as a girl in the 1960s, she longed for a girls' magazine that would feature sports stories like *Boys' Life* did. The stories in her book reflect the modern trend of stories "using sports as a natural setting in which to explore a wide array of issues and emotions " (5). The stories in *Girls Got Game* "expand the genre, presenting middle-school girls and young adults who learn about themselves and their place in the world through sports" (5). With its stories about major girls' sports like softball, basketball, and soccer and so-called minor sports like tetherball, synchronized swimming, stickball, and horseback riding, this book helps push stories about female athletes and their sports closer to the mainstream.

It is unlikely that short stories about sports will ever gain the prominence of sports novels, but as the field continues to build a reading audience, collections of sports stories will appear from time to time, and they will reflect the trends and styles of sports novel.

GAME NOVELS

Game novels are sports books whose plots revolve almost entirely around an athlete and his involvement in a sport. These books also rely on the established sports story formula: an athlete (or team) faces a challenge of some sort and must work through a number of obstacles and setbacks to meet the challenge. After a few key contests, and occasionally a loss or two, the athlete winds up in the big game. The outcome of the game remains in doubt until the closing moments of the contest when someone, usually the protagonist, secures victory through a heroic or an extraordinary effort. Though less preachy than their predecessors from the turn of the twentieth century, game novels by authors like Clair Bee, Wilfred McCormick, C. Paul Jackson, Joe Archibald, Curtis K. Bishop, William Heuman, and Matt Christopher feature wholesome boys (for the most part) engaged in conflicts related to their sport of choice, usually baseball, football, or basketball. Other than the traditional moral stances related to sport, these books avoid dealing with social issues or other heavy subplots that would distract from game action. The quality of a game novel is determined by its realistic play-by-play action. In most cases, game action—or at least some reference to sports—must take place on the first page.

A typical game novel of the 1960s is Steve Gelman's *Football Fury* (1962). It is the story of Tim Boswell, a football player in his freshman year at State U. The one-dimensional characters, wooden dialogue, and stilted writing is overshadowed by the football action that faithfully follows the sports story formula: Tim and his teammates practice and play their way toward a dramatic last-second victory in the big game. A decade later, game novels with barely distinguishable plots were still going strong. Archibald's *Phantom Blitz* (1972), is about Randy Stark, linebacker at Ogden State, and his team's efforts to overcome a number of setbacks to win the big game at the end of the season. Riddled with the same weaknesses that flaw *Football Fury*, this story sacrifices quality writing for lots of football action on the practice and playing field.

By the 1970s, however, game novels had begun to change. There were still plenty of poorly written game-action stories around, but some authors were producing better sports novels that had sports scenes complemented by subplots and better characterization. Also in the 1970s, publishers began offering game novels that weren't just for boys or just about the big three sports. A Wimbledon champion turned author, Helen Hull Jacobs, was one of the writers who expanded the range of this category with her game novel about a female tennis player, *The Tennis Machine* (1972). The sports story formula remained the same—thirteen-year-old Vicky Clifton overcomes adversity, including self-doubt, to become the surprising victor in the big Open championship—but the story is written by a woman, about a female athlete in a "minor" sport, tennis. The novel is also considerably richer than earlier game novels, with rounder characters, more background material, and more scenes off the court. Robert McKay's *The Running Back* (1979) also follows the established sports story formula, with plenty of live action that leads to the climatic last-second victory, but, like Jacobs's novel, does so with better character development and at least one subplot.

By the 1980s, most young adult game novels were series books, though a few single titles by authors like Alfred Slote, Dean Hughes, and Matt Christopher continued to be published. These books were characterized by lots of game action, some minor subplots, and faithful adherence to the sports story formula.

In recent years, game novels have changed in some important ways. Though sports fiction in general still tends to feature white male athletes, there are now more young adult sports novels about female athletes and nonwhite athletes than ever before. Another change is that today's game novels are no longer exclusively about the big three sports, and it is relatively easy to find stories about minor sports. Perhaps the biggest change in game novels is their audience. It is nearly impossible to find a game novel written for older young adults; most contemporary game novels, though often labeled young adult, are more accurately classified as middle grade books.

Here are four recent examples of game novels that typify the generalizations just discussed. Bruce Brooks's *Woodsie* (1997), the first book in the Wolfbay Wings series, is the story of a ten-year-old hockey player. One of the few hockey novels in young adult sports fiction, Brooks's fine writing sets it apart from lesser series books, but it still focuses primarily on game action. An eighth grade female tennis player is the main character in C. S. Adler's *Winning* (1999). Though the main characters in the story are white, some nonwhite characters appear in minor roles. Matt Christopher's *Soccer Duel* (2000) is about two junior high soccer players and is one of a handful of recent novels about a sport that has largely been ignored in sports literature. Finally, Brooks's *Throwing Smoke* (2001) embodies all of the changes that have taken place in recent game novels. It is a very smart story of a coed baseball team of middle school students from a variety of ethnic backgrounds. Once again, Brooks's writing skill makes this an exceptional game story, one that even strays from the traditional formula, but its focus on the game of baseball keeps it in the game novel category.

MORE-THAN-A-GAME NOVELS

The demand for sports stories that provided something more than just play-by-play action helped adolescent sports literature evolve to its next level, a category I call more-than-a-game novels. A more-than-a-game novel is sports book whose main concern is an athlete and his involvement in athletics, but it also has much more character development and some subplots that may be only tangential to sport. More-than-a-game novels still feature scenes of athletic competition and often rely on the traditional sport formula plot, but they also deal with realistic social issues that real people, not just athletes, often confront. As mentioned in the previous chapter, John R. Tunis deserves credit for moving young adult sports fiction away from game novels. His sports stories differ from game novels both in content and tone. Subplots break up the scenes of game action, but his realistic attitude toward sport, "which is seldom good and rarely clean in its effect upon those who watch and those who compete" (261–62), led to novels that were much less idealistic than most other juvenile sports stories of his time. He also altered the formula of sports fiction by having his heroes sometimes fail in the big game. Tunis preferred this kind of realism because he believed his young readers would benefit from stories about losing:

> [The reader] learns possibly that to accept defeat is an element in the coming to maturity, that you cannot always or even often have your own way, that the manner in which we face up to defeat and disappointment is a test of growth and part of the development of character. (262)

Not all writers of more-than-a-game novels share Tunis's attitude about the value of defeat, and consequently, many of these books stick to the traditional sports story formula, but authors have followed Tunis's example when it comes to better quality writing and plots with greater depth.

William R. Cox's *Home Court is Where You Find It* (1980), is an example of a late twentieth century more-than-a-game novel. It is the story of sixteen-year-old Willy Crowell, the son of rich and well-known movie stars, who has bounced from one prep school to another. Willy is a phenomenal basketball player whose lack of discipline has gotten him thrown out of a number of schools. At his latest school, he encounters a tough coach, romance, gambling, drugs, and alcohol, in addition to his struggles to help turn his team into winners. The novel has a number of scenes that feature basketball action, but more than half the book deals with issues that relate to Willy and not to basketball.

Dean Hughes is well known for his sports fiction, especially his series books, but some of his single titles are good examples of more-than-a-game novels. In *Team Picture* (1996), David is a talented thirteen-year-old pitcher who has alienated his teammates. He also struggles with his relationship with his foster father, Paul, who has a drinking problem. Because of his youth, David doesn't know how to deal with these personal conflicts, and his relationships on the team and at home deteriorate. After David and Paul both hit rock bottom, David's life on and off the field takes a turn for the better. Hughes's novel contains enough vivid sports action to please readers who enjoy sports stories, but he raises the level of his book by having it focus on the development of David as a human being instead of as an athlete.

Thomas J. Dygard was one of the best and most prolific authors of contemporary more-than-a-game novels. His book, *The Rookie Arrives* (1988), seems, at first glance, to be a game novel. All of the action centers on Ted Bell, an eighteen-year-old rookie with the Kansas City Royals. The novel's characters, action, and conflicts are all related to Ted's involvement with the Royals, and the story has lots of game action, but the book is not a game novel because it is really concerned with the emotional development of its hero. When he first joins the Royals, Ted is loaded with the naivete and confidence of youth, but the actions of his teammates and the team's enigmatic manager quickly fill him with self doubt, and for the first time in his life, Ted questions his ability to play baseball. Of course, Ted is the novel's hero, and he does ultimately perform heroically and help to lead his team to the playoffs, but the novel does not end in the World Series; instead, the story is over when Ted has conquered his doubts and when he realizes his potential and his place on the team. Baseball permeates *The Rookie Arrives*, but Dygard's focus on the development of a young man makes the novel ultimately more satisfying than a story of a young man who, according to the formula, leads his team to victory.

Like the game novels, contemporary more-than-a-game novels now feature male and female athletes in a wide range of sports, and the characters that populate these novels are more ethnically diverse than they have been in the past. With game novels now being relegated to series or middle grade fiction, most more-than-a-game novels fit comfortably in publishers' young adult category.

SPORTLERROMAN

The most sophisticated young adult sports novels are *sportlerroman*, stories that deal with the development of a young person who is an athlete. These books feature protagonists who are athletes, but the plot of the stories may have little to do with sport. Although scenes of game action frequently appear in *sportlerroman*, the stories are more concerned with the coming-of-age of the athlete-protagonist. The *sportlerroman* is a literary cousin to the *künstlerroman*, a novel "in which the protagonist is an artist struggling from childhood to maturity toward an understanding of his or her creative mission" (Harmon and Holman 285).

One of the earliest books of this type is David Guy's *Football Dreams* (1980). It is the story of Dan Keith, a senior offensive lineman at an exclusive private academy. For all of his four-year football career, Dan has had mixed feelings about football. He has some natural ability for the sport, but his heart is rarely in it; he plays because he wants to please his father, who, ironically, tells Dan several times that he doesn't have to play football to please him. Dan endures football anyway, convinced that in order to amount to something in his father's eyes, he must succeed in football. His coaches recognize Dan's misplaced motivation, but they, like Dan's father, are unable to convince him that he's playing football for the wrong reasons. Dan's father dies before Dan completes his high school career and doesn't witness his son's one moment of glory on the gridiron: a key block that allows his team to score the go-ahead touchdown in a crucial game.

Football Dreams has superbly written sports scenes that present football action and players in realistic detail, but the story is not at all about football. It is the story of a football player, Dan Keith, and his struggles to understand himself, his relationship with his father, and his place in the world. Readers who know and like football will enjoy the football flavor of the novel, but readers who care about characters will find this a compelling read because the story is about the coming-of-age of a complex, realistic adolescent. *Sportlerroman* like *Football Dreams* appeal to today's young adults more than most other forms of sports fiction because these books offer more than formula stories about games. In an article examining Will Weaver's excellent *sportlerroman*, *Striking Out* (1993) and *Farm Team* (1995), Ronald Barron describes Weaver's books in a way that places them squarely in this category of young adult sports fiction: "Baseball may serve as Weaver's 'hook' for YA readers, but his focus on family dynamics and Billy's changing relationship with his father is what makes this book a 'special read' for young adults" (9). Although sport may be the hook for many readers, writers of the *sportlerroman* recognize that, for many teenagers, sport is only one part of life, and that the real social and family issues of adolescence are always more important than athletics are.

In addition to its appeal to more sophisticated young adult readers, the *sportlerroman* also attracts serious writers who have experience or interest in sports. Unlike authors of dime novels who used sport as a vehicle for delivering sermons, contemporary writers of the *sportlerroman* use sport to help them develop interesting stories and characters. Chris Lynch, author of a number of first-rate sports novels, describes what sport adds to his books:

> The truth is, you can find almost any parable you want in sports. . . . So when a writer is in need of a handy metaphor, a microcosm of society, a model of right and wrong ways to do things, it's simply hard not to find it in the sports world. And the fact that the contemporary culture insists on making athletes our children's most recognizable icons of success . . . more through advertisements and peripheral endorsements than through game broadcasts, the opportunity for us to exploit the exploitation is tremendous. In short, we, through sports, have got their attention. (25)

Once authors like Lynch have their readers' attention, they can put their characters into complicated real-life conflicts that have little to do with sermons or winning the big game.

A more recent contributor of the *sportlerroman* to young adult literature, John H. Ritter, believes that game novels are boring. Like Lynch, Ritter sees a better use for sport in young adult novels:

> I'm more interested in using baseball scenes as metaphor, or for challenges to character, or to advance the story. I could as easily set the stories in the world of ballet, were I as knowledgeable in that arena. But the thrust would be the same. Kids dealing with hard choices. To me, that's the definition of YA lit. They're stories about that first time in life when one has to stand on one's own two feet, make a life-altering decision, then live with the consequences of that choice. If it happens on the ball field, fine. But usually it doesn't. It's just that events on the ball field may lead up to that moment and help shape the kid so that one day he can take his stand. (Crowe 6)

In a *sportlerroman*, sport is often a catalyst for crucial coming-of-age epiphanies. With the playing field as the stage for a character's self-discovery and growth, sport fades to the background as the more critical concerns of emotional and intellectual maturity take precedence.

Authors of the *sportlerroman* often use sport as a device to develop interesting and realistic characters because sports provide characters with challenges, antagonists, mentors, friends, time for introspection, opportunities for growth, and other plot elements that contribute to more sophisticated fiction. In a *sportlerroman*, it doesn't matter if sport contributes to the conflict or the resolution of the plot; its central location in modern adolescence makes sport a natural component in the contemporary coming-of-age novel.

Chris Crutcher is one of the leading writers of the *sportlerroman* and is known for the memorable and colorful characters who populate his stories. As a young man, Crutcher grew up reading Clair Bee's Chip Hilton novels and longed to be an athletic hero like Chip, but as he got older, he realized that Chip Hilton wasn't really heroic because Chip risked nothing. When Crutcher began to write books of his own, he decided he didn't want any Chip Hilton characters in his stories.

> But as much as Chip Hilton represents something to aspire to, he also represents what we can never be. A truth about humans is that we are a trial and error species, we learn from our mistakes—not just our physical mistakes, but our emotional and spiritual mistakes as well. I think true heroes aren't defined so much by what they do "right" as by how they respond to what they do "wrong." ("From Chip Hilton" 4)

Crutcher's heroes reflect the honest and realistic trend in sports fiction that began with John R. Tunis: sports stories do not have to be about winning. For writers more concerned with story than sports action, it is important that sports stories focus on character and the lessons characters learn from their involvement with athletics and with other people. Crutcher's flawed heroes, much like the protagonists in many *sportlerroman* stories, discover truth in more subtle ways than Frank Merriwell or Chip Hilton ever did.

> I have searched for my heroes among those small "t" truths. I always find them among people learning the art of acceptance—not acceptance of defeat or acceptance of some inability to influence their own futures, but rather acceptance of life on the planet, acceptance of the grays rather than the black-and-whites, acceptance of the astonishing range of human emotion and human behavior. ("From Chip Hilton" 5)

Crutcher insists that his heroes are more than just superior athletes. "I want him or her tested in an arena with less evident boundaries—no half time, no lane ropes, no marked end zone" ("Chris Crutcher" 176). By having his characters face conflicts that transcend sport, Crutcher tests them in the arena of life, the same arena authors of the *sportlerroman* and other serious novels are most interested in.

In the last two decades the *sportlerroman* field has grown substantially and now—with the exception of series books—it is the most dominant form of young adult sports fiction. Crutcher has emerged as the most successful author of the *sportlerroman* even though he doesn't consider his novels as sports fiction. He admits that sport appears in his stories, but he refuses to label himself a writer of sports fiction. Sports play important roles in his novels because he has an interest and background in athletics, but, perhaps more importantly, sport helps him tell a stronger story:

> I love that human beings of any sex, color, sexual preference, size, or religious belief can find a challenge in athletics. I love that the full range of human emotion can be touched within the structure of agreed-upon rules. . . .
>
> Athletics provides a rich background for my fiction because all of the elements of good storytelling exist in a given contest. An exciting athletic encounter snatches me straightaway from the clutches of writer's block, breathes life into dying characters, tests the limits of their will,

and mine. But I will be sad if I'm remembered only as a writer of sports fiction, because I hope that contests in the real world are as evident as those in the arena in my stories. ("Chris Crutcher" 176)

As in every *sportlerroman*, real world contests, not sports, are the focus of Crutcher's young adult novels.

Like Crutcher, many other contemporary young adult authors use sport to enrich their stories. Jan Cheripko's *Imitate the Tiger* (1996), is a *sportlerroman* about a high school football player named Chris Serbo who loves two things: football and partying. Chris has embraced the football player stereotype and lives the cocky hard life he thinks football players are supposed to live. He receives little guidance from home because his mother died when he was a child and his father is an alcoholic. Throughout the novel, Cheripko reveals the symptoms of Chris's own descent into alcoholism, but Chris does not recognize his own illness until his life bottoms out, and he winds up in a rehabilitation center. Critics praised *Imitate the Tiger* for its realistic take on teenage alcoholism and for its insight into the emotional state of a young athlete whose life is spinning out of control.

Even though soccer is one of the fastest growing sports in America, it rarely appears in young adult sports novels. One of the few soccer *sportlerroman* is Rich Wallace's *Shots on Goal* (1997). Set in the same small Pennsylvania town of Sturbridge as his first young adult novel, *Wrestling Sturbridge* (1996), this is the story of Barry Austin, a sophomore on the high school soccer team. As Barry's soccer team begins to turn their season around, his friendship with his teammate Joey deteriorates because they both like the same girl. As the story progresses, Barry learns essential lessons about friendship, love, and life.

Roughnecks (1997) by Thomas Cochran is the best novel about high school football ever written. Of course, as a *sportlerroman*, it is not really about high school football but about a high school football player, an over-achieving center named Travis Cody who plays for the Oil Camp Roughnecks, a AA team in Louisiana. The football scenes—both on the field and in the locker room—are vivid and authentic, but *Roughnecks* rises to *sportlerroman* status because of its portrayal of the mental and emotional state of a high school football player as he prepares for the last and biggest game of his career. By blending flashbacks with the big game day in the life of Travis Cody, Cochran has produced a novel that gives readers a rare balance of game action and satisfying character development.

Michael Cadnum's *Heat* (1998) features another sport that rarely appears in literature: diving. It is the story of sixteen-year-old Bonnie Chamberlain, a gifted diver everyone is sure will qualify for the Olympic trials. Her life falls apart when she hits her head on the diving platform and, for a time, loses the courage necessary to complete the most difficult—and dangerous—dives. Her life is further complicated when it is revealed that her father, a man she has always idolized, is accused of embezzlement. Cadnum shows readers Bonnie's doubts about herself and her father as she struggles to regain her former life and to find a way to understand and forgive her father.

Chris Crutcher loves iconoclasts, and his protagonist in *Whale Talk* (2001), is as iconoclastic as any of his previous characters. T. J. Jones is a multi-racial (African American, Japanese, and white) free thinker who is blessed with the most athletic ability of any student in his high school, but because he hates the mania and hypocrisy of high school sports, he refuses, much to the regret of the football and basketball coaches, to play on any school teams. In his senior year, however, driven by his desire to antagonize the athletic establishment, he organizes a group of rejects and misfits into the school's first swimming team. At the same time, T. J. crosses paths with the town's leading redneck racist, a man who regularly abuses his five-year-old mixed-race stepdaughter, a girl T. J. desperately wants to help. As he does in his other novels, Crutcher blends athletic competition with hard contemporary issues, and the result is growth for Crutcher's characters and a provocative and moving story for his readers.

In recent years, many other fine *sportlerroman* have been published. In addition to all of Chris Crutcher's young adult novels, other terrific novels include Guy's *Football Dreams*, Walter Dean Myers's *Hoops* (1981), Robert Lehrman's *Juggling* (1982), Brooks's *The Moves Make the Man*, Tessa Duder's *In Lane Three, Alex Archer* (1989), David Klass's *Wrestling with Honor* (1989), Jim Naughton's *My Brother Stealing Second* (1989), Marie G. Lee's *Finding My Voice* (1992), Carl Deuker's *Heart of a Champion* (1993), Chris Lynch's *Shadow Boxer* (1993), Will Weaver's *Striking Out*, Klass's *California Blue* (1994), Lynch's *Iceman* (1994), Randy Powell's *Dean Duffy* (1995), Myers's *Slam!* (1996), Berlie Doherty's *The Snake-Stone* (1996), Rich Wallace's *Wrestling Sturbridge* (1996), Edward Bloor's *Tangerine* (1997), Virginia Euwer Wolff's *Bat 6* (1998), Deuker's *Night Hoops* (2000), Adrian Fogelin's *Crossing Jordan* (2000), Lynch's *Gold Dust* (2000), Markus Zusak's *Fighting Ruben Wolfe* (2000), Evelyn Coleman's *Born in Sin*

(2001), A. M. Jenkins's *Damage* (2001), Neil Connelly's *St. Michael's Scales* (2002), and Randy Powell's *Three Clams and an Oyster* (2002).

At the beginning of the twenty-first century, young adult sports fiction appears to be thriving, and even the most popular novels for young readers ever published, J. K. Rowling's Harry Potter books, rely on a sport, Quidditch, for many important scenes. Rowling's novels are the only books ever to feature the sport of Quidditch, a game heretofore unknown to Muggles. Harry Potter, Gryffindor's star "Seeker" at Hogwarts School of Witchcraft and Wizardry, certainly is an athlete, at least by wizards' school standards, so his stories can be justifiably called *sportlerroman*. In all the Harry Potter stories to date, Quidditch games provide various important functions: adding exciting action, revealing conflict among characters, providing opportunities for character development, and revealing Harry's increasing maturity and development. The tension about Quidditch tournaments in the stories, and the lively Quidditch matches are undeniably important in Harry's life, and therefore to the Harry Potter books. Of course, most readers don't consider the Harry Potter novels sports stories, but nearly all readers recognize the critical role of Quidditch in every tale.

For the rest of young adult sports literature, George Plimpton's "Small Ball Theory" of sports literature (the smaller the ball in the sport, the better the literature), does not apply as generally as it does to adult sports literature. Plimpton's belief is that the very best sports books are about golf, with baseball books a close second. Because contemporary young adult sports novels cover many sports—and almost entirely ignore golf—it's not easy to use Plimpton's theory to assess the quality of young adult sports books based on their main sport.

Plimpton's observation about baseball stories, however, does correlate to young adult literature, at least in quantity. In a sample of 65 recent young adult sports novels, the greatest portion, 28 percent, featured baseball. After that, the small ball theory fizzles. The next most common sport, basketball, appeared in 14 percent of the books. Football made up 11 percent, and swimming/diving the next 9 percent. Nine different sports comprised the remaining 48 percent of the sports novels in the sample. In descending order, they were boxing, running/track and field, soccer, tennis, wrestling, gymnastics, ice hockey, softball, and Quidditch.

The strong presence of *sportlerroman* and more-than-a-game novels in the young adult market suggests that publishers will continue to produce a range of sports fiction to meet the demands and interests of teenage readers in the United States. With Americans' participation in and observation of sport reaching all-time highs, it is a safe bet to assume that their interest in sports fiction will remain strong for many years to come.

WORKS CITED

Barron, Ronald. "Will Weaver: A Grand Slam in His First At-bat." *The ALAN Review* 23.2 (Winter 1996): 8–11.
Breen, Karen, et al. "One Hundred Books that Shaped the Century." *School Library Journal* 46.1 (January 2000): 50–58.
Crowe, Chris. "An Interview with John H. Ritter." *The ALAN Review* 27.3 (Spring/Summer 2000): 5–9.
Crutcher, Chris. "Chris Crutcher on Writing Sports Fiction," in Nilsen, Alleen Pace Nilsen and Ken Donelson, *Literature for Today's Young Adults*, 4th ed. New York: HarperCollins, 1993: 176.
———. "From Chip Hilton to Bo Brewster: Some Little Truths about Heroes." *Voices from the Middle* 5.2 (April 1998): 3–6.
Donelson, Ken. "Attitudes Towards Sports: Six Representative Writers of Boys' Novels, 1900–1960." *Arizona English Bulletin* 18 (Apr. 1976): 122–32.
Forman, Jack. "Young Adult Sports Novels: Playing for Real." *Horn Book Magazine* 63.4 (July/August 1987): 500–502.
Gallo, Donald R., ed. *Ultimate Sports*. New York: Delacorte, 1995.
Harmon, William, and C. Hugh Holman. *A Handbook to Literature*, 7th ed. Upper Saddle River, NJ: Prentice Hall, 1996.
Haverstock, Mark. "Score with Sports Fiction." *Children's Writer: Newsletter of Writing and Publishing Trends* 10.4 (November 2000): 1–3.
Hulburt, Tom. "Slam Dunks and Strikeouts: The Status of Sports Fiction." *School Library Journal* 38.7 (July 1992): 30–31.
Lynch, Chris. "The Reluctant Sportswriter." *SIGNAL Journal* (Fall 1996) 21.1: 23–26.
Macy, Sue, ed. *Girls Got Game*. New York: Henry Holt, 2001.
Masin, Herman L. "Novel-ties." *Coach and Athletic Director* 68.3 (October 1998): 10.
Morse, Jean Gaalaas. *An Examination of Sports Fiction for Young Adults on its 100th Anniversary*. [M.A. Thesis] Mankato State University, 1996.
Myers, Walter Dean. "Of Games and Men." *SIGNAL Journal* (Fall 1996) 21.1: 19–22.
Oriard, Michael. *Dreaming of Heroes: American Sports Fiction, 1868–1980*. Chicago: Nelson-Hall, 1982.
———. "On the Current Status of Sports Fiction." *Arete* 1.1 (Fall 1983): 7–20.
———. "Sports History/Sports Literature: Some Future Directions and Challenges," in Wiley Lee Umphlett, ed. *The Achievement of American Sport Lit-*

erature. Rutherford: Farleigh Dickinson University Press, 1991: 184–189.
Owen, Frank, ed. *Teen-Age Sports Stories*. New York: Grosset & Dunlap, 1947.
Plimpton, George. "The Smaller the Ball, the Better the Book: A Game Theory of Literature." *New York Times Book Review*. May 31, 1992: 16, 18.
Schulman, L. M., ed. *Winners and Losers: An Anthology of Great Sports Fiction*. New York: Macmillan, 1968.
———, ed. *The Random House Book of Sports Stories*. New York: Random House, 1990.
Sherrill, Anne. "The Male Athlete in Young Adult Sports Fiction." *Arete* 2.1 (Fall 1984): 111–130.
Tunis, John R. *A Measure of Independence*. New York: Atheneum, 1964.
Vanlandingham, Michael. *Winning is Everything: Myths and Realities in Selected Contemporary Adolescent Novels of Sport*. Diss. University of Tennessee, 1983.

Chapter 4

Young Adult Sports Nonfiction and Poetry

Betty Carter and Richard F. Abrahamson's *Nonfiction for Young Adults: From Delight to Wisdom* (1990) encourages English teachers and librarians to consider including nonfiction books as part of their literature collections. Nonfiction, defined by Carter and Abrahamson as "any book that's not a novel or a short story" (xii), is a huge category of literature, many times larger than fiction. Despite the fact that nonfiction books easily outnumber novels, most literary awards recognize fiction, and best-selling young adult novels are always better known than best-selling nonfiction. This doesn't mean that readers ignore nonfiction; they merely take it for granted because nonfiction can be as common as the daily newspaper or as rare as a thin volume of sparkling poetry. Young adults read newspapers, magazines, and poetry, of course, but they also sample from the wide array of nonfiction books available to them.

Unfortunately, as librarian Ed Sullivan points out, many teachers, librarians, and readers don't view nonfiction as literature. "Because nonfiction is usually regarded in purely utilitarian terms, it does not seem to occur to some educators that a nonfiction work can simply be a 'good read'—something entertaining, fun, enjoyable, or just plain interesting" (43). This misperception leads many teachers to exclude nonfiction, or informational, books from classroom reading. This doesn't mean that teenagers don't read nonfiction on their own, but it does mean that many students, like their teachers, consider nonfiction books to be texts that have no place in English classes or literary discussion. Of course, enough poorly written nonfiction exists to give the entire genre a bad reputation, but Sullivan reminds teachers that "Good nonfiction books are as rich in possibilities for deep, thoughtful discussion as any good novel" (45).

Sullivan's statement also applies to young adult sports nonfiction. Given the popularity of sports in America, it's no surprise that sports books make up a significant portion of today's young adult nonfiction market. Publishers know there is a large audience eager to buy books about athletes, teams, games, and almost anything else related to sports. How large is this audience? The highest percentage of teenagers responding to the 2001 Teen Read Week/SmartGirl.com survey said that sports was the "activity, subject, concept, or item" they were absolutely passionate about. The next highest rated passion for these teenagers? Reading. This one-two punch of teenage interest creates a substantial demand for sports books that meet the needs and interests of these readers.

Of course, plenty of sports schlock is churned out each year. Fan books, products that publishers know will be snapped up by passionate and uncritical fans, clutter bookstore and library shelves and cheapen the reputation of young adult sports nonfiction. These current star athlete or team biographies rely on fan/readers' loyalty, not on literary quality or insight, and usually are the result of a publisher's attempt to exploit sports readers' interests in a player or team. Most fan books have little lasting value. Fortunately, the young adult sports fan books are offset by an equal number of fine works of sports nonfiction that can satisfy discriminating teachers and students.

The sports nonfiction field is constantly growing and changing, and it's difficult to categorize accurately everything being published, but here are some of the most common types of young adult sports nonfiction:

- celebrity "autobiography" (e.g., *For the Love of the Game: My Story* by Michael Jordan). Usually these books are written "as told to" an experienced author. Publishers like to capitalize on an athlete's popularity, so these books often appear immediately after a superstar's banner year. The better autobiographies are usually published some years after the athlete has retired. The distance from celebrity helps to bring objectivity and personal insight into the book.
- celebrity biography (e.g., *Mia Hamm* by John Albert Torres). Nearly all celebrity biographies are published at the height of

an athlete's career, sometimes with the athlete's cooperation, often without it. These books are even more market and event driven than the autobiographies; typically they appear immediately before or after an athlete competes in the Olympics or a major championship.
- biography (e.g., *Althea Gibson* by Tom Biracree). Biographies usually focus on an athlete whose success may have been overlooked, whose accomplishments have recently been re-recognized, or who is an icon for his or her sport. Babe Ruth and Jackie Robinson are popular subjects for baseball biographies.
- collective biography (e.g., *Champions: Stories of Ten Remarkable Athletes* by Bill Littlefield). Because baseball is populated by so many unusual characters, some authors have written books that contain several short biographies about a variety of athletes. Some of these books feature chapter-length biographies while others have shorter, encyclopedia-style entries about famous athletes.
- team biographies (e.g., Jonathan Littman's *The Beautiful Game: Sixteen Girls and the Soccer Season That Changed Everything*). Only a handful of books have been written about high school teams, so most team biographies feature professional or Olympic teams. Some of these books focus on the history of the organization while others concern themselves with the progress of a team during a particular season.
- how-to (e.g., *101 Championship Baseball Drills* by Glenn Cecchini, et al.). The level of how-to books ranges from instructions for beginners to tips for experienced athletes. Many of these books are straightforward instruction manuals and would appeal only to readers with an interest in playing a particular sport.
- encyclopedias (e.g., *Scholastic Encyclopedia of Sports in the United States* by Kevin Osborn). Osborn's encyclopedia is one of the best examples of this sort of sports nonfiction. It presents a chronology of sports in America; its articles are clear and interesting, and the text is sprinkled with historical photos of famous athletes and teams.
- history (e.g., *The Story of Baseball* by Lawrence S. Ritter). Baseball dominates this category because the American sport has long fascinated historians and writers. Sports history books may focus on the evolution of a sport, the origins of a team, or a major sporting event like the 1936 "Nazi" Olympics.

- social issues (e.g., *Steroids: Big Muscles, Big Problems* by Alvin Silverstein). Issues books are the newest entry in young adult sports nonfiction. In addition to examining the use of steroids in sports, these books explore other social issues—e.g., drugs, racism, commercialism, gender, and violence—as they are manifested in amateur and professional athletics.
- trivia (e.g., *Any Number Can Play: The Numbers Athletes Wear* by George Sullivan). Teachers and librarians who have seen kids linger—or fight—over the *Guinness Book of World Records* know that students love facts and trivia. All sports have their own statistics and trivia, but baseball is the trivia-lover's dream. Most teenagers don't read sports trivia or reference books from cover to cover; these books are for browsing.
- poetry (e.g., *American Sports Poems* edited by R. R. Knudson and May Swenson). Once again, baseball dominates this category, but a surprising number of collections of sports poetry exist, ranging from anthologies like Knudson and Swenson's to Paul Janeczko's *That Sweet Diamond: Baseball Poems*, a collection of poems about a single sport.

Young adult sports nonfiction is as diverse as sport itself, and these books provide something for nearly every teenage reader, from the serious fan, to the focused athlete, to the casual observer. The reading level and content of young adult sports nonfiction is just as varied, but many of the books in this category appeal to younger teenagers or even middle graders. Because the quality and reading level of young adult sports nonfiction is so wide-ranging, sophisticated or mature teenagers may find greater satisfaction and more depth in adult sports nonfiction.

YOUNG ADULT SPORTS POETRY

"Base-Ball."
The Ball once struck off,
Away flies the Boy
To the next destin'd Post,
And the Home with Joy.

—from *A Pretty Little Pocket Book*, 1744

"Base-Ball," assumed by sports literature historians to be the first baseball poem, appeared in *A Pretty Little Pocket Book*, published in England by John Newbery in 1744. Newbery is, of course, the British publisher for whom the American Library Association's most prestigious award, the Newbery Medal, is named. The poem documents an early literary reference to a British game called "rounders" which preceded the American pastime, and underscores the debt sports literature owes to juvenile and children's literature. It is also evidence that sports poetry may be one of the earliest forms of sports nonfiction for young readers.

Though "Base-Ball" is historically important, it's not surprising that most modern teenagers haven't read it; the historical significance of this little verse is perhaps its only redeeming value. The most famous American sports poem is one that adults and nearly all junior high and high school students have read or heard. Ernest Lawrence Thayer's "Casey at the Bat" appeared in the *San Francisco Examiner* on June 3, 1888, and went on to become the most memorized, most anthologized poem in all of sports literature. Its staying power continues in the twenty-first century, and for many young readers, "Casey at the Bat" is their first, and perhaps only, encounter with sports poetry.

Of course, other notable sports poems have been published, but none has ever reached the popularity of "Casey." A. E. Housman's "To an Athlete Dying Young" (1896) is also well-known, especially in high school and college literature classes. Maxine Kumin's "400-Meter Freestyle" (1957) and John Updike's "Ex-Basketball Player" (1958) are more contemporary poems that frequently appear in college and high school anthologies. Thanks to the literary contributions of writers like Housman, Kumin, and Updike, and to the popularity of Thayer's home run of a poem, other poets and publishers were willing to turn their attention to verse about sports.

As in other forms of sports literature, baseball is the game that catches the attention of most sports poets, and early in the twentieth century, books like William F. Kirk's *Right off the Bat: Baseball Ballads* (1910) found their way into bookstores and libraries. Even though sports poetry enjoyed some success for several years, it never reached the popularity of other sports literature. Novels, biographies, and other works of nonfiction always overshadowed poetry, and by the 1970s, sports poetry suffered from the same neglect and shrinking audience that poetry in general did. Fortunately, the decline of poetry may have reached its nadir; an increase in the number of poetry collections in the last decade suggests that sports poetry is again finding an audience. The differences between Housman's poem about the boy who "won your town the race," and Thayer's poem about "mighty Casey" suggest the basic differences between adult sports poetry and young adult sports poetry. Good young adult sports poems rely on the same attention to the craft of poetry that adult sports poems do, but young adult poetry tends to be shorter, less abstract, and more obviously connected to sport. Unlike adult sports poems which appeal to grownups who read and appreciate all kinds of poetry, most young adult sports poems will primarily interest adolescents who like sports or sports literature. Serious poetry aficionados may find young adult sports poetry too superficial or simple for their tastes.

Young adult sports poems may appear in a variety of venues: textbooks, teen magazines, Internet websites, and literature anthologies, but the most direct and reliable source is the book of poetry. One of the most notable books is R. R. Knudson and May Swenson's *American Sports Poems* (1995). It contains an impressive number of poems about sports and athletes, and a good number of the works are accessible to teenage readers. Two other noteworthy anthologies of adult sports poetry may also interest teenagers: Noah Blaustein's *Motion: American Sports Poems* (2001) and *The Sporting Life: Poems about Sports and Games* (1998) edited by Emily Buchwald and Ruth Roster. For readers who like sports better than they like poetry, Arnold Adoff, Paul B. Janeczko, and Charles R. Smith have each published collections of sports poetry targeted at middle grade and young adult readers. The undisputed champion of sports poetry for young readers is Lillian Morrison, author or editor of six such books, and, according to Baseball-Almanac, the first writer to publish a book of sports poetry. Her most recent collection is *Way to Go!: Sports Poems* (2001).

Some contemporary books of young adult sports poetry reflect the influence of successful young adult novels. Mel Glenn's *Jump Ball: A Basketball Season in Poems* (1997), Maria Testa's *Becoming Joe DiMaggio* (2002), and Ron Koertge's *Shakespeare Bats Cleanup* (2003) use the novel-in-verse form popularized by Karen Hesse's Newbery Medal–winning *Out of the Dust* (1997) to tell stories that include a sports thread. Glenn, Testa, and Koertge's books offer teen readers a sustained sports narrative in verse and are among the first of their kind. The success of these three stories may determine if poets or their publishers will release more sports novels-in-verse in the future.

Much of the recent young adult sports poetry seems to follow the same general trend of young adult literature, especially series books: a gradual move to younger readers. Indeed, the packaging and format of several of the newest books of young adult sports poetry—wide covers, rich colorful illustrations, thirty-two interior pages—make them look like children's books. But teachers and readers shouldn't be misled by the books' physical appearance. Of course, children can read these books and may even find them interesting, but adolescents will more fully appreciate the literary qualities of sports poetry. In most cases, young adult sports poetry can be enjoyed by readers of all ages.

INFORMATIONAL SPORTS BOOKS FOR YOUNG ADULTS

One of the earliest books of juvenile sports nonfiction was William Clarke's *The Boy's Own Book: A Complete Encyclopedia of All the Diversions, Athletic, Scientific, and Recreative, of Boyhood and Youth* (1828). First published in England and later in the United States, the book enjoyed steady sales on both sides of the Atlantic. According to its publisher, *The Boy's Own Book* was written to fill the needs of boys looking for something to do, and to avoid having boys "purchase publications of an objectionable character, merely because their low price placed them within his reach" (5). If that wasn't enough to convince parents to buy this book for their sons, the publishers promised that "the present Work" would be "much more amusing and instructive to the juvenile mind, than the cheap trash on which the hoarded shilling had been usually expended" (5). The book's publishers must have been convincing: By 1869, *The Boy's Own Book* had sold more than 80,000 copies and gone through more than 20 editions. An updated version was published in the United States as recently as 1996, and it remains in print.

In addition to chapters on pets, "Scientific Recreations," and card tricks, the original book contained information, mostly rules for playing, on an impressive number of nineteenth-century games and sports, including what it called "Minor sports": Games with Marbles,

Games with Tops, Games with Balls (Rackets; Fives; Foot-Ball; Hurling; Golf, or Bandy-Ball; Stool-Ball; Trap, Bat, and Ball; Northern-Spell; Rounders; Feeder; Nine-Holes or Egg-Hat; Catch-Ball). Traditional sports of the day were "Athletic Sports: Cricket; Archery; Gymnastics; Fencing; Riding; Driving." The dense print, archaic language, and forgotten games won't interest many modern teenagers, but for boys living in a century without TV, video games, computers, CDs, Little League baseball, Pop Warner football, or any of our modern diversions, this book must have been a welcome resource for solutions to boredom.

In 1834, Robin Carver's *The Book of Sports* was published in the United States, and it was the first American book to include rules for baseball. Like *The Boy's Own Book*, *The Book of Sports* was basically a guide to various games and sports for boys, and it provided some American competition for the British guide to diversions, amusements, and sports for boys.

Modern informational sports books for teenagers bear little resemblance to these two dinosaurs of young adult sports nonfiction. In today's market, the most common and most popular types of young adult sports informational books are athlete biographies and autobiographies. Dermot McEvoy's recent article in *Publisher's Weekly* reviewed the dominant presence of biographies and "autobiographies" in youth publishing. McEvoy explained that publishers know that athlete biographies sell well. Publishers also believe that the best young adult sports biographies should be instructional and entertaining, and that well-written stories from the lives of sports heroes provide an effective blend of inspiration and entertainment for teen readers.

In discussing her recent work on biographies about Hank Aaron, Lou Gehrig, and Gertrude Ederle, one editor said that she chose their stories "not just because they are about personal struggles against handicaps of illness, racial prejudices, gender prejudices. You have to extend them beyond sports fans. Do a book about Gehrig that focuses on his strength, courage, humility, terrible tragedy and how he rose above it. Hank used his faith to push through racial prejudice. . . . Each of those events is a mammoth human moment, bigger than the sport itself" (McEvoy). The best biographies and autobiographies for teenagers include moments in an athlete's life that transcend sport, while the weakest books are shallow portrayals of athletes as celebrities.

The celebrity biographies and autobiographies typically lack personal insight or introspection; these books exploit an athlete's notoriety, not his or her humanity, and the shelf life of such books rarely extends much beyond the athlete's fifteen minutes of success. Because these books must capitalize on an athlete's most recent accomplishment—for example, winning an Olympic gold medal—they are usually written quickly and rushed to press in order to be in stores before the public has forgotten the newest sports hero. Often, the rush to cash in on a figure skater's instant fame results in a poorly written, superficial biography that only the most passionate fan or the most indiscriminate reader would waste money on.

Though less popular than athlete biographies, sport and team histories have some of the same appeal as biographies because readers who are fans of a star athlete are likely to also be a fan of that player's team or sport. A number of team histories are published each year, and many of these share the same flaws as celebrity biographies. Passionate fans will read books about their teams regardless of the quality of writing or depth of content. Most team histories feature professional teams from the Major League Baseball, the National Football League, the National Basketball Association, and the National Hockey League; some books on prominent college teams, for example, Duke men's basketball or Texas football, also appear from time to time. Nearly all team histories take one of two approaches: a chronology of the team from its earliest beginnings or a more contemporary account of a single, usually championship, season.

High school teams rarely draw enough attention to merit a book, but two notable examples stand out in the field. H. G. Bissinger's *Friday Night Lights: A Town, a Team, and a Dream* (1990) is the account of 1988 season of the Permian High School football team in Odessa, Texas. Unlike some team histories, Bissinger's book is not a catalogue of football players, their statistics, and game highlights. Instead, he focuses on people and the community and how their lives are connected to and influenced by one of the best-known high school football programs in the football-mad state of Texas. Bissinger grew to love the town and the young men on the team, but his affection didn't prevent him from being honest, painfully so at times, about the people, the school, and the society of Odessa. "As I stood in that beautiful stadium on the plains week after week," he writes, "it became obvious that these kids held the town on their shoulders" (xiv). Permian football players and coaches received special privileges and attention in school and in town, but they also had to live with the incredible pressure that came from a community that considered any season without a state championship a failure. This book is not a biased fan's account of his favorite team; Bissinger's portrait of a high school football team shows the best and worst of the sport.

If few books are written about high school teams, even fewer are written about *girls'* high school teams. In part, that's what makes Madeline Blais's *In These Girls, Hope Is a Muscle: The True Story of Hoop Dreams and One Very Special Team* (1995) and Larry Colton's *Counting Coup: The True Story of Basketball and Honor on the Little Big Horn* (2000) so remarkable. High school girls' sports are nearly always overlooked—or ignored—in schools and in print, and the fact that these two books about high school girls' basketball teams received the positive attention they did is a tribute to their authors and their abilities to tell compelling and honest stories about female athletes. Blais's book follows the girls' basketball team at Amherst High School during its 1992–1993 Massachusetts state championship season. Colton's book is an account of the season he spent with the Hardin High School girls' basketball team in Crow, Montana. Both authors' fondness for their subjects is clear, but, like Bissinger, they have not allowed their affection to limit their objectivity in reporting the highs and lows of these athletes. Both books provide realistic glimpses into the lives of girls who play high school basketball and the very different communities in which they live.

Richard B. Lyttle's *The Games They Played: Sports in History* (1982) is not likely to appeal to fans of a particular team or sport, but it will interest teenagers who are curious about the origins of sport. Lyttle's history explains some of the ancient games of China, Greece, Rome, and Mexico, how they were played, and why they were played. In addition to presenting a history of various sports, the book also asks readers to consider the value of modern sports in American society.

More focused than Lyttle's book is Joanne Lannin's *A History of Basketball for Girls and Women: From Bloomers to Big Leagues* (2000), and it will certainly be popular reading among anyone interested in the women's sport. Its approach is typical of most histories of contemporary sport: a chronology from the game's origins to the modern game. This book traces the development of women's basketball from its adaptation from the men's game in 1892 to the rise of the WNBA in 1997. Lannin's text is a well-balanced blend of biography and history that is complemented by photographs and illustrations covering more than a century of the women's game. High school athletes will appreciate the book's attention to high school basketball in addition to college and professional leagues.

Lawrence S. Ritter's *The Story of Baseball*, 3rd edition (1999) uses a different approach to chronicling the history of a sport. The first half of his book uses vignettes about famous players like Ty Cobb, Babe Ruth, Jackie Robinson, and Roberto Clemente to outline the history of professional baseball from 1900 to 1980. The last three chapters of part one review some of the key issues and "magic moments" in the modern sport. The second half of the book discusses technical elements of baseball—batting, pitching, fielding, base running, and coaching strategy—using examples and statistics from some of the greatest players in the game. Ritter's wide-ranging book offers baseball fans a smorgasbord of baseball stuff: history, biography, modern issues, technical information, and trivia.

Another type of informational sports book moves from history and personality to ethical issues. The old cliché, "Sports build character," is still true, but modern sports fans are familiar with the scandals that plague sports at all levels. *The Locker Room Mirror: How Sports Reflect Society* (1993) by Nathan Aaseng offers no analysis of many of the problems in modern sports, but it does catalogue and cite specific examples of a number of problems—drug abuse, violence, cheating, race and gender discrimination, and greed—and raises questions about why these problems exist. Evaleen Hu's two books, *A Level Playing Field: Sports and Race* (1995) and *A Big Ticket: Sports and Commercialism* (1998), focus on specific modern issues in athletics. The other books in the Lerner Publications' *Sports Issues* series are similar in length and treatment. Rather than in-depth analysis, these books provide readers with an introduction and general overview of some of the problems in amateur and professional sports today.

A potpourri of informational sports books remain. Baseball fans and others who love trivia and statistics can browse books like *Baseball Oddities: Bizarre Plays and Other Funny Stuff* (1999), *The Guinness Book of Sports Records* (1992), *The Handy Sports Answer Book* (1998), or *365 Amazing Days in Sports: A Day-to-Day Look at Sports History* (1990). A variety of sports encyclopedias offer a quick reference for teenagers looking for information on a particular sport or athlete. *Scholastic Encyclopedia of Sports in the United States* (1997) is an easy-to-use general guide to sports. For more in-depth—or trivial—information about a particular sport, books like *The Official NBA Encyclopedia* (1989) and *The World Encyclopedia of Soccer* (1993) are available for almost every game. Finally, some informational sports books connect sports to science. *Science and Sports* (1988) explains the principles of physics that apply to various sports and sports equipment. For readers who want to apply these principles, books like *Sports Science Projects: The Physics of Balls in Motion* (1999) and *Science Projects About the Physics of Sports* (2000) suggest activities and experiments readers can perform to examine how scientific principles play out in sporting activities.

Not all sports nonfiction will fit comfortably into English teachers' definition of "literature" because some of the books lack the polish and care that teachers and readers come to expect from literature. Much of sports poetry, however, deserves a place at the table of literature, and many sports biographies also merit literary treatment. The rest of the field may not always have the qualities that classify a book as something worth studying in an English class, but books that provide all sorts of information on all sorts of sports will always appeal to teenagers, whether they're players themselves or merely interested observers.

WORKS CITED

Carter, Betty and Richard F. Abrahamson. *Nonfiction for Young Adults: From Delight to Wisdom.* Phoenix: Oryx Press, 1990.

The Boy's Own Book: A Complete Encyclopedia to All the Diversions, Athletic, Scientific, and Recreative, of Boyhood and Youth. New York: Sheldon & Company, 1869.

Dawson, Keith. "Playing Ball with Books." *Publishers Weekly* (February 16, 1990): 23, 25–26, 28.

McEvoy, Dermot. "In Sports, It's a Real Horse Race." *Publishers Weekly* online. (March 26, 2001). publishersweekly.reviewsnews.com/index. asp?layout=articleArchive&articleid=CA68577&publication= publishersweekly.

Sullivan, Ed. "Some Teens Prefer the Real Thing: The Case for Young Adult Nonfiction." *English Journal* 90.3 (January 2001): 43–47.

"Teen Reading Survey Results." Teen Read Week/SmartGirl.com. (July 16, 2002). www.ala.org/teenread/trw_surveyresults.pdf.

Chapter 5

Sports Literature for Young Women

In the late nineteenth and early twentieth centuries, stories about female athletes were as rare as female athletes. Everyone knew that the sporting world was a man's world, and the literature about sport reflected the male dominance of the time. This dominance, however, wasn't able to extinguish women's presence in sports, and a handful of women, usually college women, participated in sports, and a handful of stories about female athletes made their way into print.

Like men's sports literature, women's sports literature has its roots in juvenile books. In her review of the history of sports literature about or by women, Susan Bandy concludes that "Female novelists of the early 20th century were the first to use sporting themes and to create female protagonists who were athletes. Many of these works have been classified as juvenile or young adult literature" (39). One of the earliest known works of women's sports fiction was Abbe Carter's "Revenge," a short story that appeared in *College Girls* in 1895. According to Joli Sandoz, that story established a pattern for female sports fiction that lasted into the 1920s. "Early fictional women athletes," writes Sandoz, "are far from trivial. They appear as important members of girl's school and women's college communities, most often playing basketball games" ("Strong, Cool, and Brave" 36). Basketball was a new and popular sport for college women in the early 1900s, and writers like Edith Bancroft, Jessie Graham Flower, and Gertrude Morrison produced novels with female protagonists who played basketball. Morrison's series, "The Girls of Central High," was first published by Edward Stratemeyer's syndicate in 1914, establishing an early, but small market for books that featured young women playing sports (38). Michael Oriard's review of these early sports stories for women suggests that they comprised no more than one to two percent of all the juvenile sports novels published in the field's earliest years ("From Jane Allen," 10). Through most of that century, the juvenile sports literature market continued to be dominated by boys' books, but writers like Helen Hull Jacobs and Amelia Elizabeth Walden helped to maintain the presence of girls' sports stories up through the 1970s.

In the early years of young adult sports fiction, books like those in "The Girls of Central High" series were a rarity because most publishers and authors considered boys as the main audience for sports fiction. Many publishers then—and some even now—believed that teenage girls were not interested in reading about female athletes. Despite those attitudes, however, a few sports books for girls did exist, though most of them in the early twentieth century reinforced attitudes about female roles that suggested that athletes shouldn't—or couldn't—be feminine.

In her survey of sports books for young women, Maxine Grace Hunter identifies three eras of young adult sports literature for girls in the last century. She describes the period from 1900 to 1940 as the "Age of Gentility," with female characters playing sports, mostly intramural, for fun and occasional competition. In these books, girls "sped from the game room to the ball room with ease and confidence. Their personal appearance on and off the field, added to their aura of gentility. Their futures were directed toward marriage" (16). Books from Hunter's next era, "The Metaphoric Age," 1941 to 1974, replaced the genteel girl character for whom sports was merely a hobby with female athletes. These protagonists valued athletics and played a wider variety of sports at competitive levels, and in their stories, sport played a more integral role. "Sometimes sports prowess compensated for a lack of social skills, but often the girl's athletic success drew the attention of popular boys, and the girls transformed from mere athletes to stylish girl-athletes. Marriage was still the ultimate goal" (17). Hunter's last category, "The Age of New Realism," 1975 to 1982, shows the influence of feminism and other modern social trends on sports books for teenage girls. Like mainstream YA novels from this period, girls' sports novels dealt more directly with social problems that affected adolescents' lives. Girls in these books were serious athletes who played girls' sports or competed against boys, and "their conduct on or off the field was not modified by the fact that they were female." Plot resolutions were more realistic, and thus had fewer "happily ever after" resolutions. The futures of these female athletes "were far less predictable than their earlier prototypes and marriage seemed only a remote possibility" (17).

Hunter concludes by pointing out that the evolution of the girls' sports novel in the twentieth century paralleled the evolution of female athletes in American society during that time.

> The three categories mirror to some extent the change of attitudes of women toward sport and the attitudes of others toward women in sport. In the first . . ., nice-girls-who-did-something-athletic, the sport aspect was merely that, an aspect of the girl's character. It was considered something she would outgrow as she moved gracefully into womanhood and toward the inevitability of marriage. The second category, the girl-athlete, recognized that the girl may be athletic, but that her performance on and off the field of play was qualified in some way because she was a girl. In the third category, she was first of all an athlete . . . and her being female, like sport in the first category, was merely an aspect of her character. (17)

Hunter's classification of sports books for teenage girls provides a helpful overview of the relatively few such books that were available for young women in the first three-fourths of the last century.

Given that most schools provided few athletic opportunities for young women in the first seventy years of the twentieth century, it's no surprise that the market for girls' sports stories was so small. Until Title IX was passed in 1972, athletic opportunities for high school girls were almost nonexistent; girls might play high school tennis or golf, but few young women were considered, or considered themselves, athletes. Writers often assumed this lack of participation in sports a sign of girls' lack of interest, and, according to Oriard, "girls competed in juvenile novels less seriously than they dated or pursued other interests" ("From Jane Allen" 13). The scarcity of athletic opportunities for girls limited the number of females who had an interest in reading about sports, of course, but it also limited the number of girls who, when they grew up, would be able to write authentically about athletic experiences. Thus, early sports novels tended to reflect the reality of their own era: some girls participated in sports as a hobby or a school club activity, but very few young women played or thought about sports seriously.

In 1972, the adolescent sports world changed when the federal law, Title IX, mandated that schools provide equal athletic opportunities for girls; the change has been dramatic. Girls made up only seven percent of all U.S. high school athletes in 1971, the year before Title IX took effect, but in 2001, more than 2.8 million girls played varsity high school sports, accounting for 41.5 percent of all high school athletes. That's an 847 percent increase in the number of schoolgirl athletes since 1971. Now, in the twenty-first century, girls have established their rightful place in the adolescent sports world. They are no longer oddities; they are athletes. Sandoz emphasizes that contemporary society has accepted women as athletes. "Despite lingering conservative definitions of 'feminine,' everywhere we look—in print, on TV; at gyms, pools, courts, weight rooms, clubs, and playing fields—American girls and women are choosing to be themselves through sport. And loving it" (*Whole Other Ball Game* 16). Sandoz and many others emphasize that these athletes deserve their own stories.

Writing in *School Library Journal* in 1990, Renee Steinberg called for an increase in quality sports books for young women. "Girls who enjoy athletics can no longer be stereotyped as tomboys, and their sports fiction should be more than just the old story of a girl trying to prove herself capable" (62). Unfortunately, and inexplicably, despite the huge increase in girls' participation in sports, there has been no parallel increase in sports literature for young women, and the persistent low profile of female sports fiction remains a mystery to most observers. The logic seems simple. As Mary Jo Kane observes, "Given the number of adolescent girls engaging in sport, it is certainly not a stretch to suggest there is a vast audience hungry for more books in which the protagonist is an athletic female. Sports fiction that develops female protagonists can be enormously appealing to young girls" (235). Unfortunately, these kinds of books were not widely available a generation ago; before 1972, it was nearly impossible for young female athletes to find satisfying sports stories about girls like themselves. Some prominent female athletes have lamented the absence of sports books for girls during their own adolescence, and they've expressed hope for more and better sports books for today's young women.

Nancy Lieberman-Cline: "When I was a girl, I used to scour the library shelves for books about female sports stars. I couldn't find any, and so all my role models were men. I want young girls now to be able to read about someone who broke the 'rules' that say women can't compete in a 'man's world'" (quoted in Goldberg 35).

Jackie Joyner-Kersee: "While growing up, I never had the opportunity to read books about female athletes. Their struggles and accomplishments were hardly common knowledge. Female role models were at a premium" (in Cohen xiii).

Amy Van Dyken: "Hopefully we have shown that women can do whatever men can do—and probably do it better. Growing up, we didn't have as many role models as the boys did. Girls need to understand it's cool to be athletic" (quoted in Smith xvii).

These comments demonstrate the need for stories that provide positive athletic female role models for young women and also the need for validation, some sort of assurance, that it's all right to be female and to be a serious athlete.

Given that Title IX changed the nature of school sports and that female athletes are finally receiving credibility, it's important that sports fiction for women and about women present female athletes in legitimate roles. Sandoz, editor of *A Whole Other Ball Game* (1997), an anthology of fiction, essays, and poetry written by women about women's sporting experiences, stresses just how important good sports fiction for women can be:

> As long as an athlete is without her own authentic story, she remains vulnerable to scenarios written by others. So do those who oppose or belittle her, though in a different way. This individual and collective vulnerability is one consequence of ignoring women's actual experiences in sport, of choosing not to incorporate them into our definitions of 'female.' Lack of engagement with sportswomen's truths, accessible in part through their own expressive writings, simply helps to perpetuate the inequitable, and universally damaging, sports status quo.
>
> When women tell their stories, though, and are heard, by themselves and others, the story line changes. The new generations of female athletes ushered in by Title IX have begun challenging sexist athletics tradition. ("Women as Athletes" B8)

Like Sandoz, Patricia Griffin also believes that realistic sports fiction can help today's athletic girls develop as athletes and as women:

> Good sport stories written from a feminist perspective for young readers can inspire excellence and encourage participation. Strong sports heroes can support choices and raise consciousness. Undoing the internalized limitations young girls impose on their capabilities as they grow up in a sexist society is a necessary part of social change. (3)

For many years, nearly everyone with any interest in sports literature—athletes, authors, librarians, literary critics, teachers, and girls themselves—have expressed the need for more and better sports fiction for young women.

Despite the dramatic changes Title IX created in girls' sports and despite the obvious need for sports stories for young women, the market has remained surprisingly small. In a 1981 review of girls' young adult sports literature, Robert Unsworth found the field lacking: ". . . Title IX, which brought equal opportunity for girls to the playing field, hasn't brought much that is new to the sports novel" (26). A decade later, female athletes continued to be under-represented in young adult sports novels. Teri Rueth-Brandner's review of sports fiction for girls revealed that boys' sports books outnumbered girls' by six to one. A few good sports books for young women had been published, but she concludes that "there is definitely not enough of a good thing in sports fiction for adolescent girls" (89). In the same year, Brooke K. Horvath and Sharon G. Carson reported that sports literature in general had broken into the literary establishment, but "despite this growing critical interest, women's sport literature . . . continues to suffer neglect" (116). Even now, in the twenty-first century, female athletes continue to be neglected in literature, as Robin Bells Markels points out in her article in a 2000 issue of *Aethlon*. Women's sports fiction, she says, "lags significantly behind men's" (143).

So, with sports so much a part of today's popular mainstream culture, what accounts for this surprising dearth of sports books for teenage women?

No one can pinpoint the precise reasons for the shortage of sports fiction for girls, but many people have suggested possible explanations, and the feminist argument may be the most persuasive. The male-dominated sports world, it alleges, has never paid the proper attention to female athletes. Sandoz and Winans say that "sportswomen simply are not, and haven't ever been, among sport's more acceptable stories" (4). Tara VanDerveer, a successful college women's basketball coach, also believes that the media intentionally ignores women's athletics.

> The reason people don't want to have more coverage of women's athletics is because they don't want to see women doing things. The [media] coverage we have now supports an outdated status quo. When you see women who are out there on the playing field being athletic

and aggressive, it's clear that they are not home barefoot and pregnant in the kitchen. (Gottesman)

This argument is not without support. Oriard also recognized that problem: ". . . sport is, in fact, one of the firmest bastions of sexual stereotyping in our society" (*Dreaming* 172), and thus it is logical to conclude that mainstream sports media would reinforce society's dominant attitudes. Bandy adds that it's not just the news media that ignores female athletes. Literature does too. Women's writings about sport, she says, "have been ignored, marginalized, and silenced by the dominant male voice in literature. Anthologies devoted to sport, even those purported to be general and inclusive, continue to exclude women's writings. Anthologies devoted exclusively to women's writings rarely include works on sport" (38–9). This means that despite thirty years' of Title IX equity, girls' sports literature still does not match the prominence of boys' sports literature.

Literary tradition suggests that sexism probably also influences the availability of young adult sports literature for girls. After its genesis in juvenile boys' books, sports literature for adults matured, eventually gaining literary acceptance, but contemporary women's sports literature has yet to reach a level equal to men's. Oriard points out that in the twentieth century, "nearly every major male novelist of the century—from Fitzgerald, Faulkner, and Hemingway to Updike, Mailer, and Malamud—has dealt with sport either briefly or extensively, women writers until recently have been largely silent on the subject" ("From Jane Allen" 15). This silence in adult sports literature, of course, is nearly equal to the lack of contributions of female young adult writers to sports literature.

The relative paucity of female authors of sports literature may also be due to publishers' attitudes, and the feminist argument helps explain why publishers haven't recognized the potential audience for female sports literature. The following statement made in 1944 by Paul Hazard, a French critic of children's literature, typifies the old belief about what girls will and won't read:

> Girls demand books that demonstrate maternal feelings in action. Their sympathy is won by heroines who are kind to the afflicted, charitable to the poor, devoted to the sick; by those who take up bravely the daily tasks of the household so as to provide for the loved ones not only the security of affection, but well-being, material comfort, a happy life. (168)

In 1990, Steinberg suggested that publishing companies still weren't convinced that girls' sports books would sell. "Publishers and authors seem fearful that there is not a sufficient market among girls interested in sports, resulting in the relative scarcity of such selections" (63). By 1996, the situation had not improved: "Publishers are quick to produce titles about contemporary male athletes," says Goldberg, "but female sports stars are all but ignored" (34). If these critics are right, an unfortunate cause-and-effect cycle has put significant limits on young women's sports literature. If publishers don't believe girls' sports books will sell, they won't publish them. Because the availability of sports books for girls is so limited, the market remains small. And because the market is so small, publishers believe there is no demand for these kinds of books. In addition to this self-limiting cycle, the scarcity of sports books for girls also has a chilling effect on potential authors. Because sports literature for young women is so scarce, aspiring young adult writers may conclude that they would have a greater likelihood of success if they write the kinds of books that are already popular in today's market.

Gender, not sexism, may also account for the relatively small market for girls' sports literature. If young women have not accepted the male sports paradigm, if they've not been conditioned to value sports in the same ways males do, perhaps they then have less interest in, or even less need for, books about female athletes. In speculating about the audience for her magazine, *Women's Sports and Fitness*, editor Lucy Danziger offered a different view, one that may give additional reasons for the male dominance in sports literature.

> We don't do sports the way men do.... Most women don't want to be given a grade, a shot, a stat sheet. We just want to be active, healthy, and above all, enjoy ourselves. It's not the labels we give ourselves—jock, athlete, rookie, natural, couch potato—that matter, but the feeling of accomplishment, and how much we have to gain, out there, doing our thing. (316–17)

If girls and women are more interested in personal athletic activity, if they would rather be active participants instead of passive spectators, then maybe for them, reading about athletes is less interesting, less essential than it is for boys and men.

Despite the limitations that have always existed for girls' sports stories, some books have been published, and recent years have seen a slight increase in novels for young female athletes. Perhaps the most significant modern author of YA novels featuring a strong female athlete is R. R. Knudson. Her first such novel, *Zanballer* (1972), featured Zan Hagen, a high school girl who was also an exceptional athlete, a young woman who "takes herself and her sport seriously, who pushes herself to her limits, and who does not feel angst because of her status as an athlete" (Griffin 5). Knudson's novels about Zan Hagen laid the foundation for a new girls' sports story, one that would complement the kinds of young women who would grow up with the athletic advantages and opportunities provided by Title IX. Oriard says that Knudson's stories established the girls' sports novel as an equal to boys' sports novels.

> R. R. Knudson in such novels as *Zanballer* (1972) and *Zanbanger* (1977) brought Betty Friedan's type of feminism to the juvenile sports novel. Knudson offered no *alternative* to the boys' story but appropriated the male myth intact, allowing her heroines the same sort of impossible athletic triumphs fictional boys had been enjoying for decades. ("From Jane Allen" 14)

It would take nearly a decade for other female authors to produce books like Knudson's, books that presented female athletes and their stories with the same seriousness and validity as boys' sports stories.

In her 1988 analysis of ten YA sports novels for girls, Anne Sherrill points out that although the field remained small when compared to boys' sports fiction, it was improving. Part of that improvement was due to two societal changes: the acceptance of girls as serious athletes and the increase in athletic opportunities for young women. "It seems logical," writes Sherrill, "that the audience for books about female athletes has increased" (8). And the books themselves had changed. Knudson, of course, was an important part of the transformation of girls' sports stories, and her influence cleared the way for more books that presented girls' sports realistically and seriously. Sherrill characterized this new type of sports book:

> A young female reader can now experience good action detail, can see protagonists involved in non-traditional female sports, some more violent than those of past eras, and can find female protagonists going through self examination in the larger context of how sport influences life. . . . Images of females in contemporary sport books are changing. Protagonists no longer simply happen to play sports, but develop through their involvement in sports. (10)

These new books, *sportlerroman* for girls, were welcomed by readers who had hungered for realistic stories about young women who were also athletes, and many of the books from Sherrill's study are still in print. Books like these, however, represented only a small portion of YA literature at the time despite all the evidence that predicted a large potential audience for girls' sports stories.

The recent trends in sports novels for young women are surprising. For example, more girls participate in basketball, soccer, and volleyball than in any other school-sponsored sports, but very few novels about girls' team sports exist. Since 1980, novels about young women participating in baseball/softball, track/running, swimming/diving, and tennis have made up more than sixty percent of all girls' sports novels; less than fifteen young adult novels about the big three girls' team sports—basketball, soccer, and volleyball—have been published in the last twenty-five years. Of fourteen girls' sports series published since 1980, only three, "The Pink Parrots," Emily Costello's "Soccer Stars" and Tess Eileen Kindig's "Slam Dunk," focus on girls' team sports. It may not even be appropriate to consider girls' sports series in this count because, like boys' sports series books, most girls' sports series are aimed at middle grade readers rather than young adults. Nevertheless, in young adult sports novels and in sports series books for girls, the great majority of stories feature female athletes participating in individual sports. If female characters in these novels are involved in team sports, they're usually on a baseball/softball team or a boys' team.

So, even though there has been an increase in the number of sports stories for girls, it is clear that the influence of Title IX has been more obvious on the playing field than in the publishing world. The total number of *all* young adult girls' sports novels listed in Appendix A barely exceeds the number of boys' *baseball* novels contained in the same appendix. With the notable exception of Knudson's novels and a few other girls' sports books, girls appear in sports stories as cheerleaders or statisticians or girlfriends of the protagonists, but only rarely as athletes. Some modern young adult sports novels, written by men, present girls as athletes, but they are usually portrayed as athletic freaks, girls intruding into a boy's world. Kane labels these stories "lone girl novels" (236), stories in which a young woman, sometimes a talented athlete and sometimes a boy-crazy girl, breaks with local custom and perhaps even school regulations by playing on a boys' team. Dygard's *Winning Kicker* (1978) and *Forward Pass* (1989), Klass's *A Different Season* (1987), and Jerry Spinelli's *There's a Girl in My Hammerlock* (1991) are good examples of these kinds of books. Usually the young woman in a lone girl story is a serious competitor, but the plot focuses not on the girl's athletic accomplishments or abilities, but on the multiple conflicts caused by having a girl on a boys' team. Because of her athletic interests and abilities, at some point in the lone girl story, the female athlete is isolated from her teammates and peers. This creates another layer of conflict for the novel, but it also reinforces an observation made by Anne Darden that "in women's sports literature, the experience of the outsider, the excluded, is a very common theme" (1). Lone girl novels don't necessarily denigrate women as athletes, but they do trivialize the role of female athletes by suggesting that a girl who is a talented athlete is some sort of social anomaly and that in order for a girl to be taken seriously as an athlete, she must compete on a boys' team.

R. R. Knudson's novels, *Zanballer* (1972), *Zanbanger* (1977), *Zanboomer* (1978), and *Fox Running* (1975) present young women as competent athletes and offered a positive alternative to lone girl stories. Her books also established the *sportlerroman* for young women by proving that there was a market for stories that portrayed girls as serious athletes. Linnea A. Due's *High and Outside* (1980) followed the path established by Knudson. This is more than a game novel or a novel of female high school society, it is the story of Niki Etchen, a high school junior, brilliant student, star softball player—and an alcoholic. The various threads of conflict in the story affect and are affected by Niki's involvement in softball. Another early *sportlerroman* for girls is Rosemary Wells's *When No One Was Looking* (1980), a novel that blends the genres of sport and murder mystery. The heroine, Kathy, is a talented tennis player burdened by her overbearing parents and coach—and by the mysterious death of a rival player. Like *High and Outside*, *When No One Was Looking* effectively blends sports scenes and a serious athletic female character with real life complications.

Though young adult sports novels featuring girls as athletes are anything but plentiful, some good examples of the *sportlerroman* with female protagonists have been published in the last fifteen years, and hopefully more are on their way. New Zealand author Tessa Duder's *In Lane Three, Alex Archer* (1989) is the sort of well-written young adult sports novel that critics have been calling for. It tells of fifteen-year-old Alex's efforts to make the New Zealand Olympic swimming team in time for the 1960 Olympics. Alex is a dedicated elite swimmer, but this novel is about more than just swimming. In addition to the tremendous pressure she's put on herself to make the Olympic team and the intense competition she must face, Alex must also deal with the death of her boyfriend, her grandmother's declining health, and the sort of social flak that young women who excel at something attract from envious peers. The success of *In Lane Three, Alex Archer* led to a sequel, *Alex in Rome* (1991).

Ellen Sung is the fifteen-year-old protagonist in Marie G. Lee's *sportlerroman*, *Finding My Voice* (1992). Growing up, Ellen has assumed that she is accepted as part of the mainstream society in her small Minnesota town. Even though she's the only Korean American in her high school, she has friends, is a good student, and is a member of the gymnastics team, but she's also been oblivious to some of the seamier undercurrents at school. Her eyes are opened, painfully, during her senior year when she encounters romance and racism for the first time. Both experiences cause her to question her own identity and threaten to disrupt her academic focus. Additional pressure comes from her parents who expect her to attend Harvard; they're not prepared to deal with anything that might distract her from what they expect of her. Sports are less central in this story, and, as an athlete, Ellen is not in the same class as Alex Archer, but her involvement in gymnastics is an integral thread in the novel's plot.

Heat (1998), by Michael Cadnum, may be the only *sportlerroman* about a female athlete written by a male, and like other novels of this sort, it provides authentic insight into a sport, diving, and into the life of a serious athlete, sixteen-year-old Bonnie Chamberlin, who is feeling the "heat" from recent surprising twists in her life. After hitting her head on a diving platform, she must choose between a return to diving and a potential reinjury or quitting the sport she loves. Her personal world takes a dive when her father is imprisoned for embezzlement, forcing Bonnie to realize that her father is not the man she has always imagined he is. Bonnie's gradual return to competitive diving neatly parallels her reconsideration of her father and his place in her life.

Virginia Euwer Wolff, winner of the 2001 National Book Award for *True Believer*, is the author of what may be the only *sportlerroman* about softball. *Bat 6* (1998) centers its attention on a traditional softball game between the sixth grade girls of two neighboring communities in Oregon in 1949. Told in first person from the multiple perspectives of the twenty-one girls involved in the game, the novel shows the return to normalcy after World War II and some of the lingering spiritual war wounds inflicted on residents of these two small towns. Much of the commentary deals with what happens between two characters, Aki Mikami, whose family has only recently been released from an internment camp, and Shazam, a disturbed girl whose father died in Pearl Harbor. Though her family suffered greatly because of the forced imprisonment, Aki has reconciled herself with the war and looks forward to resuming her place among her friends. Shazam, however, is still smoldering over her father's death, and she blames all Japanese for killing him. In the much-awaited game, Shazam attacks Aki, and the girls take turns giving their versions of what happened. Wolff uses the softball game as a vehicle for exposing racism and some of the troubles resulting from war and as a device for showing how young women can face difficult situations and resolve them.

Nina Revoyr's remarkable sports novel, *The Necessary Hunger* (1997), has received by far the most literary praise of any sports novel that features high school girls as athletes, and some of that praise may have come because the book was not originally marketed as a young adult novel. The story has some of the most common characteristics of young adult novels: it's about Nancy Takahiro and Raina Webber, a pair of high school seniors, and it is written in the first person, with Nancy as narrator. Typical young adult plot elements, e.g., school events, peer relationships, conflicts with parents, and the sorts of troubles teenagers often get into, occupy a good portion of the plot. And ultimately, like nearly all young adult novels, this book is a coming-of-age story. Some of the novel's content, however, is more of what readers might expect in an adult novel, or at least in a novel for mature teenagers. The narrative structure is also more adult than young adult. Revoyr's narrative stance, Nancy as an adult some years later looking back on the events of her senior year in high school and frequently interjecting her adult perspective, is a stance rarely used in young adult novels. Still, the novel is brilliantly written, and it includes some superb game action along with magnificent insights into adolescent female athletes. Revoyr's book is one of those rare novels that has received praise and found readers among both adults and teenagers.

The Necessary Hunger tells of two talented and fiercely competitive basketball players, Nancy and Raina, and how their lives intertwine in unexpected ways. The girls are Division I bound, star players in their separate Los Angeles high schools, but when Nancy's father falls in love with Raina's mother and the two adults decide to live together, Nancy and Raina's lives are also linked. Though the girls have some things in common, both are outstanding basketball players and both are lesbians, in other ways they are very different. One is Japanese American, the other African American. Nancy is six feet tall; Raina is five inches shorter. Nancy often doubts her own identity and athletic abilities; Raina is supremely confident about everything she does. Throughout much of the novel, Nancy envies and pines for Raina, and although Raina becomes like a sister to Nancy, she seems oblivious to Nancy's inner feelings and angst.

Nancy's angst and reflective personality are part of what make this such a fine novel. She's constantly reconsidering basketball, herself, her family, and her future, and her musings provide interesting reading. One of the best of these passages reveals Nancy's—and Revoyr's—keen understanding of sports. After describing Raina's intensity on the basketball court, Nancy goes on to reconsider a favorite cliché of coaches and sports commentators, and in the language of an intelligent and experienced athlete, she puts a different spin on the old saw, "Sports build character."

> I've always thought it was more accurate to say that they *show* it. You live the way you play. A kid who blows an easy lay-up in the last seconds of a close game is going to choke ten years later on the witness stand. A kid who can kick a field goal to win the state football championship can be trusted to land a plane in a tornado. If there is something to be known about a person, it will become evident on the court, or on the field. People with no experience in competitive sports don't understand how revealing they can be. Or how serious. Anyone who thinks traders on Wall Street are under pressure should try shooting a free throw in a packed gym with the game on the line. (15)

Experienced athletes—teenagers or adults, female or male—will nod with understanding when they read this passage that reveals Nancy's thoughtfulness and clarifies the true nature of the effects of competitive sports. Insights such as this are too rare in sports novels, even in *sportlerroman*.

This novel also contains plenty of beautifully written game action. Sometimes Nancy describes herself in a game, but more often her attention is focused on Raina. Once again, her understanding of basketball and her skill with language are immediately apparent. In one scene, Nancy is watching Raina's team play a tournament game, and after three quarters, her team is playing poorly and seems destined to lose. With less than five minutes remaining in the game, however, Raina's intensity and talent trigger a change in momentum. Nancy provides an excellent play-by-play of the game action and then describes Raina's power:

> To put it simply, she took over the game. After her team's initial comeback surge, things even out again, and the teams traded baskets for a while. But suddenly Raina was at the center of everything. She controlled what was happening. She gathered the game into herself and parceled it out again as she saw fit. (277)

The novel goes on to follow the pattern of most sports novels by building up to the big game. Nancy and Raina's teams both make the state tournament and, to the surprise of both girls, end up playing each other. Nancy provides a marvelous account of the game where she must compete with the girl she envies and loves, the girl who is one of the most talented basketball players in California. Once again, Nancy's understanding of basketball and her ability to articulate her thoughts and feelings create a powerful scene and contribute to the overall effectiveness of this exceptional *sportlerroman*.

Despite the critical acclaim for *The Necessary Hunger*, sports fiction for young women continues to struggle for more attention from publishers and readers while girls' sports nonfiction is firmly established in the young adult market. After acknowledging the changes in girls' sports since Title IX, one editor predicts that the increase in the number of girls who played sports in high school has created a demand for more sports nonfiction for girls. David Hirshey, executive editor at HarperCollins, agrees and anticipates especially strong growth in sports biographies of popular women athletes.

> It's been 29 years since Title IX, and the first generation of girls who grew up playing organized sports their whole lives are now adults. Some of them—Mia Hamm, Venus and Serena Williams, Chamique Holdsclaw—have developed into extraordinary athletes and role models. Unlike many of their male counterparts, they radiate a wholesome, feel-good aura. After years of neglect and dismissal, they have also been embraced by Madison Avenue and the TV networks, the tent poles of any success in sports. (McEvoy)

Both editors are correct. Sports nonfiction for young women has increased in recent years, in part because a few decades ago such books were almost nonexistent and because since Title IX, there have been more prominent women's teams, events, and athletes to write about. The market has grown and is growing, but it remains dwarfed by boys' sports nonfiction. Sports autobiographies and biographies about males listed in Appendix A outnumber females by five to one, and there are three times as many team history books about men's teams as there are women's. The number of titles may be unequal, but the kinds of books for each gender are about the same; nonfiction categories for girls roughly parallels the categories for boys, with biographies and team histories comprising the majority of books for boys and girls. Like boys' sports nonfiction series, most girls' nonfiction series are targeted for middle graders, not young adults.

In addition to biographies, team histories and the other categories it shares with boys' sports nonfiction, sports nonfiction for young women has a category all its own: books about women's sports in general. Because girls' opportunities in sport have come partially as a result of the women's movement, and because women's sports and women athletes are a relatively new phenomenon, a number of books focus on topics unique to girls' sports. Some, like Jane Gottesman's *Game Face: What Does a Female Athlete Look Like?* (2001) and Dickerson and DeVillers's *Break the Tape: Women Athletes Breaking Barriers* (2003) celebrate the place of women in the sports world. Others, like *Winning Ways: A Photohistory of American Women in Sports* (1996), by Sue Macy, Ernestine Miller's *Making Her Mark: Firsts and Milestones in Women's Sports* (2002), and Saari and Gall's *Women's Firsts: Milestones in Women's History* (1998) create a history of women's athletics. These books and others in this category provide readers with a wide range of nonfiction about women's sports in general.

Biographies are the most prominent works of sports nonfiction for girls, and the books fall into two categories: serious biographies and "instant" books about the most current celebrity athlete. The writing and production quality of celebrity athlete biographies are usually as ephemeral as the athlete's fifteen minutes of media limelight. Biographies about established athletes (Althea Gibson, Wilma Rudolph, and Babe Didrickson are the most popular subjects) are generally higher quality, but because famous female athletes are still a relative novelty, sports biographies for girls make up only a small portion of the overall nonfiction market. Russell Freedman's *Babe Didrikson Zaharias: the Making of a Champion* (1999) and Susan E. Cayleff's *Babe Didrikson: The Greatest All-Sport Athlete of All Time* (2000) deserve special attention. Michelle Y. Green's biography of a woman who played in the professional men's Negro Leagues, *A Strong Right Arm: The Story of Mamie 'Peanut' Johnson* (2002), also stands out among young adult sports biographies.

Sports history and team highlights make up the second largest category of young adult sports nonfiction. Unlike the boys' books, girls' sports history and team highlights focus on college or amateur teams, not professional teams. That's because relatively few professional women's teams exist, and most of those are so new that they've yet to develop the sort of fan base that is necessary for a team history. The one exception is 1940s women's professional baseball, popularized by Penny Marshall's movie, *A League of Their Own* (1992). A number of children's, young adult, and adult books have been written about players and teams from that women's league, and one of the best of them all is a young adult edition, *A Whole New Ball Game: The True Story of the All-American Girls Professional Baseball League* (1993) by Sue Macy. In terms of recent team histories published for young women, the most popular women's team is the U.S. women's soccer team that won the 1999 World Cup.

Unlike elite-level women's teams, girls' high school teams rarely merit attention in book form, but there are a few exceptions, most notably Madeline Blais's *In These Girls, Hope Is a Muscle* (1995). Her book is an account of the championship season of a high school basketball team in Amherst, Massachusetts, is one of the few books about a high school team. Most popular women's sports are covered by team histories, but basketball is the most popular subject for girls' nonfiction, and Joanne Lannin's *A History of Basketball for Girls and Women* (2000) is a fascinating and thorough history of the sport. Other good books in this category are available, but the number of girls' sports nonfiction books is still dwarfed by the number of boys' books.

Even though it still has a long way to go to match the overall quantity and acceptance of boys' sports fiction and nonfiction, young adult sports literature for girls enjoys a prominence unimaginable a generation ago. And it's easy to be optimistic about the future. American society is now more willing than ever to accept young women as serious athletes. Publishers are beginning to recognize the demand for books for and about these athletes. And with more girls participating in competitive athletics than ever before, it's certain that an unprecedented number of young women will grow up and write about their sporting experiences. Today's young women have more sports books available to them than at any other time in history, and the next generation of young women may very likely discover that their sports literature is equal in every way to boys' sports literature.

WORKS CITED

Bandy, Susan. "Sport and Literature." *Olympic Review* 15 (June–July 1997): 38–42.

Cohen, Greta L., ed., *Women in Sport: Issues and Controversies*. Newbury Park, CA: Sage, 1993.

Darden, Anne. "Outsiders: Women in Sport and Literature." *Aethlon* 15.1 (Fall 1997): 1–10.

Danziger, Lucy. "Conclusion: A Seismic Shift in the Culture," in *Nike Is a Goddess: The History of Women in Sports*. Lissa Smith, ed. New York: Atlantic Monthly Press, 1998: 315–318.

Goldberg, Martin. "Women in Sports: Recommended Books for Children and Teenagers." *Multicultural Review* 5.3 (September 1996): 34–41.

Gottesman, Jane. "Coverage of Women in Sports: Q&A with Championship Basketball Coach Tara VanDerveer. *Extra!* (Online). November/December 1994. www.fair.org/extra/9411/women-sports.html.

Griffin, Patricia. "R. R. Knudson's Sport Fiction: A Feminist Critque." *Arete* 3.1 (Fall 1985): 3–10.

Hazard, Paul. *Books, Children and Men*. Trans. Marguerite Mitchell. Boston: The Horn Book, 1944.

Horvath, Brooke K., and Sharon G. Carson. "Women's Sports Poetry: Some Observations and Representative Texts." In *The Achievement of American Sports Literature: A Critical Appraisal*, Wiley Lee Umphlett, ed. 116–131. Rutherford: Farleigh Dickinson University Press, 1991.

Hunter, Maxine Grace. "Fair Play: The Girl Athlete in Young Adult Fiction, 1900–1980." *Proceedings of the Meeting of North American Society for Sports History*. 1982: 16–17.

Kane, Mary Jo. "Fictional Denials of Female Empowerment: A Feminist Analysis of Young Adult Sports Fiction." *Sociology of Sport Journal* 15.3 (1998): 231–262.

McEvoy, Dermot. "In Sports, It's a Real Horse Race." *Publishers Weekly* online. (March 26, 2001). publishersweekly.reviewsnews.com/index.asp?layout=articleArchive&articleid=CA68577&publication=publishersweekly.

Markels, Robin Bells. "The Conduct and Culture of Women's Basketball in *The Necessary Hunger*." *Aethlon* 17.2 (Spring 2000): 143–157.

Oriard, Michael. *Dreaming of Heroes: American Sports Fiction, 1868–1980*. Chicago: Nelson-Hall, 1982.

———. "From Jane Allen to *Water Dancer*: A Brief History of the Feminist (?) Sports Novel." *Modern Fiction Studies* 33.1 (Spring 1987): 9–20.

Revoyr, Nina. *The Necessary Hunger*. New York: Simon & Schuster, 1997.

Rueth-Brandner, Teri. "Sports Fiction for Young Women: Not Enough of a Good Thing." *VOYA* (June 1991): 89–90.

Sandoz, Joli. "'Strong, Cool, and Brave': Constructing the Female Athlete in U.S. Women's Sports Fiction through 1977." *Aethlon* 15.1 (Fall 1997): 31–66.

———. "Women as Athletes: Creating a Literature of Vindication." *The Chronicle of Higher Education* 45.37 (May 21, 1999): B7–B8.

———, ed. *A Whole Other Ball Game: Women's Literature on Women's Sport*. New York: Noonday Press, 1997.

Sandoz, Joli, and Joby Winans, eds. *Whatever It Takes: Women on Women's Sport*. New York: Farrar, Straus, and Giroux, 1999.

Sherrill, Anne. "Pandora and Hippolyta: Girls in Sports." *The ALAN Review* 15.3 (Spring 1988): 8–10.

Smith, Lissa, ed. *Nike Is a Goddess: The History of Women in Sports*. New York: Atlantic Monthly Press, 1998.

Steinberg, Renee. "Striking Out Stereotypes: Girls in Sports Fiction." *School Library Journal* (June 1990): 62–63.

Unsworth, Robert E. "First Baseperson? Heroines in YA Sports Fiction." *School Library Journal* 27 (May 1987): 26–27.

Chapter 6

Coaches in Young Adult Sports Fiction

Coaches are significant people in the lives of young adults, and not surprisingly, they are significant characters in young adult sports literature. In an editorial about the importance of coaches in today's society, Dick Crepeau points out that coaches relate to players in a variety of roles, from surrogate parent to feared dictator, but in nearly all coach–athlete relationships, the sporting lives of athletes are completely under their coaches' control (78). Crepeau goes on to say that

> This is why in youth sport the position of coach is such a critical one. Young boys and girls are still feeling their way in life, learning what is and what is not acceptable, caught up in the quest for recognition and love, willing to do anything to please those who have the power to fill the empty spaces in their developing personalities. (78)

Coaches can make or break an athlete, and in young adult fiction that means that coaches can serve as antagonists who complicate the lives of characters or as mentors who help characters navigate the rough tides of adolescence. In real life, coaches are often major characters in a young athlete's life, but in young adult sports novels, the story's focus is on the teenage character, not the adult coach, so coaches tend to be minor characters who fall into one of two categories: the villainous, demented sadist or the nurturing mentor. It's natural that these two types of coach characters appear in young adult sports novels because they reflect society's compatible but often irreconcilable dual view of coaches and their roles.

In the tradition of Frank Merriwell and other sports books from the early twentieth century, sports stories a generation ago portrayed coaches as benevolent mentors, kind-hearted men who loved the game and their players, the kind of men described by William H. Beezley as folk heroes and models for success (26). Because authors of early juvenile sports stories wanted to write positive stories that would instill in teenage readers a love of sports, respect for the nobility of athletics, and, of course, a belief in the American way to success through hard work, luck, and pluck, coaches rarely appeared as villains. The presentation of Coach Earl Molenda in Joe Archibald's *Phantom Blitz* (1972) is typical of the idealistic portrayal of coaches and suggests the staying power of the idea that sports stories had to be positive. During halftime of what would be a disappointing loss,

> Molenda calmly called for the Mustangs' attention. He was a short, chunky man with a disarmingly cherubic countenance and a pair of eyes that seemed to penetrate with the intensity of a laser beam. The players respected him. He was the kind of coach who would let a two-hundred-and-fifty pound guard knock him over in practice to prove a point. (11)

Coach Molenda is the epitome of patience and kindness, and often in the novel he sounds more like a Scoutmaster than a football coach, spinning clichés that embody the American ideal of equality, hard work, and fair play: "'The Explorers aren't supermen,' he reminded [his team]. 'They pull their pants on one leg at a time, the same as you do. Just give it all you've got'" (150). Even Little League players in the twenty-first century would have difficulty believing that this kind of Pollyanna coach still exists.

Ironically, early sports stories with Boy Scout coaches and plot formulas that guaranteed a win in the big game reflected the realistic social expectation, play to win, wrapped in idealistic stories peopled with good-natured coaches and wholesome players. Even today, society expects two things from its amateur sports coaches: to win games and to develop the character of the young people who play those games. Of course, if coaches must choose between the two goals, they know that modern American society values winning over character building every time. Still, at least on the surface, coaches are expected to show success in both areas, and those who fail at one or the other—or both—are not tolerated for long. The pressure on coaches to succeed, even in junior high–level athletics, is tremendous, and in their desperation to succeed and thus to secure their jobs, some coaches become "dementors." Television, newspapers, and sports magazines regularly report examples of these desperate, extremist, maniacal coaches who, in their efforts to produce a winner, commit crimes against their players and/or society. According to Richard D. Keller, this type of negative coach character is commonly found in adult sports literature. His review of the portrayal of coaches in contemporary literature concludes that writers rarely present coaches as "human beings with whom we can emphasize" (148).

These negative coach characters have found their way into the background of many young adult novels. Some, like the nameless football coach in Robert Cormier's *The Chocolate War*, look and act the part.

> The coach looked like an old gangster: broken nose, a scar on his cheek like a stitched shoestring. He needed a shave, his stubble like slivers of ice. He growled and swore and was merciless. But a helluva coach, they said. The coach stared at him now, the dark eyes probing, pondering. Jerry hung in there, trying not to sway, trying not to faint. (9)

This coach is as evil as he looks, giving Jerry false hope that he'll make the team and openly allowing other players, members of the school's secret society, to torment and brutalize Jerry on and off the practice field. It's obvious to Jerry and to the readers that the coach doesn't care at all about Jerry.

There are many more like him. In David Guy's *Football Dreams*, Coach Grupp, whose name suggests his personality, is the stupid and obsessed varsity football coach. Dan Keith, the protagonist/narrator describes him this way:

> He was a short round man, and stood with his arms behind his back, his belly rested before him like a great boulder. He had a bushy mustache, and a large upper lip that he characteristically pushed up and out in contemplation . . . regularly—I had already heard—exploded into violent fits of temper. (81)

For example, at one practice, Coach Grupp becomes angry over a small mistake, and "slammed his clipboard to the ground and shouted so they probably heard him at Hargrove that we were the worst team he ever coached" (16). For reasons known only to Coach

Grupp, he belittles and discourages Dan early in his career, cheats him of a starting position, and eventually drives him to quit the team.

The racist basketball coach in Bruce Brooks's *The Moves Make the Man* is bad in a different way. Black thirteen-year-old Jerome Foxworthy wants to try out for the team but is denied permission by the white coach. Hoping to impress the coach and win a tryout, Jerome throws up a trick shot; it drops in from twenty-five feet out, but the coach is not impressed. Instead, he insults and criticizes Jerome by saying: "Typical jig shot . . . Fancy, one-handed, big jump. Harlem Globetrotter stuff. You like the Globetrotters, boy?" (71). Jerome, knowing he is better than any other boy in the gym, challenges them to a two-on-one game. If he wins, he gets a uniform; if he loses, he gives up. The coach accepts the challenge and selects his two best players to face Jerome, but Jerome's experience still gives him the edge. His talent and determination, however, can't overcome the coach's consistently unfair calls that negate every basket Jerome makes. He leaves the gym defeated, cheated, and without a uniform.

Society is familiar with this type of coach. Few would condone such behavior, even fewer—only the most rabid fanatics—would recommend it for their own children or their schools. In general, society expects coaches to ensure that sports provide opportunities for growth and development for young people. Coaches should, according to Tutko and Bruns, protect an athlete's ". . . right to freedom from physical and emotional punishment . . . by the coach. . . . [because] the purpose of sports should be to help a child grow, feel expansion, and realize his or her potential" (quoted in Higgs 156). Yet society also expects coaches to win, and, because winning is more public and more easily measured, "most coaches go by the Vince Lombardi dictum that 'winning isn't everything—it's the only thing'" (Ogilvie and Tutko 63).

The pressure to win often turns a coach into a "dementor," a Vince Lombardi or Frank Kush in real life, or in young adult fiction, someone like a Coach Lednecky in Chris Crutcher's *Running Loose*. Louie Banks, the protagonist of the novel, describes his football coach:

> And one reason I didn't make it big in football before this year was that I wouldn't cream the little guys in practice. Lednecky always wanted everybody to go all out against everybody, and that meant if you came up against a 95-pounder in the meat grinder, you took his head off. (15)

Hoping to guarantee victory in a crucial game, Lednecky orders his players to injure the black star of an opposing team. The team wins the game but loses Louie, who quits in protest of the coach's unethical actions. Because of Louie's insubordination, Lednecky and the principal suspend him from all sports. Madison, the assistant coach, pleads for him to be allowed to turn out for track, but the coach and principal refuse. Lednecky, citing one of the oldest and most popular justifications for sports, explains:

> "You seem to have missed the point, Coach," he said. "We're not just producing athletes here; we're building young men. Young men we can turn out into the community or send off to college and be proud of. Somewhere along the way we obviously failed in this case, and I don't want it to spread. One person with an attitude like Banks's can destroy a whole team."
> [Louie describes this reasoning as] The Domino Theory of Rotten Apples. (155)

Many coaches, especially the dementors, fail to see the irony in their rationalization of unethical behavior that produces winning teams. The sacred myth that sports builds character (often epitomized by the Duke of Wellington's statement, "The Battle of Waterloo was won on the playing fields of Eton") is attacked by Ogilvie and Tutko. Their study of sports' effect on character found no empirical support for the tradition that sport builds character (61). Nevertheless, coaches like Lednecky still defend sports in general and their coaching methods in particular by using the old argument that participation in sports somehow improves one's character.

Perhaps in days long past, most coaches were fair men who treated athletes with respect and kindness. If the older young adult novels are any indicator, the 1950s and 1960s were a kinder, gentler era for athletes. But times have changed: Donelson and Nilsen point out that the coaching character in the young adult novels of the 1950s and 1960s, the "kindly old Pop Dugout, wily with his sports wisdom and remembered for his warm and genial backpatting" (229), is a thing of the past. Winning is more important today than it used to be: in the name of victory, Little League coaches falsify birth certificates, college football coaches castrate bulls on the practice field, track coaches administer dangerous drugs to their athletes.

Many of the coaches who appear in contemporary young adult novels reflect this ever more negative reality. Not all dementors act ruthlessly in the name of victory. Some victimize young adults because of their lack of ability. What scrawny or obese students have not been picked on by a P.E. coach at some point in their lives? These teacher/coaches wield considerable authority and are often too willing to abuse it and their students. The P.E. coach in the Yorgasons' *Chester, I Love You* humiliates Travis Tilby in front of his classmates because he could not complete the rope climb. Despite the coach's meanness, no one, not even Travis's brother Jason, dares to stand up to him. The title of "Coach" insulates him from criticism, gives him omnipotence over the boys in his charge, a power Jason knows better than to challenge.

> Jason lifted his eyes and stared into the face of Coach, a bull of a man who thought much of himself and who was not actually a coach at all but simply a one-time substitute PE teacher who had somehow taken root and flourished. Still, he liked to be called Coach, and so everyone did it. No one, no one *ever*, argued with Coach. (4)

Similarly, no one argues with a Bobby Knight or a Joe Paterno. Our society reveres coaches, especially successful ones, often granting them *carte blanche* in locker rooms and on playing fields.

Other characters suffer more subtly than Travis did. Coaches do nothing directly to harm them, but their fear of coaches, or of the coaches' activities, drives them to great extremes of avoidance. In our schools, students forge excuses from parents, "forget" their workout clothes, or ditch P.E. class. Characters in young adult novels do many of the same things for many of the same reasons. Marcy Lewis in *The Cat Ate My Gymsuit* spends much of her time dreaming up excuses to avoid dressing out for P.E. Celine, the narrator in Brock Cole's novel, *Celine*, also avoids Miss Summers, her P.E. coach. As Celine explains to the counselor who reminds her that she really ought to be in P.E. class:

> "Yes, but I'm excused. I'm in swimming this semester, and well, you know. . ." I hold my breath and tighten my stomach muscles in an attempt to blow the top of my head off. I hope that this will make me turn bright red. It may not be much of an expression, but it makes Miss Summers, my swimming coach, turn the color of a tomato herself and scribble on her clipboard. (65)

Zan Hagen, the athletic young woman in R. R. Knudson's lone girl story *Zanballer* detests P.E. class for a different reason. The class is taught by Mrs. Butor, "sloppy fat, that gym teacher" (35), who refuses to allow the girls to play basketball or some other competitive sport and instead requires them to dance. Coaches like the fictional Miss Summers and Mrs. Butor, and their counterparts in real life, inspire young adult authors to create dementors who do more to damage and confuse young people than they do to help them "grow, feel expansion, and realize his or her potential" (quoted in Higgs 156). Examples of bad coaches are plentiful, and young adult sports novelists can draw on their own school experiences or skim the sports pages to find negative coaching types to use as characters in their stories.

Even parents turned coaches can become dementors. Willie Weaver, the protagonist in *The Crazy Horse Electric Game*, is crippled in a skiing accident. Willie's ex-jock father can't accept his son's handicap and tries to rehabilitate him by teaching him to play racquetball. It's too much too soon for Willie, and the lesson/game overwhelms him. His father, however, won't let him quit. As Willie's play degenerates, his father hits the ball faster and harder, finally calling him a girl and ending the game in anger and disgust (82–85).

This type of treatment is, unfortunately, not restricted to the pages of adolescent fiction. Robert Lipsyte in *Sports World: An American Dreamland* describes the negative effects of coaches, often parent-coaches, this way:

> A million Little Leaguers stand for hours while a criminally obese 'coach' drills the joy of sports out of their souls, makes them self-conscious and fearful, teaches them technique over movement, emphasizes dedication, sacrifice, and obedience instead of accomplishment and fun. (quoted in Higgs 153)

Coaches like these and like those described in Martin Ralbovsky's *Lords of the Locker Room: The American Way of Coaching and Its Effect on Youth* clearly provide the negative models of coaches used in many young adult novels.

Characters in young adult novels and people in the world outside young adult novels are not blind to the nature of dementor coaches. In *Football Dreams*, Dan describes Coach Grupp this way: ". . . like every high school football coach he had the heart of a twelve-year-old kid, and threw a fit if he lost even the coin toss before the game"

(Guy 163). Michener, in *Sports in America*, substantiates Dan's assessment by characterizing coaches in general: "Coaches," he says, "tend to be simplistic, conservative and dictatorial, and the outstanding ones have these characteristics to a marked degree" (318). Social scientist John Massengale is even more specific:

> Coaches as a group are aggressive and highly organized, seldom paying attention to what others say. They display unusually high psychological endurance, persistence and inflexibility. Coaches appear to dislike change and tend to be very conservative politically, socially and attitudinally. (quoted in Michener 319)

None of this, of course, comes as any surprise to young adult characters and authors or to real world athletes and parents who have had firsthand experiences with the Grupps and Ledneckys, the Lombardis and Kushes.

Writing about the verbal abuse that one season cost several college basketball coaches—including the head coach at Berkeley—their jobs, Ron Fimrite explains the rationalization frequently used by these coach/educators:

> Paradoxically, the tyrant-coach cloaks himself in the robes of the educator. After all, it is *he*, the coach insists, who spends more time in the company of the student-athlete than any professor. And it is *he* who actually prepares his charges for the nasty challenges of the Real World by toughening them to the point where anything less than a bellow sounds sotto voce and anything short of a personal insult seems a kindness. (66)

Coaches, especially the dementors, often excuse their excesses by citing the multiple roles— "salesman, public relations man, counselor and psychologist" (Singer 2)—placed on them by society. Expanding their role from coach to coach/educator gives them more power, power justified by society's expectations of them, power the Ledneckys, Grupps, and other dementor coaches in young adult fiction readily abuse.

Of course, in real life not all coaches are bad. While the tyrannical coaches are hard to forget, the coaches who make a positive difference in a player's life, the true mentors, are, for very different reasons, just as memorable. Young adult literature has its share of athletic mentors, coaches who, at crucial moments in characters' lives, provide support, advice, or wisdom.

Coach Wiggins is the understanding and wise junior varsity coach in *Football Dreams* who serves as Dan Keith's mentor. Wiggins recognizes Dan's latent talent and provides instruction and encouragement to help him earn a varsity position. Later, when Dan confronts Coach Grupp, Wiggins smooths things over to allow Dan to stay on the team. As a foil for Grupp, Wiggins provides a benevolent coaching act for every one of Grupp's bad ones.

Dan's father recognizes his son's admiration for Wiggins and commends it: "No, it's good. One man can mean so much. More than all the rest of your education put together. It doesn't matter if it's on the football field, or where it is. It doesn't even matter if it's at school. He sounds like an authentic man" (Guy 117). As a father, Dr. Keith understands the positive influence a coach, especially a concerned, nurturing coach like Wiggins, can have in the life of his son. Wiggins's influence becomes even more important when Dan's father dies, leaving Wiggins as the only positive adult male role model in Dan's life. At critical points in Dan's life in the latter half of the novel, Wiggins is there to provide support and direction. This is an example of the ideal coach, the kind society hopes will take charge of its sports programs.

Max Il Song, the P.E. teacher and swimming coach in *Stotan!* is a model mentor coach. Says Walker, the narrator in the novel: "He's one of those guys you only know by what they *do*. You have to guess how they *are*" (Crutcher, *Stotan!* 3). Walker's parents are old and relatively uninvolved in his life, but Max fills the void: "I don't think I've suffered much, though," says Walker, "because, even though Max is a little removed, in a lot of ways he's been as good a parent as I could ask for" (*Stotan!* 15). It's right that Max fill Walker's need this way because, as Singer points out, coaches must also be both counselor and psychologist (2). Coaches like Wiggins and Max who provide much more than athletic instruction represent society's best hope for the positive effect coaches can have in the lives of young people.

There are many more of them, most of them minor characters, in young adult fiction. Gary Soto describes one such coach in his short story, "Baseball in April."

> Manuel [Michael and Jesse's coach] was middle-aged, patient, and fatherly. He bent down on his haunches to talk to the kids, spoke softly and listened to what they had to say. He cooed "good" when they made catches, even routine ones. The kids knew he was good to them because most of them didn't have fathers, or had fathers who were so beaten from hard work that they came home and fell asleep in front of the TV set. (23)

Manuel provided a baseball season, and opportunities for growth, for Chicano boys who otherwise would not have had either. Another of the same mold is Mr. Galanter, the softball coach in Potok's *The Chosen*, a benign, passionate coach who shows kindness and concern to Reuven after his accident in the softball game with a rival yeshiva. In *Running Loose*, Lednecky's foil is Coach Madison, the man who provides a voice of reason and stability in a year where Louie quits the football team, loses his girlfriend in a car accident, and offends the entire community at her funeral. "I owe him a lot," says Louie (Crutcher 28). The girls' basketball coach in Crutcher's *Chinese Handcuffs* is understanding, tough, and fair. Says Dillon, the male protagonist:

> The one coach in school I'd put myself on the line for—anytime, no questions asked—is Coach Sherman. . . . In my mind that lady knows what athletics is about better than anyone in the business. Her teams win and lose with grace and dignity, and her players never walk away empty-handed, never walk away without a lesson. (Crutcher, *Chinese* 17)

Coach Sherman's patience and wisdom help Dillon save the life and mind of his girlfriend, Jennifer.

Lisa, the P.E. coach and therapist in *The Crazy Horse Electric Game* helps Willie regain his confidence and proper use of his body after his crippling accident. Using a kind of tough love, she also helps him accept the cause of his accident:

> God didn't cripple you, Willie. *You* did. You stretched the rules till they broke; had to go a little faster than you could, push out there at the edge because you thought nothing would hurt you. . . . The rules don't slack off for naivete. . . . Physics doesn't work on a sliding scale. You broke the rules, you got hurt. (Crutcher, *Crazy Horse* 149)

Coaches in other novels provide a similar kind of mentoring, wise advice that has more to do with becoming an adult than with becoming a better athlete, to the young players they work with. In addition to helping them become better runners, the track coach in A. E. Cannon's *Shadow Brothers* encourages Henry and Marcus to befriend Frank, a new Native American student at the school. The coach also helps Marcus recognize his athletic and human potential. In Jerry Spinelli's *Maniac Magee*, Earl Grayson, an old ex-minor league pitcher, becomes a kind of life coach for Maniac, providing food, shelter, affection, and lessons about life and baseball for the homeless boy. From Grayson, Maniac learns some important things about baseball, but what he learns about life is even more important.

Female coaches, mentors or dementors, are rare in young adult sports stories because in real life, many coaches, even of girls' teams, are men. A recent article by Sara Steindorf reports that thirty years ago most women's collegiate teams were coached by women, but now only 44 percent of the women's teams have female coaches. Of course, female coaches never coach the major revenue sports, football and men's basketball, but they're absent from nearly all other men's sports as well, accounting for less than 2 percent of all coaches for college men's sports. Until the last decade, that trend was reflected in many of the girls' sports stories published for young adults: most of the coaches in those stories were men. Today, however, it is no longer unusual for stories and novels about girls' sports to have female coaches.

With the exception of most lone girl stories, coaches in girls' sports fiction, are more likely to be mentors than dementors. In lone girl stories, coaches occupy the role of the necessary and obvious antagonist, the characters at the center of the gender conflict of trying to prevent a girl from playing a boys' sport. In some lone girl stories, the dementor coaches may share their antagonist role with other characters, usually school administrators, but occasionally peers, male teammates, or parents will also work to thwart a girl's attempts to play on a boys' team. The coaches, though, are typically in the middle of the conflict because they have the final say in determining who will be on their teams. These coaches are nearly always sexist, but they are rarely as cruel or inhumane as the dementors in boys' sports novels.

In the better lone girl stories, the coaches' anti-girl perspectives are eventually softened by the commitment, performance, and tenacity of the female athlete. For example, the football coach in Knudson's *Zanballer* sounds like a typical dementor coach. When Zan approaches Coach O'Hara to see if she and other girls can play a real sport during P.E. instead of remaining in Mrs. Butor's dance class, she's nervous because O'Hara is the stereotypical football coach. "As always, he frightened me: those large teeth, the square jaw, the ruthless brown eyes behind thick, tinted glasses, a kelly-green baseball cap hiding one of the last of the great crew cuts. He didn't mess around" (47). But O'Hara's not as cruel as Zan thinks, and after Zan and her classmates show their determination and skill,

Coach O'Hara goes out of his way to help them organize a football team and to play against a boys' team. Coach Cappelli, the hard-nosed wrestling coach in Spinelli's *There's a Girl in My Hammerlock*, is initially against allowing Maisie to try out for his team, but even though he's tough, he's also fair-minded. He reveals this when he tells Maisie's parents,

> Once she walks into that wrestling room, as far as I'm concerned, she's the same as everybody else. I stress hard work, discipline, and a team concept. When it comes down to final cut day, I won't care if she's a boy, a girl, or a banana. If it can wrestle and keep its grades up, it's on my team. (31)

Maisie endures the criticism of her friends, the animosity of most of the wrestling team, and the brutal wrestling practices and makes the team, proving her commitment and earning Coach Cappelli's grudging respect. Near the end of the season after Maisie is injured by a snowplow while rescuing her sister's friend, Cappelli visits her on behalf of his team. Now that's she's worked with him for most of the season, Cappelli's become a very different character in Maisie's eyes. "In my living room," she says, "he didn't seem like a coach or a teacher" (193). While talking with Maisie about her accident, Cappelli shows that his anti-girl attitude has changed when he tells her, "We're all very proud of you, what you did" (193) and gives her a banner made by his team. To some degree, this kind of transformation occurs in most contemporary lone girl stories.

Why do girls' sports stories have more mentors than dementors? Several possible explanations exist. One may be that because football has not been a traditional sport for girls, the girls' sports culture has not evolved around the archetype of the drill-sergeant football coach patterned after Bear Bryant or Vince Lombardi. If young women aren't exposed to dementor coaches during their own athletic experience, it's unlikely that such characters will appear in the fiction that they write when they're adults.

Gender may also be a reason. Monica A. Frank's study about coaching style, particularly feedback, and its effects on athletes recommends that an athlete's gender ought to be considered by coaches when considering a feedback style. Frank also suggests that dementor-style negative coaching is less effective with adolescent female athletes than with teenage boys. Surely, most coaches of young women discovered this intuitively well before Frank's report, and that would mean that girls' coaches understand that their athletes benefit more from a mentor coaching style than from a dementor style. Writers of sports fiction for young women want their stories to reflect reality, and in all likelihood, the reality for most girls who play sports in school is that their coaches are mentors.

Alex Archer's swimming coach in *In Lane Three , Alex Archer*, is a good example of a mentor. Alex describes her coach, Mr. Jack, as "my teacher, and later coach and friend" (9). He helps Alex develop her Olympic-caliber swimming skills, but he also supports her through the death of her boyfriend and other calamities that befall her in the course of the novel. At the end of Alex's story, Mr. Jack intervenes with officials at the national meet to allow Alex to compete despite rumors swirling through the meet that suggest she will be disqualified. Bonnie Chamberlin's coach in *Heat* is similar to Alex's Mr. Jack. Miss Petrossian is a successful diving coach whose reputation for discipline is legendary, and she provides the kind of structure and support that Bonnie needs in order to recover her form after a diving accident and to stay focused on her sport as her father's life unravels. In both novels, the coaches provide the same sort of mentoring as mentor-coaches do in boys' sports stories.

This is not to suggest that girls' mentors are soft. Like coaches in boys' sports stories, girls' mentor-coaches know how to balance the requisite toughness with the right amount of sincere, personal concern. In Linnea Due's short story "Cream Puff," Jen is at an elite basketball camp and being grilled by Coach Brandt because Jen won't stand up to a bigger girl driving on her. The coach screams at Jen, accusing her of being a wuss, a cream puff, a player who's afraid of her own shadow and saying things to Jen that "make you laugh in real life or get up in someone's face just to show you can" (22). Coach Brandt's harangue troubles Jen and temporarily makes her play even worse. But the coach's toughness also pushes Jen to a point where she examines her own performance and motivation for playing basketball and discovers a way to become the kind of player Coach Brandt expects her to be.

In girls' sports stories, a coach's toughness often temporarily masks her mentor qualities from the athlete. At the beginning of the basketball camp, Jen takes her coach's criticism as a sign that she doesn't like her. Jen eventually realizes that Coach Brandt's style was the best way to help Jen discover her own potential. A similar situation occurs in Sue Macy's story, "Batting after Sophie." Becky is a star softball player struggling to adjust to Coach Janssen, a new coach, a coach who demands that players obey her orders. In a crucial game when Becky ignores Coach Janssen's bunt signal and swings away, the coach comes down hard on Becky, threatening to throw her off the team. Becky assumes that her coach is taking a hard line with her because she dislikes Becky and doesn't appreciate her softball talent. Later Becky realizes that the coach wants her to play in a way that will benefit the team. By the end of the story, Becky admires her new coach and recognizes her as a valuable mentor.

These coach/mentors, these positive forces in the lives of various boys and girls, are both ideal and real. Their presence in young adult sports novels reflects society's hope of what coaches should be. Such positive adult role models are valuable because many young adult novels tend to, as Donelson and Nilsen point out, cast parents and other adults in negative roles (94). For young adult readers, coach/mentor characters provide hope, and perhaps reminders, that worthwhile, trustworthy adults still exist in today's increasingly unstable society.

Neither the mentors nor the dementors play a major role in any of these young adult sports novels, but in the novels as in real life, each of these coaches in some way shapes the lives of the characters they interact with. It's tempting to dismiss coaches in young adult literature as mere stereotypes, but they are more than that. As mentors and dementors, they reflect the very real good and bad coaches that exist in society today, driven by the mixed values society places on coaches and sports.

WORKS CITED

Archibald, Joe. *Phantom Blitz*. Philadelphia: Macrae Smith, 1972.
Beezley, William H. "Coach: Locker Room Folk Hero, Champion of Faith, Family and Football." *Proceedings of the North American Society for Sport History*, 1980: 25–26.
Brooks, Bruce. *The Moves Make the Man*. New York: Harper, 1984.
Cadnum, Michael. *Heat*. New York: Viking, 1998.
Cannon, A. E. *Shadow Brothers*. New York: Dell, 1990.
Cole, Brock. *Celine*. New York: Farrar, Straus and Giroux, 1989.
Cormier, Robert. *The Chocolate War*. New York: Bantam, 1974.

Crepeau, Dick. "Coaching and the Abuse of Authority." *Aethlon* 20.1 (Fall 2002): 77–79.
Crutcher, Chris. *Chinese Handcuffs*. New York: Greenwillow, 1989.
———. *The Crazy Horse Electric Game*. New York: Dell, 1987.
———. *Running Loose*. New York: Dell, 1983.
———. *Stotan!* New York: Greenwillow, 1986.
Danziger, Paula. *The Cat Ate My Gymsuit*. New York: Delacorte, 1974.
Donelson, Kenneth L., and Alleen Pace Nilsen. *Literature for Today's Young Adults*, 3rd ed. Glenview, IL: Scott, Foresman, 1989.
Duder, Tessa. *In Lane Three, Alex Archer*. Boston: Houghton Mifflin, 1989.
Due, Linnea. "Cream Puff." *Girls Got Game: Sports Stories and Poems*, ed. Sue Macy. New York: Henry Holt, 2001: 22–30.
Fimrite, Ron. "Epitaph for Epithets," *Sports Illustrated*. 8 March 1993: 66.
Frank, Monica A. "Feedback, Self-Efficacy, and the Development of Motor Skills." Behavioral Consultants.com (online)www.behavioralconsultants.com/feedback.htm. May 9, 2003.
Guy, David. *Football Dreams*. New York: Signet, 1980.
Higgs, Robert J. *Sports: A Reference Guide*. Westport, CT: Greenwood Press, 1982.
Keller, Richard D. "The Man in Charge: Coaches in Modern Literature." *Arete* 1.2 (Spring 1984): 139–150.
Knudson, R. R. *Zanballer*. New York: Puffin Books, 1972.
Macy, Sue. "Batting after Sophie." *Girls Got Game: Sports Stories and Poems*, ed. Sue Macy. New York: Henry Holt, 2001: 7–21.
Michener, James A. *Sports in America*. New York: Fawcett, 1976.
Ogilvie, Bruce C., and Thomas A. Tutko. "Sport: If You Want to Build Character, Try Something Else," *Psychology Today*. October 1971: 61–63.
Potok, Chaim. *The Chosen*. New York: Simon & Schuster, 1967.
Ralbovsky, Martin. *Lords of the Locker Room: The American Way of Coaching and Its Effect on Youth*. New York: P. H. Hyden, 1974.
Steindorf, Sara. "Women Make the Team, But Less Often Coach It." *The Christian Science Monitor* (online). March 12, 2002. www.csmonitor.com/2002/0312/p13s01-lehl.html.
Singer, Robert N. *Coaching, Athletics, and Psychology*. New York: McGraw, 1972.
Soto, Gary. "Baseball in April," *Baseball in April and Other Stories*. New York: Odyssey, 1990: 16–28.
Spinelli, Jerry. *Maniac Magee*. New York: Scholastic, 1990.
———. *There's a Girl in My Hammerlock*. New York: Simon & Schuster, 1991.
Yorgason, Blaine M., and Brenton G. Yorgason. *Chester, I Love You*. Salt Lake City: Bookcraft, 1983.

Resources on Sports and Sports Literature: An Introduction to the Appendixes

A wealth of information on sports and sports literature is available from a number of sources. The following four appendixes offer additional material for students, teachers, librarians, or anyone else interested in sports or books about sports.

Appendix A is a short bibliography of books about sports literature. Most of the titles on this list are academic, but a few are anthologies of sports literature or autobiographies of famous sports novelists.

Appendix B lists more than 3,000 titles of sports books for young adults. The titles are divided into two main categories, books for boys and books for girls. Within each of those categories, books are subdivided into fiction and nonfiction and then arranged by sport.

Appendix C is my personal list of the best one hundred young adult sports books—fiction and nonfiction—ever written.

Appendix D contains a wide range of websites on sports and sports literature arranged in seven categories: authors' websites; bibliographies, reference sources, and archives; full-text documents on the Web; journals and articles; sports halls of fame; sports news and commentary; and sports organizations. The website addresses were all current at the time of this writing, but internet sites often change, and some of the links I provided may no longer be active. If you encounter a dead link, type in the name of the site in your favorite search engine to be directed to the current home of that webpage.

Appendix A
For Further Reading

Bandy, Susan J., et al., eds. *Crossing Boundaries: An International Anthology of Women's Experiences in Sport.* New York: Human Kinetics, 1999.

Cohen, Greta L., ed. *Women in Sport: Issues and Controversies.* Newbury Park, CA: Sage, 1993.

Dawidoff, Nicholas, ed. *Baseball: A Literary Anthology.* New York: Library of America, 2002.

Emra, Bruce, ed. *Sports in Literature: Experiencing Literature through Poems, Stories, and Nonfiction about Sports.* Chicago, IL: National Textbook Company, 1991.

Gallo, Donald R., ed. *Ultimate Sports.* New York: Delacorte, 1995.

Macy, Sue, ed. *Girls Got Game.* New York: Henry Holt, 2001.

Morris, Timothy. *Making the Team: The Cultural Work of Baseball Fiction.* Champaign, IL: University of Illinois Press, 1997.

Oriard, Michael V. *Dreaming of Heroes: American Sports Fiction, 1868–1980.* Chicago: Nelson-Hall, 1982.

Patten, Gilbert. *Frank Merriwell's Father: An Autobiography of Gilbert Patten ("Burt L. Standish").* Norman: University of Oklahoma Press, 1964.

Plimpton, George, ed. *The Norton Book of Sports.* New York: W. W. Norton, 1992.

Sandoz, Joli, ed. *A Whole Other Ball Game: Women's Literature on Women's Sport.* New York: Noonday Press, 1997.

Sandoz, Joli, and Joby Winans, eds. *Whatever It Takes: Women on Women's Sport.* New York: Farrar, Straus and Giroux, 1999.

Smith, Lissa, ed. *Nike is a Goddess: The History of Women in Sports.* New York: Atlantic Monthly Press, 1998.

Tunis, John R. *A Measure of Independence.* New York: Atheneum, 1964.

Umphlett, Wiley Lee, ed. *The Achievement of American Sports Literature: A Critical Appraisal.* Rutherford: Farleigh Dickinson University Press, 1991.

Appendix B

Thousands of Young Adult Sports Books Classified by Gender, Sport, and Other Categories

BOYS' FICTION

Series

Alden All Stars: *Breaking Loose; Power Play; Duel on the Diamond; Jester in the Backcourt; Last Chance Quarterback; Shot from Midfield*

Armstrong, Rob. *Runnin' with the Big Dawgs; In Your Face!; Got Game?; Stuffin' It; Schoolin'; Trashmaster; Large and in Charge!*

Bee, Clair. Chip Hilton Sports Series: *Touchdown Pass; Championship Ball; Strike Three!; Clutch Hitter; A Pass and a Prayer; Hoop Crazy; Pitchers' Duel; Dugout Jinx; Freshman Quarterback; Backboard Fever; Fence Busters; Ten Seconds to Play!; Fourth Down Showdown; Tournament Crisis; Hardcourt Upset; Pay-off Pitch: No-Hitter; Comeback Cagers*

Bowen, Fred. AllStar SportStory: *T.J.'s Secret Pitch; Off the Rim; Playoff Dreams; The Golden Glove; Full Court Fever; The Final Cut; On the Line; The Kid Coach, Winners Take All*

Brooks, Bruce. The Wolfbay Wings (hockey): *Woodsie; Zip; Cody; Boot; Prince; Shark; Billy; Dooby; Reed; Subtle; Barry*

Brouwer, Sigmund. Lightning on Ice (hockey): *Rebel Glory; All-Star Pride; Thunderbird Spirit; Winter Hawk Star; Blazer Drive; Chief Honor;* Sports Mystery Series: *Cobra Threat* (football); *Hurricane Power* (track); *Scarlet Thunder* (auto racing); *Tiger Heat* (baseball); *Titan Clash* (basketball); Short Cuts Series: *Cliff Dive: Mountain Biking . . . to the Extreme; Off the Wall: Scuba Diving . . . to the Extreme; 'Chute Roll: Sky Diving . . . to the Extreme*

Deegan, Paul J. Dan Murphy Sports Stories: *Important Decision; Dan Moves Up; The Tournaments*

Franklin, Lance, and Tommy Hallowell. Varsity Coach: *Fourth and Goal; Takedown; Out of Bounds; Double Play*

Gorman, S. S. The High Fives: *Soccer Is a Kick; Home Run Stretch; Skiing for the Prize; Daredevil Bladers*

Guest, Jacqueline. *Hat Trick; Free Throw; Lightning Rider; Rookie Season; Triple Threat*

Gutman, Dan. Baseball Card Adventure: *Jackie and Me; Honus and Me; Babe and Me; Shoeless Joe and Me; Mickey and Me*

Herman, Hank. Super Hoops: *Crashing the Boards; In Your Face!; Trash Talk; Monster Jam; One on One; Show Time!; Slam Dunk!; Ball Hog; Hang Time; Foul!; Above the Rim; Who's the Man?; Rebound!*

Howard, Tristan. *Strike Out!; Catch Flies!; Use Their Heads!; Reach Their Goal!; Fast Break!*

Hughes, Dean. Angel Park All-Stars: *Making the Team; Big Base Hit; Winning Streak; What a Catch!; Rookie Star; Pressure Play; Line Drive; Championship Game; Superstar Team; Stroke of Luck; Safe at First; Up to Bat; Play-Off; All Together Now*; Angel Park Football Stars: *Quarterback Hero*; Angel Park Hoop Stars: *Nothing but Net; Point Guard; Go to the Hoop!; On the Line*; Angel Park Karate Stars: *Find the Power!*; Angel Park Soccer Stars: *Kickoff Time; Defense!; Victory Goal; Psyched!; Backup Goalie; Total Soccer; Shake Up; Quick Moves*; Scrappers: *Play Ball!; Home Run Hero; Team Player; Now We're Talking; Bases Loaded; No Easy Out; Take Your Base; No Fear; Grand Slam*

Italia, Bob. Action Sports Library: *Bungee Jumping; Rock Climbing; Hang Gliding*

Korman, Gordon. Slapshots: *The Stars from Mars; All-Mars All-Stars; The Face-Off Phony; Cup Crazy*; NFL/ABC Monday Night Football Club: *Quarterback Exchange: I Was John Elway; Running Back Conversion: I Was Barry Sanders; Super Bowl Switch: I Was Dan Marino; Heavy Artillery: I Was Junior Seau; Ultimate Scoring Machine: I Was Jerry Rice; NFL Rules!: Bloopers, Pranks, Upsets, and Touchdowns*

Marshall, Kirk. Hoops: *Fast Breaks; Longshot Center; Backboard Battle; Tourney Fever; Halfcourt Hero; Pressure Play*

MacGregor, Roy. The Screech Owls: *Mystery at Lake Placid; The Night They Stole the Stanley Cup; The Screech Owls Northern Adventure; Murder at the Hockey Camp; Kidnapped in Sweden; Terror in Florida; The Quebec City Crisis; The Screech Owls' Home Loss; Nightmare in Nagano; Danger in Dinosaur Valley; The Ghost of the Stanley Cup; The West Coast Murders; Sudden Death in New York City; Horror on River Road; Death Down Under; Power Play in Washington; The Secret of the Deep Woods*

Montgomery, Robert. Gary Carter's Iron Mask: *Home Run!; The Show!; Hitting Streak; Grand Slam; Triple Play; MVP*

The Warwick Sports Young Adult Novels Series: *The Mystery of Wagner Whacker; The Youngest Goalie: The Adventures of a Hockey Legend*

Selman, Matty. The Jersey: *No Girly-Girls Allowed; This Rocks!; The Girlfriend; Team Player*

Trembath, Don. The Black Belt Series: *Frog Face and the Three Boys; One Missing Finger; The Bachelors*

Baseball

Bennett, James W. *Plunking Reggie Jackson.* Simon & Schuster, 2001.
Bosworth, Richard. *Box Seat Dream.* Boz Imagineering, 2000.
Brock, Darryl. *If I Never Get Back.* Crown, 1990.
Brooks, Bruce. *Throwing Smoke.* HarperCollins, 2000.
———. *What Hearts.* HarperCollins, 1990.
Brooks, Walter. *Freddy and the Baseball Team from Mars.* Overlook, 1999.
Butcher, Kristin. *Cairo Kelly and the Mann.* Orca, 2002.
Carlson, Ron. *The Speed of Light.* HarperCollins, 2003.
Carter, Alden R. *Bull Catcher.* Scholastic, 1997.
Carter, Ron. *Me & the Geezer.* Harbour, 1996.
Chabon, Michael. *Summerland,* Talk Miramax, 2002.
Cottonwood, Joe. *Babcock.* Scholastic, 1996.
Cochrane, Mick. *Sport.* University of Minnesota Press, 2003.
Coyle, Daniel. *Hardball.* Putnam, 1993.
Crutcher, Chris. *The Crazy Horse Electric Game.* Greenwillow, 1987.
Deuker, Carl. *Heart of a Champion.* Little, Brown, 1993.
———. *Painting the Black.* Houghton Mifflin, 1997.
———. *High Heat.* Houghton Mifflin, 2003.
Dygard, Thomas. *Infield Hit.* Morrow Junior Books, 1995.
———. *The Rookie Arrives.* Morrow, 1988.
Gaetz, Dayle Campbell. *No Problem.* Orca, 2003.
Gantos, Jack. *Joey Pigza Loses Control.* Farrar Straus Giroux, 2000.
Garfield, Henry. *Tartabull's Throw.* Atheneum, 2001.
Grosser, Morton. *The Fabulous Fifty.* Atheneum, 1990.
Hamill, Pete. *Snow in August.* Little, Brown, 1997.
Hite, Sid. *Cecil in Space.* Henry Holt, 1999.
Hughes, Dean. *Hooper Haller.* Deseret, 1981.
———. *Team Picture.* Atheneum, 1996.
Hurwitz, Johanna. *Baseball Fever.* Beech Tree, 1981.
Jenkins, Jerry B. *Rookie.* Wolgemuth & Hyatt, 1991.
Johnson, Scott. *Safe at Second.* Philomel, 1999.
Johnston, Tim. *Never So Green.* Farrar Straus Giroux, 2002.
Kid, Ronald. *Who Is Felix the Great?* Dutton, 1983.
King, Stephen. *The Girl Who Loved Tom Gordon.* Scribner, 1999.
Kinsella, W. P. *Shoeless Joe.* Houghton Mifflin, 1982.
Klass, David. *The Atami Dragons.* Scribner, 1984.
Kluger, Steve. *Last Days of Summer.* Bard, 1998.
Koertge, Ron. *Shakespeare Bats Cleanup.* Candlewick, 2003.
Korman, Gordon. *The Toilet Paper Tigers.* Scholastic, 1995.
Lipsyte, Robert. *Jock and Jill.* Harper & Row, 1982.
Lynch, Chris. *Gold Dust.* HarperCollins, 2000.
Lytle, Robert A. *A Pitch in Time.* EDCO, 2002.

Appendix B

Manes, Stephen. *An Almost Perfect Game*. Scholastic, 1995.
Minor, Roy. *In the Fall*, Sterling House, 1999.
Murphy, Claire Rudolf. *Free Radical*. Houghton Mifflin, 2002.
Myers, Walter Dean. *Me, Mop, and the Moondance Kid*. Delacorte, 1992.
———. *The Journal of Biddy Owens: The Negro Leagues*. Scholastic, 2001.
Naughton, Jim. *My Brother Stealing Second*. Harper & Row, 1989.
Nixon, Joan Lowery. *Playing for Keeps*. Delacorte, 2001.
Norman, Rick. *Fielder's Choice*. August House, 1991.
Park, Barbara. *Skinnybones*. Random House, 1997.
Patneaude, David. *Haunting at Home Plate*, Whitman & Co., 2000.
Peck, Robert Newton. *Extra Innings*. HarperCollins, 2001.
Peers, Judi. *Shark Attack*. Lorimer, 1998.
Powell, Randy. *Dean Duffy*. Farrar Straus Giroux, 1995.
Rallison, Janette. *Playing the Field*. Walker, 2002.
Ritter, John H. *The Boy Who Saved Baseball*, Philomel, 2003.
———. *Choosing Up Sides*. Philomel, 1998.
———. *Over the Wall*. Philomel, 2000.
Romain, Joseph. *The Mystery of the Wagner Whacker*. Warwick, 1997.
Salisbury, Graham. *Under the Blood-Red Sun*. Delacorte, 1994.
Scholz, Jackson. *Fielder from Nowhere*. Beech Tree, 1993.
Slote, Alfred. *Finding Buck McHenry*. HarperCollins, 1991.
———. *Rabbit Ears*, Lippincott, 1982.
Smith, Robert Kimmel. *Bobby Baseball*. Delacorte, 1989.
Walker, Paul Robert. *The Sluggers Club*. Harcourt, Brace, Jovanovich, 1992.
Weaver, Will. *Farm Team*. HarperCollins, 1995.
———. *Hard Ball*. HarperCollins, 1998.
———. *Striking Out*. HarperColins, 1993.
Williams, Karen Lynn. *Baseball and Butterflies*. Lothrop Lee & Shepard, 1990.
Wooldridge, Frosty. *Strike Three! Take Your Base*. Brookfield, 2001.

Basketball

Almon, Russell. *The Kid Can't Miss!* Avon Flare, 1992.
Bates, Cynthia. *Courage on the Line*. Formac, 1999.
Bennett, James. *Blue Star Rapture*. Simon & Schuster, 1998.
———. *The Squared Circle*. Scholastic, 1995.
Brooks, Bruce. *The Moves Make the Man*. HarperCollins, 1984.
Carter, Alden. *Sheila's Dying*. Penguin, 1987.
Christopher, Matt. *The Basket Counts*. Little, Brown, 1991.
Coy, John. *Strong to the Hoop*. Lee & Low, 1999.
Cheripko, Jan. *Rat*. Boyds Mills, 2002.
Deuker, Carl. *Night Hoops*. Houghton Mifflin, 2000.
———. *On the Devil's Court*. Little, Brown, 1988.

Draper, Sharon M. *Tears of a Tiger*. Atheneum, 1994.
Dygard, Thomas J. *The Rebounder*. Morrow, 1994.
———. *Rebound Caper*. Morrow, 1983.
———. *Tournament Upstart*. Morrow, 1984.
Ellison, James W. *Finding Forrester*. Newmarket, 2000.
Farside, Daniel Joseph. *Slow Death. Three Point Land*, 1999.
Gostick, Adrian Robert. *Impressing Jeanette*. Bookcraft, 1997.
Gutman, Dan. *The Million Dollar Shot*. Hyperion, 1998.
Kehret, Peg. *I'm Not Who You Think I Am*. Dutton, 1999.
Kidd, Ronald. *Dunker*. Dutton, 1982.
Klass, David. *Danger Zone*. Scholastic, 1996.
Myers, Walter Dean. *Hoops*. Dell, 1983.
———. *Slam!* Scholastic, 1996.
———. *The Outside Shot*. Laurel Leaf, 1987.
Rapp, Adam. *Missing the Piano*. Viking, 1994.
Ripslinger, Jon. *How I Fell in Love and Learned to Shoot Free Throws*. Simon & Schuster, 2003.
Russon, Marisabina. *House of Sports*. Greenwillow, 2002.
Smith, Charles R., Jr. *Tall Tales: Six Amazing Basketball Dreams*, Dutton, 2000.
Smith, Geof. *Above 95th Street and Other Basketball stories*. Lowell, 2001.
Soto, Gary. *Taking Sides*. Harcourt, Brace, Jovanovich, 1991.
Spinelli, Jerry. *Maniac Magee*. Little, Brown, 1990.
Sweeney, Joyce. *Players*. Winslow Press, 2000.
Telander, Rick. *String Music*, Cricket, 2002.
Wallace, Rich. *Playing without the Ball*. Knopf, 2000.
Weesner, Theodore. *Winning the City*. Summit Books, 1990.

Boxing

Cadnum, Michael. *Redhanded*. Viking, 2000.
Karr, Kathleen. *The Boxer*. Farrar Straus Giroux, 2000.
Leonard, Todd. *Squaring Off*. Viking, 1990.
Lipsyte, Robert. *The Brave*. HarperCollins, 1991.
———. *The Chief*. HarperCollins, 1993.
———. *The Contender*. HarperCollins, 1967.
———. *Warrior Angel*. HarperCollins, 2003.
Lynch, Chris. *Shadow Boxer*. HarperCollins, 1993.
Vance, Steve. *Pound for Pound*. Royal Fireworks Press, 1999.
Zusak, Markus. *Fighting Ruben Wolfe*. Arthur A. Levine, 2001.

Dance

Ure, Jean. *You Win Some, You Lose Some*. Delacorte, 1986.

Football

Bertrand, Diane Gonzales. *Lessons of the Game*. Pinata / Arte Public, 1998.
Blacker, Terrence. *Homebird*. Bradbury, 1993.
Blessing, Richard. *A Passing Season*. Little, Brown, 1982.
Boushell, Mike. *Freshman Flash*. Royal Fireworks, 2002.
Brancato, Robin. *Winning*. Bantam, 1984.
Cheripko, Jan. *Imitate the Tiger*. Boyd Mills, 1996.
Christopher, Matt. *Tackle without a Team*. Little, Brown, 1989.
Cochran, Thomas. *Roughnecks*. Harcourt Brace, 1997.
Crowe, Chris. *Two Roads*. Bookcraft, 1994.
Crutcher, Chris. *Running Loose*. Greenwillow, 1983.
Dygard, Thomas J. *Backfield Package*. Morrow Junior Books, 1992.
———. *Game Plan*. Morrow, 1993.
———. *Halfback Tough*. Morrow, 1986.
———. *Quarterback Walk-on*. Morrow, 1982.
———. *Running Wild*. Morrow, 1996.
———. *Second Stringer*. Morrow, 1998.
Eaton, Edgar E. *Linemen Don't Score Touchdowns*. Deseret, 1987.
Gutman, Bill. *Gridiron Scholar*. Turman, 1990.
Guy, David. *Football Dreams*. Seaview, 1980.
Hallowell, Tommy. *Varsity Coach: Fourth and Goal*. Bantam, 1986.
Jenkins, A. M. *Damage*. HarperCollins, 2001.
Johnson, Annabel, and Edgar Johnson. *Gamebuster*. Cobblehill, 1990.
Korman, Gordon. *No More Dead Dogs*. Hyperion, 2000.
Lee, Marie G. *Necessary Roughness*. HarperCollins, 1996.
Lipsyte, Robert. *The Chemo Kid*. HarperCollins, 1992.
MacGregor, Rob. *Hawk Moon*. Simon & Schuster, 1996.
Mackel, Kathy. *Eggs in One Basket*, HarperCollins, 2000.
Marek, Margot. *Matt's Crusade*. Four Winds, 1988.
Miklowitz, Gloria. *Anything to Win*. Delacorte, 1989.
Powell, Randy. *My Underrated Year*. 1991.
———. *Three Clams and an Oyster*, Farrar Straus Giroux, 2002.
Rushford, Patricia H. *Dying to Win*. Bethany, 1995.
Scholz, Jackson. *Rookie Quarterback*. Morrow, 1993.
———. *The Football Rebels*. Morrow, 1993.
Sommers, Beverly. *What Do Girls Want?* Fawcett Juniper, 1992.
Wallace, Rich. *Restless: A Ghost's Story*. Viking, 2003.
Wright, Randy. *The Interception*. Claycomb Press, 1991.
Wunderli, Steven. *The Heartbeat of Halftime*. Holt, 1996.

Golf

Coyne, Tom. *A Gentleman's Game: A Novel*. Atlantic Monthly, 2001.
Hollingsworth, Alan B. *Flatbellies: It's Not about Golf, It's about Life*. Sleeping Bear Press, 2001.

Shrake, Edwin, and Bud Shrake. *Billy Boy: A Novel.* Simon & Schuster, 2001.

Hockey

Book, Rick. *Necking with Louise: Stories.* Harper, 1999.
Bossley, Michele Martin. *Danger Zone.* Lorimer, 2003.
DeClements, Barthe. *Tough Loser.* Viking, 1994.
Drumtra, Stacy. *Face-Off.* Avon Flare, 1992.
Foon, Dennis. *Skud.* Groundwood, 2003.
Godfrey, Martin. *Please Remove Your Elbow from My Ear.* Avon Flare, 1993.
Gostick, Adrian. *Eddy and the Habs.* Deseret, 1994.
Guest, Jacqueline. *A Goal in Sight.* Lorimer, 2003.
Korman, Gordon. *The Chicken Doesn't Skate.* Scholastic, 1998.
Lynch, Chris. *Iceman.* HarperCollins, 1994.
MacIntyre, R. P. *Yuletide Blues.* Thistledown, 1991.
McFarlane, Brian. *The Youngest Goalie: The Adventures of a Hockey Legend.* Warwick, 1997.
Riddell, Ruth. *Ice Warrior.* Atheneum, 1992.
Rivers, Camilla Reghelini. *Red-Line Blues.* Lorimer, 2002.
Romain, Joseph. *Two Minutes for Roughing.* Formac, 1995.
Vandervelde, Beatrice. *Ice Attack.* Lorimer, 2002.
Wieler, Diana. *Bad Boy.* Delacorte, 1992.

Skiing

MacLean, John. *When the Mountain Sings.* Houghton Mifflin, 1992.

Soccer

Avi. *S. O. R. Losers.* Bradbury, 1984.
Bloor, Edward. *Tangerine.* Scholastic Inc., 1997.
Chapin, Kim. *The Road to Wembley.* Farrar Straus Giroux, 1994.
Cottonwood, Joe. *The Adventures of Boone Barnaby.* Scholastic, 1990.
Dygard, Thomas J. *The Soccer Duel.* Morrow, 1981.
Gutman, Dan. *The Million Dollar Kick.* Hyperion, 2001.
Jarzyna, Dave. *Slump.* Delacorte, 1999.
Ketchum, Liza. *Blue Coyote.* Simon & Schuster, 1997.
Klass, David. *Breakaway Run.* Dutton, 1987.
———. *Home of the Braves.* Farrar, Straus, and Giroux, 2002.
Kordon, Klaus. *Brothers Like Friends.* Trans. Elizabeth D. Crawford. Philomel, 1992.
Lehrman, Robert. *Juggling.* Harper, 1982.
McGinley, Jerry. *Joaquin Strikes Back.* Tudor, 1998.

Murrow, Liza Ketchum. *Twelve Days in August*. Holiday House, 1993.
Quies, Werner. *Soccer Shots*. Frontier, 1995.
Wallace, Rich. *Shots on Goal*. Knopf, 1997.
Yee, Paul. *Breakaway*. Groundwood, 2000.

Swimming/Diving

Behrens, Michael A. *At the Edge*. Avon / Flare, 1988.
Bowler, Tim. *River Boy*. Simon & Schuster, 2000.
Crutcher, Chris. *Staying Fat for Sarah Byrnes*. Greenwillow, 1993.
———. *Stotan!* Greenwillow, 1986.
———. *Whale Talk*. Greenwillow, 2001.
Deford, Frank. *An American Summer*. Sourcebooks, 2002.
Doherty, Berlie. *The Snake Stone*. Orchard, 1996.
Gelb, Alan. *Real Life: My Best Friend Died*. Archway, 1994.
MacLean, John. *When the Mountain Sings*. Houghton Mifflin, 1992.
Maloney, Ray. *Impact Zone*. Delacorte, 1986.
Marino, Jan. *Like Some Kind of Hero*. Little, Brown, 1992.
Shannon, George. *Unlived Affections*. Harper & Row, 1989.
Singleton, Linda Joy. *Almost Perfect*. Bantam, 1992.
West, Callie. *My First Love*. Bantam, 1995.
Winton, Tim. *Lockie Leonard: Human Torpedo*. Pan Macmillan, 1995.

Tennis

Batten, Jack. *Tie-Breaker*. Irwin, 1984.
Corbet, Robert. *Fifteen Love*. Walker, 2003.
Kelgard, Todd. *Outside In*. Royal Fireworks Press, 2001.
Powell, Randy. *My Underrated Year*. Farrar, Straus and Giroux, 1988.
Weaver, Will. *Claws*. HarperCollins, 2003.

Track/Running/Triathlon

Cannon, A. E. *Shadow Brothers*. Delacorte, 1990.
Carter, Peter. *Bury the Dead*. Farrar, Straus and Giroux, 1987.
Crutcher, Chris. *Chinese Handcuffs*. Greenwillow, 1989.
———. *Ironman*. Greenwillow, 1995.
Deans, Sis Boulos. *Racing the Past*. Holt, 2001.
Hill, David. *Time Out*. Cricket Books, 2001.
Hoffius, Stephen. *Winners and Losers*. Simon & Schuster, 1993.
Hughes, Dean. *End of the Race*. Atheneum, 1993.
Jackson, Jeremy. *Life at These Speeds*. Thomas Dunne, 2002.
Klass, David. *California Blue*. Scholastic, 1994.

Knudson, R. R. *Frankenstein's 10 K.* Viking, 1986.
———. *Speed.* Dutton, 1983.
MacKellar, William. *Terror Run.* Dodd, Mead, 1982.
Neumann, Peter J. *Playing a Virginia Moon.* Houghton Mifflin, 1994.
Platt, Kin. *Brogg's Brain.* Lippincott, 1981.
Schwandt, Stephen. *The Last Goodie.* Free Spirit, 1995.
Voigt, Cynthia. *The Runner.* Mass Market, 1985.
Wallace, Rich. *Losing Is Not an Option.* Knopf, 2003.
———. *Restless: A Ghost's Story.* Viking, 2003.

Wrestling

Benjamin, E. M. J. *Takedown.* Banks Channel Books, 1999.
Connelly, Neil. *St. Michael's Scales.* Arthur A. Levine/Scholastic, 2002.
Davis, Terry. *Vision Quest.* Viking, 1979.
Gutman, Dan. *The Secret Life of Dr. Demented.* Simon and Schuster, 2001.
Hayes, Daniel. *No Effect.* David R. Godine, 1993.
Killien, Christi. *Rusty Fertlanger, Lady's Man.* Houghton Mifflin, 1988.
Klass, David. *Wrestling with Honor.* Lodestar/Dutton, 1988.
Wallace, Rich. *Wrestling Sturbridge.* Knopf, 1996.

Other

Brown, Susan M. *You're Dead, David Borelli.* Atheneum/Simon & Schuster, 1995.
Bruchac, Joseph. *The Warriors.* Darby Creek, 2003.
Choyce, Lesley. *Skateboard Shakedown.* Formac, 1989.
———. *Wave Watch.* Formac, 1990.
Christopher, Matt. *Mountain Bike Mania.* Little, Brown, 1998.
———. *Olympic Dream.* Little, Brown, 1996.
Davis, Terry. *If Rock and Roll Were a Machine.* Delacorte, 1992.
Godfrey, Martyn. *Can You Teach Me to Pick My Nose?* Avon Flare, 1990.
Halvorson, Marilyn. *Bull Rider.* Orca, 2003.
Henry, Sue. *Murder on the Iditarod Trail.* Atlantic Monthly Press, 1991.
Hyde, Dayton O. *The Major, The Poacher, and the One-Trout River.* Boyds Mills, 1997.
Kent, Richard. *The Mosquito Test.* Windswept House, 1994.
Lynch, Chris. *Slot Machine.* HarperCollins, 1995.
Meredith, Don. *Dog Runner.* Western Producer Prairie Books, 1989.
Mulford, Philippa Greene. *The World Is My Eggshell.* Delacorte, 1986.
Prill, David. *The Unnatural.* St. Martin's, 1995.
St. Pierre, Stephanie. *Project Boyfriend.* Bantam, 1991.
Salisbury, Graham. *Jungle Dogs.* Delacorte, 1998.
Tamar, Erika. *Fair Game.* Harcourt Brace, 1993.

Westall, Robert. *Falling into Glory*. Farrar, Straus and Giroux, 1993.
Zimmerman, Zoe. *Danny*. Bantam, 2000.

Anthologies and Short Story Collections

Brooks, Bruce. *Boys Will Be*. Henry Holt, 1993.
The Boys' Life Book of Sports Stories. New York: Random House, 1965.
Chapin, Henry B., ed. *Sports in Literature*. McKay, 1976.
Crutcher, Chris. *Athletic Shorts*. Greenwillow, 1991.
Dawidoff, Nicholas, ed. *Baseball: A Literary Anthology*. Library of America, 2002.
Durant, Alan, ed. *Sports Stories*. Larousse Kingfisher Chambers, 2001.
Emra, Bruce, ed. *Sports in Literature: Experiencing Literature through Poems, Stories, and Nonfiction about Sports*. National Textbook, 1991.
Gallo, Donald R., ed. *Ultimate Sports: Short Stories by Outstanding Writers for Young Adults*. Delacorte, 1995.
Gutman, Bill. *"My Father the Coach" and Other Stories*. New York: Simon & Schuster, 1976.
Paulsen, Gary. *How Angel Peterson Got His Name: And Other Outrageous Tales about Extreme Sports*. Wendy Lamb Books, 2003.
Plimpton, George, ed. *The Norton Book of Sports*. New York: W. W. Norton, 1992.
Schinto, Jeanne, ed. *Show Me a Hero*. Persea Books, 1995.
Skipper, John C. *Umpires: Classic Baseball Stories from the Men Who Made the Calls*. McFarland, 1997.
Smith, Charles Jr. *Tall Tales: Six Amazing Basketball Dreams*. Dutton, 2000.
Soto, Gary. *Baseball in April*. Harcourt Brace Jovanovich, 1990.
Schulman, L. M., ed. *The Random House Book of Sport Stories*. Random House, 1990.
———. *Winners and Losers*. New York: Macmillan, 1968.
Wimmer, Dick, ed. *The Fastest Game: An Anthology of Hockey Writings*. Masters, 1997.
Young, Scott. *Seven Parts of a Ball Team and Other Sports Stories*. HarperCollins, 1990.

BOYS' NONFICTION

Autobiography and Biography

Series

Baseball Superstars: *Derek Jeter: the Yankee Kid; Ken Griffey, Jr.: the Home Run Kid; Randy Johnson: Arizona Heat!: Sammy Sosa: Slammin' Sammy; Bernie*

Williams: Quiet Superstar; Omar Vizquel: The Man with the Golden Glove; Mo Vaughn: Angel on a Mission; Pedro Martinez: Throwing Strikes!; Juan Gonzalez: Juan Gone!; Tony Gwynn: Mr. Padre; Kevin Brown: Kevin with a K; Larry Walker: Canadian Rocky; Nomar Garciaparra: High 5!; Mark Grace: Winning with Grace; Curt Schilling: Phillie Phire!; Alex Rodriguez: A+ Shortstop; Roger Clemens: Rocket!

Omnigraphics. Biography Today Sports Series (10 volumes).

Fast Breaks: Jason Kidd Story; Kobe Bryant Story

Football Superstars: Jake Plummer: Comeback Cardinal; Marshall Faulk: Rushing to Glory; Peyton Manning: Passing Legacy; Mark Brunell: Super Southpaw; Junior Seau: Overcoming the Odds; Ed McCaffery: Catching a Star; Drew Bledsoe: Patriot Rifle

Gutman, Bill. Millbrook Sports World: Emmett Smith: NFL Super Runner; Hakeem Olajuwon: Superstar Center; Juan Gonzalez: Outstanding Outfielder; Shaquille O'Neal: Basketball Sensation; Jim Abbott: Star Pitcher; Tiger Woods: Golf's Shining Young Star; Troy Aikman: Super Quarterback; Scottie Pippen: The Do-Everything Superstar; Tara Lipinski: Queen of the Ice; Greg Maddux: Master on the Mound; Reggie White: Star Defensive Lineman; Michael Jordan: Basketball Champ; Steve Young: NFL Passing Wizard; Magic Johnson: Hero On and Off the Court; Jennifer Capriati: Teenage Tennis Star; Barry Sanders: Football's Rushing Champ; Larry Johnson: King of the Court; Cal Ripken, Jr.: Baseball's Iron Man; Ken Griffey, Sr., and Ken Griffey, Jr.: Father and Son Teammates; Mario Lemieux: Wizard with a Puck; Brett Favre: Leader of the Pack; Grant Hill: Basketball's High Flier; Deion Sanders: Mr. Prime Time; David Robinson: NBA Super Center; Frank Thomas: Power Hitter

Hockey Heroes: Pewter Forsberg; Paul Kariya; Jaromir Jagr; Patrick Roy; Mats Sundin; Teemu Selanne; Dominik Hasek

Latinos in Baseball: Roberto Alomar; Moises Alou; Bobby Bonilla; Vinny Castilla; Ramon Martinez; Tino Martinez; Manny Ramirez; Alex Rodriguez; Ivan Rodriguez; Bernie Williams

Male Sports Stars Series: Superstars of Men's Tennis; Superstars of Men's Pro Wrestling; Superstars of Men's Track and Field; Superstars of Men's Figure Skating; Superstars of Men's Soccer; Superstars of Men's Swimming and Diving

Rising Stars: The 10 Best Young Players in the NBA; The 10 Best Young Players in the NFL; The 10 Best Young Players in the NHL; The 10 Best Young Players in Baseball

Baseball

Aaseng, Nathan. *True Champions: Great Athletes and Their Off-the-Field Heroics.* Walker, 1993.

Andryszewski, Tricia. *The Amazing Life of Moe Berg: Catcher, Scholar, Spy.* Millbrook Press, 1996.

Appel, Marty. *Joe DiMaggio.* Chelsea House, 1990.

———. *Yogi Berra*. Chelsea House, 1992.
Bjarkman, Peter C. *Roberto Clemente*. Chelsea House, 1991.
Bloom, Barry. *Sandy and Alomar: Baseball Brothers*. Sports Publishing, 2000.
Brandt, Ed. *Rafael Palmiero: At Home with the Baltimore Orioles*. Mitchell Lane, 1997.
Clayton, Bruce. *Praying for Base Hits: An American Boyhood*. University of Missouri, 1998.
Copley, Robert E. *The Tall Mexican: The Life of Hank Aguirre, All-Star Pitcher, Businessman, Humanitarian*. Pinata / Arte Publico, 1998.
Craig, Robert. *Derek Jeter: A Biography*. Archway, 1999.
Davidson, Margaret. *The Story of Jackie Robinson: Bravest Man in Baseball*. Yearling, 1988.
Devaney, John. *Bo Jackson, a Star for All Seasons*. Walker, 1992.
Dingle, Derek T. *First in the Field: Baseball Hero Jackie Robinson*. Hyperion, 1998.
Duden, Jane. *Baseball*. Crestwood House, 1991.
Dunham, Montrew. *Roberto Clemente: Young Baseball Player*. Aladdin, 1997.
Gilbert, Thomas. *Damn Yankees: Casey, Yogi, Whitey, and the Mick*. Franklin Watts, 1997.
Gutman, Bill. *Bo Jackson*. Archway, 1991.
———. *Sammy Sosa: A Biography*. Pocket Books, 1998.
Hall, Jonathon. *Mark McGwire: A Biography*. Archway, 1998.
James, Bill. *The Baseball Book 1990*. Villard, 1990.
Jeter, Derek. *Game Day: My Life On and Off the Field*. Crown, 2001.
Kernan, Kevin. *Mariano Rivera: Panama Express*. Sports Publishing, 2000.
Leavy, Jane. *Sandy Koufax: A Lefty's Legacy*. HarperCollins, 2002.
Macht, Norman L. *Christy Mathewson (Baseball Legends)*. Chelsea House, 1991.
———. *Frank Robinson*. Chelsea House, 1991.
O'Neill, Paul. *Me and My Dad: A Baseball Memoir*. Morrow, 2003.
Pallone, Dave. *Behind the Mask: My Double Life in Baseball*. Viking Penguin, 1990.
Rains, Rob. *Baseball Samurais: Ichiro Suzuki and the Asian Invasion*. St. Martins, 2001.
Reiser, Howard. *Jackie Robinson: Baseball Pioneer*. Watts, 1992.
Ripken, Cal, and Mike Bryan. *Cal Ripken, Jr.: My Story*. Adapted by Dan Gutman. Dial, 1999.
Ripken, Cal and Greg Brown. *Count Me In*. Taylor, 1995.
Robinson, Jackie. *I Never Had It Made: An Autobiography*. Ecco, 1997.
Robinson, Frazier "Slow." *Catching Dreams: My Life in the Negro Baseball Leagues*. Syracuse University Press, 2000.
Robinson, Sharon. *Jackie's Nine: Jackie Robinson's Values to Live By*. Scholastic, 2002.
Savage, Jeff. *Home Run Kings*. Raintree/Steck-Vaughn, 1999.

Shcechter, Gabriel. *Unhittable! Baseball's Greatest Pitching Seasons.* Charles April, 2002.
Scott, Richard. *Henry Aaron.* Chelsea House, 1993.
Shields, David. *Baseball Is Just Baseball: The Understated Ichiro.* TNI Books, 2001.
———. *Satchel Paige: Baseball Great.* Chelsea House, 1993.
Simon, Scott. *Jackie Robinson and the Integration of Baseball.* John Wiley, 2002.
Stewart, Mark. *Derek Jeter: Substance and Style.* Millbrook, 1999.
Sullivan, George. *Baseball's Boneheads, Bad Boys and Just Plain Crazy Guys.* Millbrook, 2003.
Thornley, Stew. *Mark McGwire: Star Home Run Hitter.* Enslow, 1999.
———. *Sports Great Greg Maddux.* Enslow, 1997.
Weidhorn, Manfred. *Jackie Robinson.* Atheneum, 1993.
Winter, Jonah. *Fair Ball! 14 Great Stars from Baseball's Negro Leagues.* Scholastic, 1999.
Wolff, Rick. *Brooks Robinson.* Chelsea House, 1990.
Yastrzemski, Carl, and Gerald Eskenazi. *Yaz: Baseball, the Wall, and Me.* Doubleday, 1990.
Young, Ken. *Cy Young Award Winners.* Walker, 1994.
Zimmer, Don, and Bill Madden. *Zim: A Baseball Life.* Total Sports, 2001.

Basketball

Abdul-Jabbar, Kareem. *Kareem.* Random House, 1990.
Bird, Larry. *Drive: The Story of My Life.* Doubleday, 1989.
Chamberlain, Wilt. *A View from Above.* Villard, 1991.
Dolan, Sean. *Michael Jordan.* Chelsea House, 1994.
Duden, Jane, and Susan Osberg. *Basketball.* Crestwood House, 1991.
Fortunato, Frank. *Sports Great Alonzo Mourning.* Enslow, 1997.
Frisaro, Joe. *Reggie Miller: From Downtown.* Sports Publishing, 2000.
Gutman, Bill. *Grant Hill: A Biography.* Archway/Simon & Schuster, 1997.
———. *Michael Jordan.* Archway, 1991.
———. *Michael Jordan.* Archway, 1995.
———. *Sammy Sosa: A Biography.* Archway, 1998.
———. *Shaquille O'Neal.* Archway, 1993.
———. *Teammates: Michael Jordan and Scottie Pippen.* Millbrook, 1998.
Johnson, Earvin "Magic" with William Novak. *My Life, Earvin "Magic" Johnson.* Random House, 1992.
Joravsky, Ben. *Hoop Dreams.* Perennial, 1996.
Jordan, Michael. *I Can't Accept Not Trying.* Harper San Francisco, 1994.
Jordan, Michael, and Mark Vancil. *For the Love of the Game: My Story.* Crown, 1998.
Kavanaugh, Jack. *Sports Great Larry Bird.* Enslow, 1992.
Kernan, Kevin. *Keith van Horn: Nothing but Net.* Sports Publishing, 1999.

———. *Tim Duncan: Slam Duncan*. Sports Publishing, 1999.
Knapp, Ron. *Michael Jordan: Star Guard*. Enslow, 1994.
Kornbluth, Jesse. *Airborne: The Triumph and Struggle of Michael Jordan*. MacMillan/Simon & Schuster, 1995.
Lipsyte, Robert. *Michael Jordan: A Life above the Rim*. Harper Trophy, 1994.
Lovitt, Chip. *Michael Jordan*. Scholastic, 1998.
Marvis, Barbara J. *Tommy Nuñez: NBA Referee/Taking My Best Shot*. Mitchell Lane, 1996.
Naughton, Jim. *Taking to the Air: The Rise of Michael Jordan*. Warner, 1992.
Pascarelli, Peter F. *The Courage of Magic Johnson*. Bantam, 1992.
Rappoport, Ken. *Grant Hill*. Walker, 1996.
———. *Shaquille O'Neal*. Walker, 1994.
———. *Guts and Glory: Making It in the NBA*. Walker, 1997.
Riffenburgh, Beau, and David Boss. *Great Ones: NFL Quarterbacks from Baugh to Montana*. Viking, 1989.
Rivers, Glenna, and Bruce Brooks. *Those Who Love the Game*. Henry Holt, 1994.
Rodman, Dennis, Pat Rich, and Alan Steinberg. *Rebound: The Dennis Rodman Story*. Crown, 1994.
Sakamoto, Bob. *Michael "Air" Jordan*. Signet, 1991.
Savage, Jeff. *Grant Hill: Humble Hotshot*. Lerner, 1997.
———. *Sports Great Juwan Howard*. Enslow, 1999.
———. *Top 10 Basketball Point Guards*. Enslow, 1997.
———. *Top 10 Basketball Power Forwards*. Enslow, 1997.
Shaw, Mark. *Larry Legend*. NTC, 1998.
Sirak, Ron. *Juwan Howard*. Chelsea House, 1998.
Wilker, Josh. *Julius Irving*. Chelsea House, 1995.

Boxing

Bacho, Peter. *Boxing in Black and White*. Henry Holt, 1999.
Duplacey, James. *Muhammad Ali: Athlete, Activist, Ambassador*. Warwick Publishing, 1999.
Jakoubeck, Robert. *Jack Johnson*. Chelsea House, 1990.
———. *Joe Louis*. Chelsea House, 1990.
Lipsyte, Robert. *Joe Louis: A Champ for All America*. Harper Trophy, 1994.
Myers, Walter Dean. *The Greatest: Muhammad Ali*. Scholastic, 2001.
Tessitore, John. *Muhammad Ali: The World's Champion*. Watts, 1998.

Dance

Ford, Carin T. *Legends of American Dance and Choreography*. Enslow, 2000.
Glover, Savion, and Bruce Weber. *Savion: My Life in Tap*. Morrow, 2000.
Lewis-Ferguson, Julinda. *Alvin Ailey, Jr.: A Life in Dance*. Walker, 1994.

Encylopedias of Sports Biography

Great Athletes: The Twentieth Century. Salem, 1994. (23 volumes)
Lincoln Library of Sports Stars, 6th ed. Frontier, 1993. (14 volumes)
Paré, Michael A. *Sports Stars*. Gale, 1994.
———. *Sports Stars II*. Gale, 1996.
Porter, David L., ed. *African-American Sports Greats: A Biographical Dictionary*. Greenwood, 1995.

Football

Aaseng, Nathan. *Barry Sanders: Star Running Back*. Enslow, 1994.
Bowden, Bobby with Bill Smith. *More than Just a Game*. Thomas Nelson, 1994.
Christopher, Matt. *In the Huddle With—John Elway*. Little, Brown, 1999.
———. *In the Huddle With—Steve Young*. Little, Brown, 1996.
Cohn, Lowell. *Rough Magic: Bill Walsh's Return to Stanford Football*. Harper Collins, 1994.
Duden, Jane, and Susan Osberg. *Football*. Crestwood House, 1991.
Frisaro, Joe. *Peyton Manning: Passing Legacy*. Sports Publishing, Inc., 1999.
Gutman, Bill. *Bo Jackson*. Archway, 1991.
Kavanaugh, Jack. *Sports Great Joe Montana*. Enslow, 1992.
Haley, Charles, and Joe Layden. *All the Rage: The Life of an NFL Renegade*. Andrews McMeel, 1997.
Klein, Aaron. *Deion Sanders: This Is Prime Time*. Walker, 1995.
Majewski, Stephen. *Sports Great Jerome Bettis*. Enslow, 1997.
Prieto, Jorge. *The Quarterback Who Almost Wasn't*. Arte Publico, 1994.
Priseo, Peter. *Mark Brunell: Super Southpaw*. Sports Publishing, 1999.
Rains, Rob. *Marshall Faulk: Rushing to Glory*. Sports Publishing, 1999.
Rekela, George R. *Sports Great Kurt Warner*. Enslow, 2003.
Savage, Jeff. *Peyton Manning: Precision Passer*. Lerner, 2001.
———. *Thurman Thomas: Star Running Back*. Enslow, 1995.
Sullivan, George. *Football Kids*. Cobblehill, 1990.
Warner, Kurt. *All Things Possible: My Story of Faith, Football, and the Miracle Season*. Harper, 2000.
Wells, Robert W. *Vince Lombardi: His Life and Times*. Prairie Oak Press, 1997.

Golf

Boyd, Aaron. *Tiger Woods*. Morgan Reynolds, 1997.
Durbin, William C. *Tiger Woods*. Chelsea House, 1998.
Edwards, Nicholas. *Tiger Woods: An American Master*. Scholastic, 2001.
Gilbert, Thomas W. *Lee Trevino*. Chelsea House, 1991.
Lace, William W. *Tiger Woods: Star Golfer*. Enslow, 1999.

Rasaforte, Time. *Tiger Woods: The Making of a Champion.* St. Martin's, 1997.
Tait, Alistair. *Golf: The Legends of the Game.* Firefly Books, 1999.
Teague, Allison L. *Prince of the Fairway: The Tiger Woods Story.* Avisson Press, 1997.
Uschan, Michael V. *Tiger Woods.* Lucent, 1999.

Hockey

Schabner, Dean. *Jaromir Jagr.* Chelsea House, 1998.
———. *Sergei Federov.* Chelsea House, 1999.
Schnakenberg, Robert E. *Martin Brodeur.* Chelsea House, 1999.
Taylor, Jim. *Wayne Gretsky: The Authorized Pictorial Biography.* Firefly Books, 1994.
Wilker, Josh. *Wayne Gretsky.* Chelsea House, 1998.

Skating

Boitano, Brian with Suzanne Harper. *Boitano's Edge: Inside the Real World of Figure Skating.* Simon & Schuster, 1997.
Jansen, Dan. *Full Circle.* Villard Books, 1994.
Lang, Thomas. *Going for the Gold: Apolo Anton Ohno,* HarperCollins, 2002.
Layden, Joe. *All about Apolo.* Aladdin, 2002.
Ohno, Apolo Anton. *Apolo Anton Ohno: My Story.* Simon & Schuster, 2002.
Styles, Alicia. *Gold! The Todd Eldredge Story.* Xlibris, 2001.

Soccer

Arnold, Caroline. *Pele: The King of Soccer.* Watts, 1992.
Goodall, Lian. *Maradona: The Man with the Magic Feet.* Firefly, 1999.
Urigs, Timothy. *Superstars of Men's Soccer.* Chelsea House, 1998.

Tennis

Collins, David R. *Arthur Ashe against the Wind.* Dillon, 1994

Track

Gentry, Tony. *Jesse Owens.* Chelsea House, 1990.
Klots, Steve. *Carl Lewis.* Chelsea House, 1995.
Knapp, Ron. *Top Ten American Sprinters.* Enslow, 1999.
Rosenthal, Bert. *Michael Johnson: Sprinter Deluxe.* GHB, 2000.
Rutledge, Rachel. *The Best of the Best in Track and Field.* Millbrook, 1999.
Streissguth, Thomas. *Jesse Owens.* Lerner, 1999.

Wrestling

Cohen, Daniel. *Wrestling Superstars*. Archway, 1985.
Holland, Stephen T. *Talkin' Dan Gable*. Limerick, 1983.
Lewin, Ted. *I Was a Teenage Professional Wrestler*. Orchard, 1993.
Rock, and Joe Layden. *The Rock Says—: The Most Electrifying Man in Sports Entertainment*. Regan, 2000.
Zavoral, Nolan. *A Season on the Mat: Dan Gable and the Pursuit of Perfection*. Simon & Schuster, 1998.

Other

Armstrong, Lance, and Sally Jenkins. *It's Not about the Bike: My Journey Back to Life*. Penguin, 2000.
Boga, Steven. *Cyclists: How the World's Most Daring Riders Train and Compete*. Stackpole, 1992.
Duden, Jane. *The Olympics*. Crestwood House, 1991.
Deford, Frank. *The Heart of a Champion: Celebrating the Spirit and Character of America's Sports Heroes*. Northwood Press, 2002.
Egan, Terry, et al. *The Good Guys of Baseball: Sixteen True Sports Stories*. Simon & Schuster, 1997.
Halberstam, David, ed. *The Best American Sports Writing of the Century*. Houghton Mifflin, 1999.
Hawk, Tony. *Tony Hawk: Between Boardslides and Burnout: My Notes from the Road*. HarperCollins, 2002.
———. *Hawk: Occupation Skateboarder*. HarperCollins, 2001.
———. *Tony Hawk: Professional Skateboarder*. HarperCollins, 2002.
Hoffman, Mat. *Testimony: My Life on the Edge*, HarperCollins, 2003.
Hoffman, Mat, and Mark Lewman. *The Ride of My Life*. HarperCollins, 2002.
Johnson, Dave with Verne Becker. *Aim High*. Zondervan, 1994.
Johnstone, Mike. *NASCAR: The Need for Speed*. Lerner, 2002.
Lipsyte, Robert. *Jim Thorpe: 20th Century Jock*. HarperCollins, 1993.
Masoff, Joy. *Snowboard! Your Guide to Freeriding, Pipe and Park, Jibbing, Backcountry, Alpine, Boardercross and More*. National Geographic, 2002.
Milan, Garth. *Freestyle Motocross 2 Air Sickness: More Jump Tricks for the Pros*. MBI, 2002.
Philobus. *Twisted Yoga*. Sea Star, 2002.
Pollack, Pamela. *Ski! Your Guide to Jumping, Racing, Skiboarding, Nordic, Backcountry, Aerobatics, and More*. National Geographic, 2002.
Rutledge, Rachel. *The Best of the Best in Gymnastics*. Millbrook, 1999.
Savage, Jeff. *Top 10 In-Line Skaters*. Enslow, 1999.
Schatz, Howard. *Athlete*. HarperCollins, 2002.

Seate, Mike. *Streetbike Extreme*. MBI, 2002.
Stewart, Mark. *Sweet Victory: Lance Armstrong's Incredible Journey*. Millbrook, 2000.
Uschan, Michael V. *Male Olympic Champions*. Lucent Books, 2000.

History and Team Highlights

Series

Scarecrow Press. American Sports History: *The Fierce Fun of Ducky Medwick; Effa Manley and the Newark Eagles; The League That Failed; Jimmie Foxx: The Pride of Sudlersville; Baseball's Radical for All Seasons: A Biography of John Montgomery Ward; College Basketball's National Championships: The Complete Record of Every Tournament Ever Played; Chris von Der Ahe and the St. Louis Browns; For Pride, Profit, and Patriarchy: Football and the Incorporation of American Cultural Values; Sunday at the Ballpark: Billy Sunday's Professional Baseball Career, 1883–1890; Major Leagues; Whose Baseball?: The National Pastime and Cultural Diversity in California, 1859–1941; The United States and World Cup Soccer Competition: An Encyclopedic History of the United States in International Competition; The Encyclopedia of American Soccer History; Football's Stars of Summer: A History of the College All-Star Football Game Series of 1934–1976; Major League Champions, 1871–2001; Biographical Directory of Professional Basketball Coaches; Mel Ott: The Gentle Giant; Slide, Kelly, Slide: The Wild Life and Times of Mike "King" Kelly, Baseball's First Superstar; Baseball by the Numbers: A Guide to the Uniform Numbers of Major League Teams; Roller Skating for Gold; Baseball's Biggest Blunder: The Bonus Rule of 1953–1957; Lights On!: The Wild Century-long Saga of Night Baseball; Windy City Wars: Labor, Leisure, and Sport in the Making of Chicago; American Soccer League, 1921–1931: The Golden Years of American Soccer*

Baseball

Baseball as America: Seeing Ourselves through Our National Game. National Geographic, 2002.
Baseball's Best Shots: The Greatest Baseball Photography of All Time. DK, 2002.
Brashler, William. *The Story of Negro League Baseball*. Ticknor & Fields, 1994.
Burgan, Michael. *Great Moments in Baseball*. World Almanac Library 2002.
Chadwick, Bruce, and David M. Spindel. *The Giants: Memories and Memorabilia from a Century of Baseball*. Abbeville, 1993.
Collins, Ace, and John Hillman. *Blackball Superstars: Legendary Players of the Negro Baseball Leagues*. Avisson Press, 1999.
Curran, William. *Strikeout: A Celebration of the Art of Pitching*. Crown, 1995.

Duden, Jane. *Baseball.* Crestwood House, 1991.
Feinstein, John. *Play Ball: The Life and Troubled Times of Major League Baseball.* Villard, 1993.
Ford, Whitey, and Phil Pepe. *Few and Chosen: Defining Yankee Greatness across the Eras.* Triumph, 2001.
Fremon, David. *The Negro Baseball Leagues.* New Discovery, 1994.
Gardner, Robert, and Dennis Shortelle. *The Forgotten Players: The Story of Black Baseball in America.* Walker, 1993.
Gay, Douglas, and Kathlyn Gay. *The Not-So-Minor Leagues.* Millbrook, 1996.
Gent, Peter. *The Last Magic Summer: A Season with My Son.* William Morrow, 1996.
Gilbert, Bill. *They Also Served: Baseball and the Home Front, 1941–1945.* Crown, 1992.
Gilbert, Thomas. *Baseball at War: World War II and the Fall of the Color Line.* Franklin Watts, 1997.
———. *Dead Ball: Major League Baseball before Babe Ruth.* Watts, 1996.
———. *Baseball and the Color Line.* Watts, 1995.
Gutman, Bill. *Baseball Super Teams.* Archway, 1992.
Gutman, Dan. *Banana Bats and Ding Dong Balls: A Century of Unique Baseball Inventions.* Macmillan, 1995.
———. *Baseball's Biggest Bloopers: The Games That Got Away.* Viking, 1993.
———. *World Series Classics.* Viking, 1994.
Gunther, Marc. *Basepaths: From the Minor Leagues to the Majors and Beyond.* Scribner's, 1984.
Honig, Donald. *The American League: An Illustrated History.* Crown, 1987.
———. *American League Most Valuable Players,* Bantam, 1989.
———. *American League Rookies of the Year.* Bantam, 1989.
———. *Baseball America: The Heroes of the Game and the Times of Their Glory.* Simon & Schuster, 1985.
———. *Baseball in the 30's: A Decade of Survival.* Crown, 1989.
———. *Baseball in the 50's: A Decade of Transition.* Crown, 1987.
———. *Baseball: The Illustrated History of America's Game.* Crown, 1990.
———. *Baseball's Ten Greatest Teams.* Macmillan, 1982.
———. *The Boston Red Sox: An Illustrated History.* Prentice Hall, 1990.
———. *The Boston Red Sox: An Illustrated Tribute.* St. Martin's, 1984.
———. *The Brooklyn Dodgers: An Illustrated Tribute.* St. Martin's, 1981.
———. *The Chicago Cubs: An Illustrated History.* Simon & Schuster, 1991.
———. *The Cincinnati Reds: An Illustrated History.* Simon & Schuster, 1992.
———. *The Dodgers: The Complete Record of Dodgers Baseball.* Macmillan, 1986.
———. *The Greatest Catchers of All Time.* Brown & Benchmark, 1991.
———. *The Greatest First Basemen of All Time.* Haynes, 1988.
———. *The Greatest Pitchers of All Time.* Crown, 1988.
———. *The Greatest Short Stops of All Time.* Brown & Benchmark, 1992.

———. *The Los Angeles Dodgers: The First Quarter Century.* St. Martin's, 1983.
———. *Mays, Mantle, Snider: A Celebration.* Macmillan, 1987.
———. *The National League: An Illustrated History.* Crown, 1987.
———. *The New York Mets: The First Quarter Century.* Crown, 1986.
———. *The New York Yankees: An Illustrated History.* Dilithium, 1987.
———. *October Heroes: Great World Series Games Remembered by the Men Who Played Them.* University of Nebraska, 1996.
———. *The Philadelphia Phillies: An Illustrated History.* Prentice Hall, 1992.
———. *The Plot to Kill Jackie Robinson.* Dutton, 1992.
———. *Power Hitters.* Outlet, 1989.
———. *Shadows of Summer: Classic Baseball Photographs, 1869–1947.* Penguin, 1994.
———. *The St. Louis Cardinals: An Illustrated History.* Simon & Schuster, 1991.
———. *The World Series: An Illustrated History from 1903 to the Present.* Crown, 1986.
Hoppett, Leonard. *The Man in the Dugout.* Crown, 1993.
Kaufman, Alan S. and James C. Kaufman. *The Worst Baseball Pitchers of All Times.* McFarland, 1993.
Kisseloff, Jeff. *Who Is Baseball's Greatest Hitter?* Henry Holt, 2000.
———. *Who Is Baseball's Greatest Pitcher?* Cricket, 2003.
Kravitz, Bob. *Mile High Madness.* Times Books, 1994.
McKissack, Patricia, and Frederick McKissak, Jr. *Black Diamond: The Story of the Negro Baseball Leagues.* Scholastic, 1994.
Margolies, Jacob. *The Negro Leagues: The Story of Black Baseball.* Franklin Watts, 1993.
Pietrusza, David, *The San Francisco Giants Baseball Team.* Enslow, 2000.
———. *The Baltimore Orioles Baseball Team.* Enslow, 2000.
Ritter, Lawrence S., and Donald Honig. *The Image of Their Greatness: An Illustrated History of Baseball From 1900 to the Present.* Crown, 1992.
Ritter, Lawrence S. *The Story of Baseball.* 3rd ed. Morrow, 1999.
Snelling, Dennis. *A Glimpse of Fame: Brilliant but Fleeting Major League Careers.* McFarland, 1993.
Ward, Geoffrey C., et al. *Who Invented the Game?* Knopf, 1994.
———. *Shadow Ball: A History of the Negro Leagues.* Knopf, 1994.
———. *25 Great Moments.* Knopf, 1994.

Basketball

Basketball's Best Shots: Grace, Passion, Energy, Athleticism Captured in Spectacular NBA Photography. DK, 2002.
Blatt, Howard. *The NBA's 10 Greatest Teams Ever.* Scholastic, 1999.
Burgan, Michael. *Great Moments in Basketball.* World Almanac Library, 2002.
Cebulash, Mel. *Fast Break: Great Basketball of the 20th Century.* New Readers, 1993.

Feinstein, John. *Forever's Team*. Villard, 1990.
Frey, Darcy. *The Last Shot: City Streets, Basketball Dreams*. Touchstone, 1994.
Jones, Ron. *B-Ball: The Team That Never Lost a Game*. Bantam Starfire, 1990.
Layden, Joe. *Dream Team USA Basketball*. Scholastic, 1996.
———. *NBA Game Day*. Scholastic, 1997.
McKissack, Frederick, Jr. *Black Hoops: The History of African Americans in Basketball*. Scholastic, 1999.
O'Shei, Tim. *The Duke Blue Devils Men's Basketball Team*. Enslow, 1999.
Reynolds, Bill. *Fall River Dreams: A Team's Quest for Glory—A Town's Search for Its Soul*. St. Martins, 1995.
Salzberg, Charles. *From the Set Shot to the Slam Dunk: The Glory Days of Basketball in the Words of Those Who Played It*. University of Nebraska Press, 1998.
Telander, Rick. *Heaven Is a Playground*. University of Nebaska Press, 1995.

Dance

Haskins, James. *Black Dance in America*. Crowell, 1990.

Football

Armstrong, John. *The Way We Played the Game: A True Story of One Team and the Dawning of American Football*. Sourcebooks, 2002.
NFL Best Shots: The Greatest NFL Photography of the Century. DK, 1999.
NFL's Greatest: Pro Football's Best Players, Teams, and Games. DK, 2002.
Bissinger, H. G. *Friday Night Lights: A Town, a Team, and a Dream*. HarperCollins, 1990.
Buckley, James. *America's Greatest Game: The Real Story of Football and the NFL*. Hyperion, 1998.
———. *Great Moments in Football*. World Almanac Library, 2002.
Duden, Jane, and Susan Osberg. *Football*. Crestwood House, 1991.
King Football: Greatest Moments in Texas High School Football. Houston Chronicle/Epic Sports, 2002.
Layden, Joe. *Notre Dame Football A–Z*. Taylor, 1997.
Lightle, William. *Made or Broken: Football and Survival in the Georgia Woods*. 1stBooks, 2002.
Molzahn, Arlene Bourgeois. *The Green Bay Packers Football Team*. Enslow, 1999.
Mottley, Chuck and Sandra B. Ghost. *The Turnaround from 0–10 to 10–0*. Jubilee, 1999.
NFL Football Top 10. DK, 2002.
Rawlings, Russell. *Cyclone Country: The Time, the Town, the Team*. Wilson Daily Times, 2000.
Yaeger, Don, and Douglas S. Looney. *Under the Tarnished Dome: How Notre Dame Betrayed Its Ideals for Football Glory*. Simon & Schuster, 1993.

General

Ash, Russell. *The Top 10 of Sports*. DK, 2002.
Aymar, Brandt, ed. *Men in Sports: Great Sport Stories of All Time, From the Greek Olympic Games to the American World Series*. Crown, 1994.
Brooke, Michael. *The Concrete Wave: The History of Skateboarding*. Warwick, 1999.
Gutman, Bill. *Great Sports Upsets 2*. Archway, 1993.
Krull, Kathleen. *Lives of the Athletes: Thrills, Spills (and What the Neighbors Thought)*. Harcourt, 1997.
LaBlanc, Michael, ed. *Professional Sports Team Histories*. 4 Volumes. Gale, 1994.
Lyttle, Richard B. *The Games They Played: Sports in History*. Atheneum, 1982.
McComb, David G. *Sports: An Illustrated History*. Oxford University Press, 1998.
Rowling, J. K. (Kennilworthy Whisp). *Quidditch through the Ages*. Arthur A. Levine, 2001.
Venables, Stephen. *To the Top: The Story of Everest*. Candlewick, 2003.
Wulffson, Don L. *When Human Heads Were Footballs: Surprising Stories of How Sports Began*, Aladdin, 1998.

Hockey

Allen, Kevin, and Bob Duff. *Without Fear: Hockey's 50 Greatest Goaltenders*. Triumph, 2002.
Buckley, James. *Great Moments in Hockey*. World Almanac, 2002.
Hockey's Best Shots: The Greatest NHL Photography of the Century. DK, 2001.
McDonell, Chris. *Hockey All Stars: The NHL Honor Roll*. Firefly, 2000.

Olympics

Anderson, Dave. *The Story of the Olympics*. HarperCollins, 2000.
Bachrach, Susan D. *Nazi Olympics: Berlin 1936*. Little, Brown, 2000.
Chronicle of the Olympics 1986–1996. Dorling Kindersley, 1996.
Burgan, Michael. *Great Moments in the Olympics*. World Almanac, 2002.
Dheenshaw, Cleve. *Olympics 100: Canada at the Summer Games*. Orca, 1996.
Dinn, Sheila. *Hearts of Gold: A Celebration of Special Olympics and Its Heroes*. Blackbirch, 1996.
Duden, Jane. *The Olympics*. Crestwood House, 1991.
Greenspan, Bud. *Frozen in Time: The Greatest Moments at the Winter Olympics*. General Publishing Group, 1998.

Series

The Composite Guide: *The Composite Guide to Track and Field; The Composite Guide to Soccer; The Composite Guide to Basketball; The Composite Guide to*

Wrestling; *The Composite Guide to Lacrosse; The Composite Guide to Baseball; The Composite Guide to Strongman Competition; The Composite Guide to Football; The Composite Guide to Golf; The Composite Guide to Hockey; The Composite Guide to Tennis; The Composite Guide to Martial Arts; The Composite Guide to Volleyball; The Composite Guide to Gymnastics; The Composite Guide to Bodybuilding; The Composite Guide to Softball; The Composite Guide to Strongman Competition; The Composite Guide to Auto Racing*

Great Sports Teams: *The San Francisco Giants; The Notre Dame Fighting Irish; The Green Bay Packers; The San Francisco 49ers; The Boston Celtics; The New York Rangers; The Montreal Canadiens; The Pittsburgh Steelers; The Seattle Supersonics; The Georgetown Hoyas; The Michigan Wolverines; The Philadelphia 76ers; The Los Angeles Dodgers; The Detroit Pistons; The Detroit Red Wings; The Baltimore Orioles; The New York Yankees; The Philadelphia Flyers; The Chicago Bears Football Team; The Duke Blue Devils Men's Basketball Team; The Houston Rockets Basketball Team; The Denver Broncos Football Team; The St. Louis Cardinals Baseball Team; The Cleveland Indians Baseball Team; The Phoenix Suns Basketball Team; The New York Knicks Basketball Team; The Los Angeles Lakers Basketball Team; The Dallas Cowboys Football Team; The San Antonio Spurs Basketball Team; The Chicago Bulls Basketball Team; The Miami Dolphins Football Team; The Boston Red Sox Baseball Team; The Atlanta Braves Baseball Team*

Layden, Joseph. Fast Breaks: *Rising Stars; Against the Odds*

The NHL Series: *Goals; Saves; Make-a-Play; Posterbook; Body Checks; Stats; A Century of Hockey Heroes: 100 of the Greatest All-time Stars; Suit Up; Game Face; Cup Crazy: Great Stanley Cup Series; The Autobiography of Willie O'Ree: Hockey's Black Pioneer*

Owens, Thomas S., and Diana Star Helmer. Game Plan: *Football; Baseball; Basketball; Hockey; Soccer; NASCAR*

Stout, Glenn, ed. The Best American Sports Writing. Annual editions from 1991 to 2002.

Soccer

Goldblatt, David. *World Soccer Yearbook 2003: The Complete Guide to the Game.* DK, 2002.

Stewart, Mark. *Soccer: A History of the World's Most Popular Game.* Scholastic, 1998.

Wrestling

Chapman, Mike. *A History of Wrestling in Iowa: From Gotch to Gable.* University of Iowa, 1981.

DeVito, Basil, and Joe Layden. *Wrestlemania: The Official Insider's History.* Regan, 2000.

HOW-TO

Baseball

Bagonzi, John. *The Act of Pitching: A Tutorial for All Levels by a Master Technician—Detailing Every Aspect of Pitching.* Hedgehog Hill, 2001.
Cecchini, Glenn, et al. *101 Championship Baseball Drills.* Coaches Choice, 2000.
Dorfman, H. A. *The Mental ABC's of Pitching: A Handbook for Performance Enhancement.* Diamond Communications, 2000.
House, Tom. *Fit to Pitch.* Human Kinetics, 1996.
———. *The Pitching Edge.* Human Kinetics, 1999.
Hughes, Dean, and Tom Hughes. *Baseball Tips.* Random House, 1993.
Johnson, Randy, and Jim Rosenthal. *Randy Johnson's Power Pitching: The Big Unit's Secrets to Domination, Intimidation, and Winning.* Three Rivers, 2003.
Krasner, Steven. *Play Ball Like the Pros: Tips for Kids from 20 Big League Stars.* Peachtree, 2002.
Kreutzer, Peter, and Ted Kerley. *Little League's Official How-to-Play Baseball Book.* Doubleday, 1990.
Mazzone, Leo, and Jim Rosenthal. *Pitch Like a Pro.* Griffin, 1999.
Maitland, William J. *Young Ball Player's Guide to Safe Pitching.* Maitland, 1992.
Ryan, Nolan, and Tom House. *Nolan Ryan's Pitcher's Bible: The Ultimate Guide to Power, Precision, and Long-Term Performance.* Fireside, 1991.
Seaver, Tom, and Lee Lowenfish. *The Art of Pitching.* William Morrow, 1994.
Williams, Ted, and John Underwood. *The Science of Hitting.* Simon & Schuster, 1986.

Basketball

Krause, Jerry V. *Basketball Skills and Drills.* Human Kinetics, 1999.
St. Martin, Ted. *The Art of Shooting Baskets: From the Free Throw to the Slam Dunk.* NTC, 1992.
Wissell, Hal. *Basketball: Steps to Success.* Human Kinetics, 1994.

In-Line Skating

Edwards, Chris. *The Young Inline Skater.* DK, 1996.
Powell, Mark, and John Svensson. *In-Line Skating.* Human Kinetics, 1992.

Football

Banks, Carl. *Carl Banks' Football Training Program: A Conditioning and Total Health Program for the Young Athlete.* Penguin, 1991.
Brown, Michael. *Football Techniques in Pictures.* Perigree, 1992.
Wilkinson, Bud. *Football: Winning Defense.* Sports Illustrated, 1995.

Golf

Andrisani, John. *The Tiger Woods Way: Secrets of Tiger Woods' Power Swinging Technique*. Crown, 1997.
Ballingall, Peter. *101 Essential Tips on Golf*. Dorling Kindersley, 1996.

Skiing/Snowboarding

Bartelski, Konrad with Robin Neillands. *Learn Downhill Skiing in a Weekend*. Knopf, 1992.
Guillion, Laurie. *Nordic Skiing: Steps to Success*. Human Kinetic Publishers, 1992.
Haxhurst, Chris. *Snowboarding! Shred the Powder*. Rosen, 2000.
McKenna, Anne T. *Big-Air Snowboarding*. High/Low Books/Capstone Press, 1999.

Soccer

Luongo, Albert M. *Soccer Drills: Skill Builders for Field Control*. McFarland, 2000.
Luxbacher, Joe. *Soccer Practice Games: 120 Games for Technique, Training, and Tactics*. Human Kinetics, 1994.
———. *Soccer: Steps to Success*. Human Kinetics, 1996.
Sullivan, George. *All About Soccer*. Putnam, 2001.

Tennis

Chu, Donald A. *Power Tennis Training*. Human Kinetics, 1995.
Deegan, Paul J. *Basic Strokes*. Child's World, 1976.
Douglas, Paul, and Deni Bown. *101 Essential Tips on Tennis*. Dorling Kindersley, 1996.
Douglas, Paul. *Learn Tennis in a Weekend*. Knopf, 1991.
Jordan, Robert H. *Tennis for Winners! All about Becoming a Much Better Player: What It Takes and How to Do It*. Robert H. Jordan, 1991.

Volleyball

Lucas, Jeff. *Pass, Set, Crush: Volleyball Illustrated*. Euclid Northwest, 1992.

Wrestling

Jarman, Tom, and Reid Hanley. *Wrestling for Beginners*. McGraw-Hill, 1983.
Johnson, Dennis A. *Wrestling Drill Book*. Human Kinetics, 1991.
Mysnyk, Mark, et al. *Winning Wrestling Moves*. Human Kinetics, 1994.
Ryan, Thomas, and Julie Sampson. *Beginning Wrestling*. Sterling, 2002.

Other

Falla, Jack. *Hockey: Learn to Play the Hard Way*. Rev. ed. Sports Illustrated, 1995.
Kittleson, Stan. *Racquetball: Steps to Success*. Leisure Press, 1991.
Knudson, R. R. *Punch!* Avon, 1983.
Murdock, Tony, and Nik Stuart. *Gymnastics, A Practical Guide for Beginners*. Watts, 1989.
Reiser, Howard. *Skateboarding*. Watts, 1989.
Sprague, Ken, and Chris Sprague. *Weight and Strength Training for Kids and Teenagers*. Tarcher, 1991.

POETRY

Adoff, Arnold. *The Basket Counts*. Simon & Schuster, 2000.
———. *Sports Pages*. J. B. Lippincott, 1986.
Blaustein, Noah, ed. *Motion: American Sports Poems*. University of Iowa Press, 2001.
Buchwald, Emily, and Ruth Roster, eds. *The Sporting Life: Poems about Sports and Games*. Milkweed, 1998.
Burleigh, Robert. *Hoops*. Harcourt Brace, 1997.
Carney, Gene. *Romancing the Horsehide: Baseball Poems on Players and the Game*. McFarland, 1993.
Fehler, Gene. *Center Field Grasses: Poems from Baseball*. McFarland, 1991.
———. *Dancing on the Basepaths: Baseball Poetry*. McFarland, 2001.
———. *I Hit the Ball!: Baseball Poems for the Young*. McFarland, 1996.
———. *The Silly (and Sometimes Serious) Side of Sports: Sports Poems*. Mailbox, 1999.
Gardner, Martin, ed. *The Annotated Casey at the Bat: A Collection of Ballads about the Mighty Casey*. Dover, 1995.
Glenn, Mel. *Jump Ball: A Basketball Season in Poems*. Lodestar, 1997.
Hopkins, Lee Bennett, ed. *Extra Innings: Baseball Poems*. Harcourt, 1993.
———. *Opening Days: Sports Poems*. Harcourt, 1996.
Janeczko, Paul B. *That Sweet Diamond: Baseball Poems*. Atheneum, 1999.
Knudson, R. R., and May Swenson, eds. *American Sports Poems*. Orchard Books, 1995.
Korman, Gordon. *Last-Place Sports Poems of Jeremy Bloom*. Scholastic, 1996.
Mathis, Sharon Bell. *Red Dog, Blue Fly: Football Poems*. Viking, 1991.
Morrison, Lillian, ed. *At the Crack of the Bat: Baseball Poems*. Hyperion, 1992.
———. *Sprints and Distances: Sports in Poetry and the Poetry of Sports*. Crowell, 1965.
———. *Rhythm Road*. Lothrop, Lee & Shepard Books, 1988.
———. *The Break Dance Kids: Poems of Sport, Motion, and Locomotion*. Lothrop, Lee & Shepard Books, 1985.
———. *Slam Dunk: Basketball Poems*. Hyperion, 1995.

———. *Way to Go!: Sports Poems.* Wordsong/Boyds Mills, 2001.
Smith, Charles R. *Rimshots: Basketball Pix, Rolls, and Rhythms.* Dutton, 1999.
———. *Short Takes: Fast Break Poetry.* Dutton, 1991.
Testa, Maria. *Becoming Joe DiMaggio.* Candlewick, 2002.
Thayer, Ernest Lawrence. *Casey at the Bat: A Ballad of the Republic Sung in the Year 1888.* Handprint, 2000.

MISCELLANEOUS NONFICTION

College and Careers

Abramson, Hilary S. *Student Athletes' Guide to College.* Princeton Review/Random, 1999.
Blumenthal, Howard J. *Careers in Baseball: You Can Do It!* Little, Brown, 1993.
Fisher, David. *50 Coolest Jobs in Sports.* Macmillan, 1997.
Fossey, Keith R. *Football Scholarship Guide.* Pigskin Press, 1992.
Heitzmann, William R. *Opportunities in Sports Medicine Careers.* VGM Career Horizons, 1991.
———. *Careers for Sports Nuts & Other Athletic Types.* VGM Career Horizons, 1990.
———. *Opportunities in Sports and Athletic Careers.* VGM, 1993.
Kaplan, Andrew. *Careers for Sports Fans.* Millbrook, 1991.
Laney, David. *Athletic Scholarships: Making Your Sports Pay.* Warwick, 1993.
McDaniels, Pellom, III. *So, You Want to Be a Pro?* Addax Publishing Group, 1999.
Nagle, Jeanne. *Careers in Coaching.* Rosen, 2000.
Nelson, Cordner. *Careers in Pro Sports.* Rosen, 1990.
Nuwer, Hank. *Recruiting in Sports.* Watts, 1989.
Walker, Ron, ed. *Peterson's Sports Scholarships.* Peterson's Guide, 1994.
Weiss, Ann E. *Money Games: The Business of Sports.* Houghton Mifflin, 1993.

Issues in Sports

Aaseng, Nathan. *Locker Room Mirror: How Sports Reflect Society.* Walker, 1993.
Ashe, Arthur R. *A Hard Road to Glory: The African-American Athlete in Basketball.* Amistad, 1988.
Berger, Gilda. *Violence in Sports.* Franklin Watts, 1990.
Bryant, Howard. *Shut Out: A Story of Race and Baseball in Boston.* Routledge, 2002.
Clayton, Laurence, and Betty Sharon Smith. *Coping with Sports Injuries.* Rosen, 1992.
Dolan, Edward F. *Drugs in Sports.* Watts, 1992.
Dudley, William. *Sports in America: Opposing Viewpoints.* Greenhaven, 1994.
Funk, Gary D. *A Balancing Act: Sports and Education.* Lerner, 1995.

Good Sports: Fair Play and Foul. Rosen, 1992.
Guttmann, Allen. *A Whole New Ball Game: An Interpretation of American Sports.* University of North Carolina, 1988.
Hu, Evaleen. *A Big Ticket: Sports and Commercialism.* Lerner, 1998.
———. *A Level Playing Field: Sports and Race.* Lerner, 1995.
Layden, Joe. *The Great American Baseball Strike.* Millbrook, 1995.
Margolis, Jeffrey A. *Violence in Sports.* Enslow, 1999.
Morgan, Joe, and Richard Lally. *Long Balls, No Strikes: What Baseball Must Do to Keep the Good Times Rolling.* Crown, 1999.
Nuwer, Hank. *Sports Scandals.* Watts, 1994.
———. *Steroids.* Watts, 1990.
Putnam, Douglas. *Controversies of the Sports World.* Greenwood, 1999.
Richardson, Allen F. *Sports.* Peterson's, 1993.
Ryan, Joan. *Little Girls in Pretty Boxes: The Making and Breaking of Elite Gymnasts and Figure Skaters.* Doubleday, 1995.
Savage, Jeff. *A Sure Thing? Sports and Gambling.* Lerner, 1997.
Shaw, Lisa Angowski Rogak. *Steroids: Dangerous Game.* Lerner, 1992.
Silverstein, Alvin, et al. *Steroids: Big Muscles, Big Problems.* Enslow, 1992.
Stiefer, Sandy. *A Risky Prescription: Sports and Health.* Lerner, 1997.
Steiner, Andy. *A Sporting Chance: Sports and Gender.* Lerner, 1995.
Williams, Aeneas. *It Takes Respect.* Multnomah, 1998.
Young, Perry Deane. *Lesbians and Gays and Sports.* Chelsea House, 1995.

A LITTLE OF EVERYTHING AND MISCELLANEOUS

Adrian, Lorne A., ed. *The Most Important Thing I Know™ about the Spirit of Sport: 101 Inspiring Messages from Athletes, Coaches, Sports Writers, and Commentators.* Morrow, 1999.
Baddiel, Ivor. *Soccer: The Ultimate World Cup Companion.* DK, 1998.
Barnes, Ernie. *From Pads to Palette.* WRS, 1995.
Berra, Yogi, and Dave Kaplan. *When You Come to a Fork in the Road, Take It!: Inspiration and Wisdom from One of Baseball's Greatest Heroes.* Hyperion, 2001.
Brown, Fern G. *Special Olympics.* Watts, 1992.
Bussell, Darcey. *The Young Dancer.* Dorling Kindersley, 1994.
Cohen, Steven A., ed. *The Games We Played: A Celebration of Childhood and Imagination.* Simon & Schuster, 2001.
Coffland, Jack, and David A. Coffland. *Basketball Math: Slam Dunk Activities and Projects.* Pearson, 2001.
Gardner, Robert. *Science and Sports.* Franklin Watts, 1988.
———. *Science Projects about the Physics of Sports.* Enslow, 2000.
Gay, Kathlyn. *They Don't Wash Their Socks!: Sports Superstitions.* Walker, 1990.
Goodstein, Madeline. *Sports Science Projects: The Physics of Balls in Motion.* Enslow, 1999.

Gutman, Dan. *Gymnastics*. Viking, 1996.
———. *Ice Skating: From Axels to Zambonis*. Viking, 1995.
Gutman, Bill. *Blazing Bladers*. TOR, 1992.
Hegedus, Alannah, and Kaitlin Rainey. *Shooting Hoops and Skating Loops: Great Inventions in Sports*. Tundra Books, 1999.
Herbst, Dan. *Soccer: The Complete Player*. Sports Illustrated, 1995.
James, Bill. *The Baseball Book 1990*. Villard, 1990.
Kaminsky, Marty. *Uncommon Champions: Fifteen Athletes Who Battled Back*. Boyds Mills, 2000.
Karolyi, Bela, and Nancy Ann Richardson. *Feel No Fear: The Power, Passion, and Politics of a Life in Gymnastics*. Hyperion, 1994.
Kellogg, David. *True Stories of Baseball's Hall of Famers*. Bluewood Books, 2000.
Madden, John. *The First Book of Football*. Crown, 1991.
Malafronte, Victor A. *The Complete Book of Frisbee: The History of the Sport and the First Official Price Guide*. American Trends Publishing, 1998.
Miller, J. David. *The Super Book of Football*. Sports Illustrated for Kids, 1990.
Ontario Sports Centre. *Sportworks: More than 50 Fun Games and Activities That Explore the Science of Sports*. Addison-Wesley, 1989.
Osborn, Kevin. *Scholastic Encyclopedia of Sports in the United States*. Scholastic, 1997.
Paulsen, Gary. *Father Water, Mother Woods: Essays on Fishing and Hunting in the North Woods*. Delacorte, 1994.
Resciniti, Angelo, and Ann Steinburg. *Incredible Super Bowl Action*. Willowisp Press, 1991.
Resciniti, Angelo, et al. *Super Bowl Excitement*. Willowisp, 1994.
Stewart, Wayne. *Baseball Oddities: Bizarre Plays and Other Funny Stuff*. Sterling, 1999.
Sullivan, George. *All about Basketball*. Putnam, 1991.
———. *Any Number Can Play: The Numbers Athletes Wear*. Millbrook, 2000.
———. *Don't Step on the Foul Line: Sports Supersitions*. Millbrook, 2000.
Swirsky, Seth, ed. *Every Pitcher Tells a Story: Letters Gathered by a Devoted Baseball Fan*. Times Books/Random, 1999.
Thatcher, Kevin J., and Brian Bannon. *Thrasher: The Radical Skateboard Book*. Random House, 1992.
Winegardner, Mark. *Prophet of the Sandlots: Journeys with a Major League Scout*. Athletic Monthly, 1990.
Wordlaw, Lee. *Cowabunga: The Complete Book of Surfing*. Avon, 1991.

TRIVIA AND REFERENCE

Cataneo, David, ed. *Peanuts & Crackerjacks: A Treasury of Baseball Legends and Lore*. Harcourt, 1994.
Dickson, David, ed. *Baseball's Greatest Quotations*. HarperCollins, 1992.

Gifford, Clive. *Soccer: The Ultimate Guide to the Beautiful Game.* Kingfisher, 2002.
Gould, Stephen Jay. *Triumph and Tragedy in Mudville.* W. W. Norton, 2003.
Gutman, Dan. *Baseball's Biggest Bloopers: The Games That Got Away.* Viking, 1993.
Hillstrom, Kevin, et al. *The Handy Sports Answer Book.* Invisible Ink, 1998.
Hollander, Phyllis, and Zander Hollander, eds. *Touchdown! Football's Most Dramatic Scoring Feats.* Random House, 1982.
Hollander, Zander, and Alex Sachare. *The Official NBA Basketball Encyclopedia.* Villard, 1989.
Jarrett, William. *Timelines of Sports History: Baseball.* Facts on File, 1989.
———. *Timetables of Sports History: The Olympic Games.* Facts on File, 1990.
Korch, Rick. *The Official Pro Hall of Fame Playbook.* Little Simon, 1990.
La Blanc, Michael L., and Richard Henshaw. *The World Encyclopedia of Soccer.* Gale, 1993.
Levenson, David, and Karen Christensen, eds. *Encyclopedia of World Sport: From Ancient Times to the Present.* ABC-CLIO, 1996.
Meserole, Mike. *The Ultimate Book of Sports Lists.* DK, 1999.
Nash, Bruce, et al. *The Sports Hall of Shame: Young Fans' Edition.* Archway, 1990.
Nash, Bruce, and Allan Zallo. *The Baseball Hall of Shame 3: Young Fans' Edition.* Archway, 1992.
Scholastic Visual Sports Encyclopedia. Scholastic, 2003.
Sherman, Eric. *365 Amazing Days in Sports: A Day-to-Day Look at Sports History.* Sports Illustrated for Kids, 1990.
Smith, Don R. *The Official Pro Hall of Fame Book of Superstars.* Little Simon, 1990.
Sobol, Donald J. *Encyclopedia Brown's Book of Wacky Sports.* Morrow, 1984.
Toropov, Brandon. *50 Biggest Baseball Myths.* Carol, 1997.
Young, Mark, ed. *The Guiness Book of Sports Records, 1991.* Facts on File, 1991.
———. *The Guinness Book of Sports Records, 1992.* Facts on File, 1992.

GIRLS' FICTION

Series

Betancourt, Jean. Cheer USA: *Go, Girl, Go!; Fight, Bulldogs, Fight!; We've Got Spirit!*
Cebulash, Mel. Ruth Marini on the Mound: *Ruth Marini of the Dodgers; Ruth Marini World Series Star; Ruth Marini, Dodger Ace.*
Costello, Emily. Soccer Stars: *Foul Play; On the Sidelines; Against the Rules; Best Friend Face-Off; Lottery Blues; Tournament Trouble; Calling the Shots; Teaming Up;* Ballet School: *Becky at the Barre; Jillian on Her Toes; Katie's Last Class; Megan's Nutcracker Prince; Moms in Tutus*
Holohan, Maureen. The Broadway Ballplayers: *Friday Nights; Everybody's Favorite; Left Out; Sideline Blues; Don't Stop; Ice Cold; Catch Shorty*

Kindig, Tess Eileen. Slam Dunk: *Muggsy Makes an Assist; Sixth Man Switch; Zip, Zero, Zilch; Gimme an "A"; March Mania; Spider McGee and the Hoopla; Double Whammy*

Levy, Elizabeth. The Gymnasts: *Beginners; First Meet; Nobody's Perfect; The Winner; Trouble in the Gym; Bad Break; Tumbling Ghosts; Captain of the Team; Crush on the Coach; Boys in the Gym; Mystery at the Meet; Out of Control; First Date; World Class Gymnast; Nasty Competition; Fear of Falling; Gymnast Commandos; The New Coach; Tough at the Top; The Gymnast's Gift; Team Trouble; Go for the Gold*

Lewis, Beverly. Girls Only (gymnastics): *Only the Best; Better than the Best; Reach for the Stars*

Lowell, Melissa. Silver Blades (skating): *A Leap Ahead; The Ice Princess; Wedding Secrets; The Competition; The Perfect Pair; Skating Camp; Spring Break; Center on Ice; The Big Audition; A Surprise Twist; Double Dare; The Winning Spirit; In the Spotlight; More than Friends; On the Edge; Chance of a Lifetime; Breaking the Ice; Rumors at the Rink; Nutcracker on Ice; A New Move; Ice Magic; Natalia Comes to America; The Only Way to Win; Wanted: One Perfect Boy; Rival Roommates; Gold Medal Dreams: Now or Never*

Malcolm, Jahnna N. Bad News Ballet: *Blubberina; The King and Us; The Terrible Tryouts; Battle of the Bunheads; Drat! We're Rats!; Save Dad; Stupid Cupids; Who Framed Mary Bubnik?; Camp Clodhopper; Boo Who?*

The Pink Parrots (baseball): *The Girls Strike Back: The Making of the Pink Parrots; Change Up; Fielder's Choice; No-Hitter; Mixed Signals; All That Jazz.*

Singleton, Linda Joy. Cheer Squad: *Crazy for Cartwheels; Spring to Stardom; Boys Are Bad News; Camp Confessions*

Sports Stories (James Lorimer & Co.): *Off the Wall; Sink or Swim; Great Lengths; Face Off; Fast Finish; Brothers on Ice; Queen of the Court; Pool Princess; Heads Up; Cutting It Close; Hockey Heat Wave; The Winning Edge; Rookie Season; Breathing Not Required; Power Hitter; Sayonara, Sharks; Shark Attack!; Shooting Stars; Power Play; Rink Rivals; Home Court Advantage; Mikayla's Victory; Shadow Ride; Hockey Heroes; Taking a Dive; Water Fight!; Triple Threat; A Leap of Faith.* (Most of these books feature female athletes, but the series also includes stories about male athletes)

Thacker, Nola. Michelle Kwan Presents Skating: *The Turning Point; Staying Balanced; Skating Backward; Champion's Luck; The Winning Edge; Coach's Choice*

Tocher, Timothy. *Long Shot; Playing for Pride*

Girls on Boys' Teams

Baseball

Butler, Dori Hillestad. *Sliding into Home*. Peachtree, 2003.
Fowler, Karen Joy. *The Sweetheart Season*. Holt, 1996.
Gregorich, Barbara. *She's on First*. Contemporary Books, 1987.

Herzig, Alison. *The Boonsville Bombers*. Viking, 1991.
Klass, David. *A Different Season*. Lodestar, 1987.

Basketball

Barwin, Steven, and Gabriel David Tick. *Slam Dunk*. Lorimer, 1998.
Carbone, Elisa. *Sarah and the Naked Truth*. Yearling, 2002.
Jackson, Alison. *Blowing Bubbles with the Enemy*. Dutton, 1993.
Moore, Elaine. *Who Let the Girls in the Boys' Locker Room?* Troll, 1994.

Football

Baczewski, Paul. *Just for Kicks*. Lippincott, 1990.
Dygard, Thomas. *Winning Kicker*. Morrow, 1978.
———. *Forward Pass*. Morrow, 1989.
Korman, Gordon. *The Zucchini Warriors*. Scholastic, 1988.

Hockey

Fisher, Lois. *Sarah Dunes, Weird Person*. Putnam, 1981.

Soccer

Molarsky, Osmond. *Scrappy*. Putnam, 1983.
Wallace, Bill. *Never Say Quit*. Holiday House, 1993.

Wrestling

Spinelli, Jerry. *There's a Girl in My Hammerlock*. Simon & Schuster, 1991.

Girls' Teams

Baseball/Softball

Conly, Jane Leslie. *What Happened on Planet Kid*. Henry Holt, 2000.
Due, Linnea. *High and Outside*. Harper & Row, 1980.
Fraustino, Lisa Rowe. *Grass and Sky*. Orchard Books, 1994.
Killien, Christi. *The Daffodils*. Scholastic, 1992.
Koss, Amy Goldman. *Strike Two*, Dial, 2001.
Lewen, Michael Z. *Cutting Loose*. Henry Holt, 1999.
Lord, Betty. *The Year of the Boar & Jackie Robinson*. HarperCollins, 1984.
Mackel, Kathy. *A Season of Comebacks*. Putnam, 1997.
Morse, Janey. *Easy Out*. 1st Books Library, 2000.

Ripslinger, Jon. *Triangle*. Harcourt Brace, 1994.
Springstubb, Tricia. *With a Name Like Lulu, Who Needs More Trouble?* Delacorte, 1989.
Van Draanen, Wendelin. *Sammy Keyes and the Search for Snake Eyes*. Knopf, 2002.
———. *Sammy Keyes and the Sisters of Mercy*. Random House, 1999.
Wolff, Virginia Euwer. *Bat 6*. Scholastic Press, 1998.

Basketball

Bledsoe, Lucy Jane. *Hoop Girlz*. Holiday House, 2002.
Cossi, Olga. *The Magic Box*. Pelican, 1990.
Gutman, Bill. *Smitty II The Olympics*. Turman, 1990.
King, Tabitha. *One on One*. Dutton, 1993.
Mead, Alice. *Soldier Mom*. FSG, 1999.
Oates, Joyce Carol. *Big Mouth, Ugly Girl*. HarperCollins, 2002.
Revoyr, Nina. *The Necessary Hunger*. Simon & Schuster, 1997.
Roberts, Nadine. *These Are the Best Years?* Fawcett, 1989.

Hockey

Corbett, Scott. *The Hockey Girls*. Dutton, 1976.
Fisher, Lois. *Sarah Dunes, Weird Person*. Putnam, 1981.

Soccer

Brashares, Ann. *The Sisterhood of the Traveling Pants*. Delacorte, 2001.
Jorgenson, Dan. *Dawn's Diamond Defense*. Chariot, 1988.
Shreve, Susan Richards. *The Goalie*. Morrow, 1996.

Volleyball

Christopher, Matt. *Spike It!* Little, Brown, 1999.
Pascal, Francine. *Win One for Sandra*. Bantam, 1996. (Sweet Valley Series)
Voigt, Cynthia. *Tell Me If Lovers Are Losers*. Atheneum, 1982.

Individual Sports

Dance

Betancourt, Jeanne. *Kate's Turn*. Scholastic, 1992.
Hewett, Lorri. *Dancer*. Dutton, 1999.
Hurwin, Davida Wills. *A Time for Dancing*. Little, Brown, 1995.

Jessel, Camilla. *Ballet School*. Viking, 2000.
Southgate, Martha. *Another Way to Dance*. Delacorte, 1996.

Gymnastics

Hermann, Spring. *Flip City*. Orchard, 1988.
Kennemore, Tim. *The Fortunate Few*. Coward, 1981.
Lee, Marie G. *Finding My Voice*. Bantam Doubleday Dell, 1992.

Skating

Bennett, Cherie. *Girls in Love*. Point Press, 1996.
Levenbron, Steven. *The Luckiest Girl in the World*. Penguin, 1998.
Levy, Elizabeth. *Cold as Ice*. Morrow Junior Books, 1988.

Swimming/Diving

Cadnum, Michael. *Heat*. Viking, 1998.
Coleman, Evelyn. *Born in Sin*. Atheneum, 2001.
Donovan, Stacey. *Dive*. Puffin, 1996.
Duder, Tessa. *Alex in Rome*. Houghton Mifflin, 1992.
———. *In Lane Three, Alex Archer*. Houghton Mifflin, 1989.
Levin, Jenifer. *Water Dancer*. Poseidon, 1982.
Mango, Karin. *Just for the Summer*. Harper, 1990.
McVeity, Jen. *On Different Shores*. Orchard, 1998.
Rottman, S. L. *Head above Water*. Peachtree Press, 1999.

Tennis

Adler, C. S. *Winning*. Clarion, 1999.
Byalick, Marcia. *It's a Matter of Trust*. Harcourt, 1995.
Hoh, Diane. *Slow Dance*. Scholastic, 1989.
Jacobs, Helen Hull. *The Tennis Machine*. Scribner's, 1972.
Lehrman, Robert. *Separations*. Viking, 1990.
Lamott, Anne. *Crooked Little Heart*. Doubleday, 1998.
Powell, Randy. *The Whistling Toilets*. Farrar Straus Giroux, 1996.
Towne, Mary. *First Serve*. Atheneum, 1976.
Wells, Rosemary. *When No One Was Looking*. Dial, 1980.

Track/Running

Anderson, Laurie Halse. *Catalyst*. Penguin Putnam, 2002.
Cadnum, Michael. *Rundown*. Penguin Putnam, 2001.
Fogelin, Adrian. *Crossing Jordan*. Peachtree Press, 2000.

Harlan, Elizabeth. *Footfalls*. Atheneum, 1982.
Harrison, Mette Ivie. *The Monster in Me*. Holiday House, 2003.
Knudson, R. R. *Zan Hagen's Marathon*. Farrar, Straus & Giroux, 1984.
Levine, Anna. *Running on Eggs*. Front Street/Cricket Books, 1999.
Levy, Marilyn. *Run for Your Life*. Houghton Mifflin, 1996.
Lewis, Catherine. *Postcards to Father Abraham*. Atheneum, 2000.
McKay, Robert. *The Girl Who Wanted to Run the Boston Marathon*. Elsevier/Dutton, 1982.
Rue, Nancy. *Janis Project*. Crossway Books, 1988.
Snyder, Zilpha Keatley. *Cat Running*. Delacorte, 1994.
Woodson, Jacqueline. *Hush*. Penguin Putnam, 2002.
Woolverton, Linda. *Running before the Wind*. Houghton Mifflin, 1987.

Other

Emerson, Mark. *The Mean, Lean Weightlifting Queen*. Tudor, 1992.
Hall, Lynn. *Tin Can Tucker*. Scribners, 1982.
Murphy, Claire Rudolf. *To the Summit*. Morrow, 1998.
Nicholson, Joy. *The Tribes of Palos Verdes*. St. Martin's, 1998.
Savage, Deborah. *To Race a Dream*. Houghton Mifflin, 1994.
Towne, Mary. *Boxed In*. Crowell, 1982.

Anthologies

Knudson, R. R., and May Swenson, eds. *American Sports Poems*. Orchard, 1988.
Macy, Sue, ed. *Girls Got Game: Sports Stories and Poems*. Henry Holt, 2001.
Nauen, Elinor, ed. *Diamonds Are a Girl's Best Friend: Women Writers on Baseball*. Faber and Faber, 1993.
Sandoz, Joli, ed. *A Whole Other Ball Game: Women's Literature on Women's Sport*. Noonday Press, 1997.

GIRLS' NONFICTION

Autobiography and Biography

Series

Fast Breaks: *She's Got Game; Chamique Holdsclaw Story; Raise the Roof! WNBA Superstars*
Greenberg, Doreen, and Michael Greenberg. Anything You Can Do . . . New Sports Heroes for Girls: *A Drive to Win: The Story of Nancy Lieberman-Cline; Sword of a Champion: The Story of Sharon Monplaisil; Fast Lane to Victory: The Story of Jenny Thompson*

Brill, Marlene Targ. Sports Success: *Winning Women in Soccer; Winning Women in Ice Hockey; Winning Women in Basketball; Winning Women in Baseball and Softball*

Layden, Joe. Women Athletes of the 2000 Olympics: *Superstars of the USA Women's Basketball; Superstars of USA Women's Soccer; Superstars of USA Women's Gymnastics*

Rutledge, Rachel. Women of Sports: *The Best of the Best in Basketball; The Best of the Best in Figure Skating; The Best of the Best in Soccer; The Best of the Best in Tennis; The Best of the Best in Gymnastics; The Best of the Best in Track and Field*

Sports Girl: *Competitive Track and Field for Girls; Competitive Volleyball for Girls; Competitive Figure Skating for Girls; Competitive Soccer for Girls*

Women Who Win: *Cynthia Cooper; Mia Hamm; Martina Hingis; Chamique Holdsclaw; Michelle Kwan; Lisa Leslie; Sheryl Swoopes; Venus and Serena Williams; Anna Kournikova; Martina Hingis; Gabrielle Reece; Lindsay Davenport; Dorothy "Dot" Richardson; Marion Jones; Laila Ali*

Baseball

Goodwin, Doris Kearns. *Wait until Next Year: Summer Afternoons with My Father and Baseball*. Simon and Schuster, 1998.

Green, Michelle Y. *A Strong Right Arm: The Story of Mamie "Peanut" Johnson*. Dial, 2002.

Basketball

Anderson, Joan. *Rookie: Tamika Whitmore's First Year in the WNBA*. Dutton, 2000.

Cooper, Cynthia. *She's Got Game: My Personal Odyssey*. Warner, 2000.

Gogol, Sara. *Katy Steding: Pro Basketball Pioneer*. Lerner, 1998.

Holdsclaw, Chamique. *Chamique: On Family, Focus, and Basketball*. Scribner, 2000.

Lieberman-Cline, Nancy. *Lady Magic*. Sagamore, 1992.

Savage, Jeff. *Rebecca Lobo*. Enslow, 2001.

Smith, Michele. *She's Got Game*. Scholastic, 1999.

Vanderveer, Tara. *Shooting from the Outside: How a Coach and Her Olympic Team Transformed Women's Basketball*. Avon, 1998.

Dance

Arnold, Sandra Martin. *Alicia Alonso: First Lady of Ballet*. Walker, 1993.

Dominy, Jeannine. *Katherine Dunham: Dancer and Choreographer*. Chelsea House, 1992.

Ford, Carin T. *Legends of American Dance and Choreography*. Enslow, 2000.

Freedman, Russell. *Martha Graham: A Dancer's Life*. Clarion Books, 1998.

Gregory, Cynthia. *Cynthia Gregory Dances Swan Lake*. Simon & Schuster Books for Young Readers, 1990.
Levine, Ellen. *Anna Pavlova: Genius of the Dance*. Scholastic, 1995.
Sandomir, Larry. *Isadora Duncan: Revolutionary Dancer*. Raintree Steck-Vaughn, 1995.

Golf

Blalock, Jane. *The Guts to Win*. Golf Digest, 1977.
Cayleff, Susan E. *Babe Didrikson: The Greatest All-Sport Athlete of All Time*. Conari, 2000.
Freedman, Russell. *Babe Didrikson Zaharias: The Making of a Champion*. Houghton Mifflin, 1999.
Knudson, R. R. *Babe Didrikson: Athlete of the Century*. Viking, 1985.
Lopez, Nancy. *The Education of a Woman Golfer*. Simon & Schuster, 1979.
Vold, Mona. *Different Strokes: The Lives and Teachings of the Game's Wisest Women*. Simon & Schuster, 1999.
Wakeman, Nancy. *Babe Didrikson Zaharis: Driven to Win*. Lerner, 2000.

Skating

Ashby, Ruth. *Going for the Gold: Sarah Hughes, America's Sweetheart*. Avon, 2002.
Chataigneau, Gerald. *Figure Skating Now*. Firefly Books, 2001.
Coffey, Frank and Joe Layden. *Thin Ice: The Complete, Uncensored Story of Tonya Harding, America's Bad Girl of Ice Skating*. Windsor, 1994.
Coffey, Wayne, and Phillip Bondy. *Dreams of Gold: The Nancy Kerrigan Story*. St. Martin's, 1994.
Epston, Edward Z. *Born to Skate: The Michelle Kwan Story*. Ballantine, 1997.
Gutman, Bill. *Tara Lipinski: Queen of the Ice*. Millbrook, 1999.
Hamill, Dorothy. *Dorothy Hamill On and Off the Ice*. Knopf, 1983.
Kelly, Evelyn B. *Katerina Witt*. Chelsea House, 1999.
Kerrigan, Nancy. *Nancy Kerrigan: In My Own Words*. Hyperion, 1996.
Krawiec, Richard. *Sudden Champion: The Sarah Hughes Story*. Avisson Press, 2002.
Kwan, Michelle. *Heart of a Champion: An Autobiography*. Scholastic, 1997.
Poynter, Margaret. *Top 10 American Women's Figure Skaters*. Enslow, 1999.
Trenary, Jill with Dale Mitch. *Jill Trenary: The Day I Skated for the Gold*. Simon & Schuster, 1991.

Soccer

Akers, Michelle. *The Game and the Glory*. Zondervan, 2000.
Hamm, Mia. *Go for the Goal: A Champion's Guide to Winning in Soccer and Life*. Quill, 2000.

Sharkey, John. *Mia Hamm*. Warwick, 2000.
Torres, John Albert. *Mia Hamm*. Mitchell Lane, 1999.

Tennis

Aronson, Virginia. *Venus Williams*. Chelsea House, 1999.
Biracree, Tom. *Althea Gibson*. Chelsea House, 1989.
Davidson, Sue. *Changing the Game: The Stories of Tennis Champions Alice Marble and Althea Gibson*. Seal Press Feminist, 1997.
Fillon, Mike. *Young Superstars of Tennis: The Venus and Serena Williams Story*. Avisson Press, 1999.
Gutman, Bill. *Venus & Serena: The Grand Slam Williams Sisters*. Scholastic, 2001.
King, Billie Jean. *Billie Jean*. Harper, 1974.
Knudson, R.R. *Martina Navritalova, Tennis Power*. Viking, 1986.
Lannin, Joanne. *Billie Jean King: Tennis Trailblazer*. Lerner, 1999.
Layden, Joe. *Return of a Champion: The Monica Seles Story*. St. Martin's, 1996.
Lloyd, Chris Evert. *Chrissie, My Own Story*. Simon & Schuster, 1982.
Rineberg, Dave. *Venus & Serena*. Frederick Fell, 2002.
Spencer, Bev. *Martina Hingis: Teen Tennis Sensation*. Warwick Publishing, 1999.
Teitelbaum, Michael. *Grand Slam Stars: Martina Hingus and Venus Williams*. Harper Active, 1998.

Track

Biracree, Tom. *Wilma Rudolph*. Chelsea House, 1991.
Benoit, Joan. *Running Tide*. Knopf, 1987.
Coffey, Wayne. *Wilma Rudolph*. Blackbirch, 1993.
Connolly, Pat. *Coaching Evelyn: Fast, Faster, Fastest Woman in the World*. HarperCollins, 1991.
Davis, Michael. *Black American Women in Olympic Track and Field*. McFarland, 1992.
Flanagan, Alice K. *Wilma Rudolph*. Ferguson, 2000.
Gibson, Althea. *I Always Wanted to Be Somebody*. Harper, 1958.
Gutman, Bill. *Marion Jones: The Fastest Woman in the World*. Pocket Books, 2000.
Knudson, R. R. *Julie Brown: Racing against the World*. Viking Kestrel, 1988.
Rapoport, Ron. *See How She Runs: Marion Jones and the Making of a Champion*. Algonquin, 2000.
Rutledge, Rachel. *Marion Jones: Fast and Fearless*. Millbrook, 2000.
Wickham, Martha. *Superstars of Women's Track and Field*. Chelsea House, 1997.

Volleyball

Reece, Gabrielle, and Karen Karbo. *Big Girl in the Middle*. Crown, 1997.

Other

Allen, Jennifer. *Fifth Quarter: The Scrimmage of a Football Coach's Daughter*. Random House, 2000.
Condon, Robert J. *Great Women Athletes of the 20th Century*. McFarland, 1991.
Da Silva, Rachel, ed. *Leading Out: Mountaineering Stories of Adventurous Women*. Seal, 1998.
Gaines, Ann. *Sports and Athletics*. Chelsea House, 1999.
Hasday, Judy L. *Extraordinary Women Athletes*. Children's Press, 2000.
Littlefield, Bill. *Champions: Stories of Ten Remarkable Athletes*. Little, Brown, 1993.
McMane, Fred, and Catherine Wolf. *Winning Women*. Bantam, 1995.
Olsen, Marilyn. *Women Who Risk: Profiles of Women in Extreme Sports*. Hatherleigh Press, 2003.
Powe-Allred, Alexandra. *Quiet Storm: A Celebration of Women in Sport*. Masters Press, 1997.
Savage, Jeff. *Julie Krone: Unstoppable Jockey*. Lerner, 1996.
Wilds, Mary. *A Forgotten Champion: The Story of Major Taylor, Fastest Bicycle Racer in the World*. Avisson Press, 2002.

History and Team Highlights

Baseball

Galt, Margot Fortunato. *Up to the Plate: The All-American Girls Professional Baseball League*. Franklin Watts, 1993.
Hanmer, Trudy J. *All-American Girls Professional Baseball League*. New Discovery, 1994.
Helmer, Diana Star. *Belles of the Ballpark*. Millbrook, 1993.
Macy, Sue. *A Whole New Ball Game: The True Story of The All-American Girls Professional Baseball League*. Henry Holt, 1993.

Basketball

Blais, Madeline. *In These Girls, Hope Is a Muscle: The True Story of Hoop Dreams and One Very Special Team*. Warner, 1995.
Colton, Larry. *Counting Coup: The True Story of Basketball and Honor on the Little Big Horn*. Warner Books, 2000
Corbett, Sara. *Venus to the Hoop: A Gold Medal Year in Women's Basketball*. Anchor, 1998.

Kessler, Lauren. *Full Court Press: A Season in the Life of a Winning Basketball Team and the Women Who Made It Happen*. Dutton, 1997.

Lannin, Joanne. *A History of Basketball for Girls and Women: From Bloomers to Big Leagues*. Lerner Sports, 2000.

Summitt, Pat. *Raise the Roof: The Inspiring Inside Story of the Tennessee Lady Vols' Undefeated 1997–98 Season*. Broadway, 1998.

Cheerleading

McElroy, James T. *We've Got Spirit: The Life and Times of America's Greatest Cheerleading Team*. Simon & Schuster, 1999.

Football

Spenser, Teena. *The Girlfriend's Guide to Football*. Firefly Books, 2001.

General

Hasday, Judy L. *Extraordinary Women Athletes*. Children's Press, 2000.

Kramer, S. A. *Wonder Women of Sports*. Grosset & Dunlap, 1997.

Teitelbaum, Michael. *Great Moments in Women's Sports*. World Almanac Library, 2002.

Golf

Glenn, Rhonda. *The Illustrated History of Women's Golf*. Taylor, 1991.

Vaughan, Roger. *Golf: The Woman's Game*. Stewart Tabori and Chang, 2001.

Hockey

Spenser, Teena. *The Girlfriend's Guide to Hockey*. Firefly Books, 2001.

Turco, Mary. *Crashing the Net: The U.S. Women's Olympic Ice Hockey Team and the Road to Gold*. HarperCollins, 1999.

Running

Pont, Sally. *Finding Their Stride: A Team of Young Runners and Their Season of Triumph*. Harcourt, 2000.

Skating

Boo, Michael. *The Story of Figure Skating*. Morrow, 1998.

Soccer

Coffey, Wayne R. *Meet the Women of American Soccer: An Inside Look at America's Team.* Scholastic, 1999.
Gregg, Lauren. *The Champion Within.* JTC Sports, 1999.
Littman, Jonathan. *The Beautiful Game: Sixteen Girls and the Soccer Season That Changed Everything.* Avon, 1999.
Longman, Jere. *Girls of Summer: The U.S. Women's Soccer Team and How They Changed the World.* HarperCollins, 2000.
Miller, Marla. *All American Girls: The USA National Soccer Team.* Archway, 1999.
Trecker, Jim, and Charles Miers, eds. *Women's Soccer: The Game and the World Cup.* Universe/Rizzoli, 1999.

Nonfiction

Bandy, Susan, and Anne Darden. *Crossing Boundaries: An International Anthology of Women's Experiences in Sports.* Human Kinetics, 1999.
Berry, Flynn, et al., eds. *New Moon Sports: What Sports Can Do for You and What You Can Do for Sports.* Crown, 1999.
Cohen, Greta L. *Women in Sport: Issues and Controversies.* Sage, 1993.
Dickerson, Karle, and Julia DeVillers. *Break the Tape: Women Athletes Breaking Barriers.* Darby Creek, 2003.
Doren, Kim, and Charlie Jones. *You Go Girl!: Winning the Woman's Way.* Andrews McNeel, 2000.
Edelson, Paula. *A to Z of American Women's Sports.* Facts on File, 2002.
Gottesman, Jane. *Game Face: What Does a Female Athlete Look Like?* Random House, 2001.
Guttmann, Allen. *Women's Sports.* Columbia University Press, 1991.
Greenberg, Judith E. *Getting into the Game: Women in Sports.* Franklin Watts, 1997.
Hasday, Judy L. *Extraordinary Women Athletes.* Children's Press, 2000.
Hastings, Penny. *Sports for Her: A Reference Guide for Teenage Girls.* Greenwood, 1999.
Haven, Kendall. *Amazing American Women.* Libraries Unlimited, 1995.
Layden, Joe. *Women in Sports: The Complete Book on the World's Greatest Female Athletes.* General, 1997.
Lessa, Christina. *Women Who Win: Stories of Triumph in Sport and in Life.* Universe Publishing, 1998.
Liebman, Glenn. *Women's Sports Shorts: 1001 One-Liners by and about Women in Sports.* McGraw-Hill, 2000.
Macy, Sue, and Jane Gottesman, eds. *Play Like a Girl: A Celebration of Women in Sports.* Henry Holt, 1999.
Macy, Sue. *Winning Ways: A Photohistory of American Women in Sports.* Holt, 1996.

Markel, Robert, and Nancy Brooks. *For the Record: Women in Sports.* World Almanac, 1985.

Markel, Robert. *The Women's Sports Encyclopedia.* Holt, 1998.

Miller, Ernestine Girchner. *Making Her Mark: Firsts and Milestones in Women's Sports.* McGraw-Hill, 2002.

Nelson, Marian Burton. *Are We Winning Yet? How Women Are Changing Sports and Sports Are Changing Women.* Random House, 1991.

Pasternack, Cel, and Linda Thornburg. *Cool Careers for Girls in Sports.* Impact, 1999.

Powe-Allrod, Alexandra, and Michelle Powe. *The Quiet Storm: A Celebration of Women in Sport.* Masters Press, 1997.

Saari, Peggy, Tim Gall, and Susan Gall, eds. *Women's Firsts: Milestones in Women's History.* Gale, 1998.

Sandoz, Joli, and Joby Winans, eds. *Whatever It Takes: Women on Women's Sport.* Farrar, Straus and Giroux, 1999.

Smith, Lissa, ed. *Nike Is a Goddess: The History of Women in Sports.* Atlantic Monthly Press, 1998.

Sparhawk, Ruth M., et al., eds. *American Women in Sport, 1887–1987.* Scarecrow, 1989.

Steiner, Andy. *Girl Power on the Playing Field.* Lerner, 2000.

Welden, Amelie. *Girls Who Rocked the World: Heroines from Sacagawea to Sheryl Swoopes.* Beyond Words, 1998.

How-To

Dufort, Anthony. *Ballet Steps: Practice to Performance.* Clarkson N. Potter, 1990.

Crisfield, Deborah W. *Winning Volleyball for Girls.* Facts on File, 1995.

Ford, Dennis R. *An Introduction to Softball Pitching Mechanics.* McGraw-Hill, 1990.

Frost, Shelley, and Ann Troussieux. *Throw Like a Girl: Discovering the Body, Mind, and Spirit of the Athlete in You.* Beyond Words, 2001.

Gaede, Katrina. *Fitness Training for Girls: A Teen Girl's Guide to Resistance Training, Cardiovascular Conditioning and Nutrition.* Tracks, 2001.

Hastings, Penny. *Sports for Her: A Reference Guide for Teenage Girls.* Greenwood, 1999.

Konzak, Burt. *Girl Power: Self-Defense for Teens.* Sport Book, 1999.

Kempf, Cheri. *The Softball Pitching Edge.* Human Kinetics, 2002.

Knudson, R. R. *Muscles!* Avon, 1983.

Lieberman-Cline, Nancy, and Robin Roberts. *Basketball for Women.* Human Kinetics, 1995.

Manley, Claudia B. *Competitive Volleyball for Girls.* Rosen, 2001.

Reber, Deborah. *Run for Your Life: A Book for Beginning Women Runners.* Berkley, 2002.
Sammons, Barry, and Lisa Fernandez. *Fastpitch Softball: The Windmill Pitcher.* Contemporary Books, 1997.
Vicario, Arantxa Sanchez. *The Young Tennis Player.* Dorling Kindersley, 1996.
Viera, Barbara L., and Bonnie Jill Ferguson. *Volleyball: Steps to Success.* Human Kinetics, 1996.
Weatherspoon, Teresa. *Teresa Weatherspoon's Basketball for Girls.* John Wiley, 1999.

1980 AND EARLIER

Authors

Alex B. Allen (1972–1975) *Basketball Toss Up; No Place for Baseball; Fifth Down; The Tennis Menace*
Bob Allison and Frank E. Hill (1951) *The Kid Who Batted 1.000*
Joe Archibald (1947–1974) *Rebel Halfback; Touchdown Glory; Hold That Line!; Inside Tackle; Block That Kick; Fighting Coach; Double Play Rookie; Fullback Fury; Full Count; Go, Navy, Go; Circus Catch; Mr. Slingshot; Catcher's Choice; Fight, Team, Fight; Bonus Kid; Falcons to the Fight; First Base Hustler; Crazy Legs McBain; Outfield Orphan; Red-Dog Center; Shortstop on Wheels; Backfield Twins; Big League Busher; Hard Nosed Halfback; Old Iron Glove; Quarterback and Son; The Easy Out; Southpaw Speed; West Point Wingback; The Long Pass; Right Field Rookie; The Scrambler; Fast Break Fury; Mitt Maverick; Pro Coach; Two Time Rookie; Backcourt Commando; Powerback; Payoff Pitch; Phantom Blitz; Right Field Runt; The Fifth Base; Three-Point Hero; Centerfield Rival*
Edith Bancroft (1917–1922) *Jane Allen of the Sub-Team; Jane Allen, Right Guard; Jane Allen, Center; Jane Allen, Junior; Jane Allen, Senior*
Ralph Henry Barbour (1899–1942) *The Half-Back; For the Honor of the School; Behind the Line; Weatherby's Inning; On Your Mark; The Crimson Sweater; The Spirit of the School; Forward Pass; Double Play; Kingsford, Quarter; The New Boy at Hilltop, and Other Stories; Winning His "Y"; Finkler's Field; For Yardley; Team-Mates; Change Signals; Crofton Chums; Around the End; The Junior Trophy; The Brother of Hero; Left End Edwards; Danforth Plays the Game; Left Tackle Thayer; The Lucky Seventh; Left Guard Gilbert; The Purple Pennant; Rivals for the Team; The Secret Play; Center Rush Rowland; Hitting the Line; Winning His Game; Keeping His Course; Fullback Foster; Guarding His Goal; The Play That Won; Quarter-Back Bates; Kick Formation; Left Half Harmon; Three-Base Benson; Tod Hale on the Nine; Right End Emerson; The Turner Twins; For the Good of the Team; Nid and Nod; Right Guard Grant; The Fighting Scrub; Follow the Ball; Infield Rivals; Right Tackle Todd; Barry Locke, Halfback; Bases*

Full; Hold 'em Wyndham!; Right Half Hollins; The Last Play; The Winning Year; The Long Pass; The Relief Pitcher; The Fortunes of the Team; Hunt Holds the Center; Lovell Leads Off; Substitute Jimmy; Tod Hale on the Scrub; Grantham Gets On; Candidate for the Line; Danby's Error; Fourth Down!; The Fumbled Pass; Squeeze Play; The Cub Battery; Skate, Glendale!; Beaton Runs the Mile; Goal to Go; The Scoring Play; Southworth Scores; The Glendale Five; Merritt Leads the Nine; Watch That Pass!; The School That Didn't Care; The Score Is Tied; Fighting Guard; Ninth Inning Rally; The Infield Twins; The Target Pass; Barclay Back

Clair Bee (1942–1968) *Championship Ball; Touchdown Pass; Clutch Hitter!; Strike Three!; Hoop Crazy; Pitchers' Duel; A Pass and a Prayer; Dugout Jinx; Freshman Quarterback; Backboard Fever Fence Busters; Ten Seconds to Play!; Fourth Down Showdown; Tournament Crisis; Hardcourt Upset; Pay-Off Pitch; No-Hitter; Triple-Threat Trouble; Backcourt Ace; Buzzer Basket; Comeback Cagers; Home Run Feud; Hungry Hurler*

Curtis Bishop (1950–1968) *Teamwork; Banjo Hitter; Saturday Heroes; Football Fever; Hero at Halfback; Larry of the Little League; Fighting Quarterback; Larry Leads Off; Goal to Go; Larry Comes Home; Dribble Up; Half-Time Hero; Little Leaguer; The Little League Way; Lank of the Little League; Little League Heroes; The Lost Eleven; The Playmaker; Sideline Pass; Sideline Quarterback; Little League Double Play; Rebound; The Big Game; Field Goal; Little League Amigo; Lonesome End; Little League Stepson; Gridiron Glory; Little League Visitor; Fast Break; Little League Victory; Hackberry Jones, Split End; Little League Little Brother*

Mary G. Bonner (1931–1959) *Out to Win; The Base Stealer; The Dugout Mystery; Two-Way Pitcher; Spray Hitter; Baseball Rookies Who Made Good; Big Baseball Book for Boys; How to Play Baseball; Real Book about Sports*

Robert Bowen, aka J. R. Richards (1948–1969) *The Winning Pitch; Fourth Down; Player-Manager; Ball Hawk; Blocking Back; Hot Corner; Touchdown Kid; Behind the Bat; Infield Spark; Million-Dollar Fumble; The Big Inning; The Last White Line; The Big Hit; Triple Play; Pennant Fever; No Hitter; Bat Boy; Perfect Game; Hot Corner Blues; Rebel Rookie; Lightning Southpaw; Infield Flash;* "J. R. Richards": *The Club Team; The Fighting Halfback; Quarterback, All-American;* "Billy Boxer": Serials in New York Five Cent Library

Howard Brier (1948–1954) *Phantom Backfield; Backboard Magic; Shortstop Shadow; Cinder Cyclone; Fighting Heart*

Noah Brooks (1884) *Freddy Plays Football; Freddy and the Baseball Team from Mars; Our Base Ball Club and How It Won the Championship; The Boys of Fairport*

William Butterworth (1966–1968) *Tiger Rookie; Li'l Wildcat; Maverick on the Mound*

Walter Camp (1883–1927) *American Football; Athletes All: Training, Organization, and Play; Base Ball; The Book of Foot-Ball; Book of Sports and Games; Football for the Spectator; Get Ready!; Drives and Putts; The Substitute; Jack Hall at*

Yale; Old Ryerson; Danny Fists; Captain Danny; Danny the Freshman; Football Facts and Figures

Terry Carr (1977) *The Infinite Arena: Seven Science Fiction Stories about Sports*

Roch Carrier (1979) *The Hockey Sweater and Other Stories*

John F. Carson (1957–1964) *Floorburns; The Twenty-Third Street Crusaders; The Coach Nobody Liked; Hotshot; Court Clown; The Mystery of the Tarnished Trophy*

Robin Carver (1834) *The Book of Sports*

Betty Cavanna (1956) *The Boy Next Door*

Allen Chapman (1913–1915) *The Heroes of the School; Fred Fenton on the Lines, or, The Football Boys of Riverport School; Fred Fenton the Pitcher, or, The Rivals of Riverport School; Fred Fenton on the Track, or, The Athletes of Riverport School; Fred Fenton on the Crew, or, The Young Oarsmen of Riverport School; Fred Fenton, Marathon Runner, or, The Great Race at Riverport School*

B. J. Chute (1944–1966) *Blocking Back; Shift to the Right; Teen-Age Sports Parade*

William Clarke (1828) *The Boy's Own Book: A Complete Encyclopedia of All the Diversions, Athletic, Scientific, and Recreative, of Boyhood and Youth.*

Matthew Colton (1911–1914) *Frank Armstrong, Drop Kicker; Frank Armstrong, Captain of the Nine; Frank Armstrong at College; Frank Armstrong's Second Team*

Charles Coombs (1948–1977) *Young Infield Rookie; Sleuth at Shortstop; Teen-age Sports Stories; Be a Winner in Baseball; Be a Winner in Basketball; Be a Winner in Football; Be a Winner in Ice Hockey; Be a Winner in Soccer; Be a Winner in Tennis; Be a Winner in Track and Field*

John R. Cooper (1947–1953) *The Mystery at the Ball Park; The Southpaw's Secret; First Base Jinx; The Phantom Homer; The College League Mystery; The Fighting Shortstop*

Scott Corbett (1965–1976) *The Baseball Trick; The Baseball Bargain; The Home Run Trick; The Hockey Trick; The Hockey Girls*

William Robert Cox (1956–1978) *Five Were Chosen; Gridiron Duel; The Wild Pitch; Tall on the Court; Third and Eight to Go; Big League Rookie; Trouble at Second Base; Goal Ahead!; The Valley Eleven; Jump Shot Joe; Rookie in the Backcourt; Big League Sandlotters; Third and Goal; Gunner on the Court; Playoff; The Unbeatable Five; Game, Set, and Match; Home Court Is Where You Find It*

John Craig (1973–1979) *Power Play; Superdude; All G.O.D.'s Children (autobiography); Chappie and Me*

Don Creighton (1965–1968) *Little League Giant; The Secret Little Leaguer; Little League Old-Timer; Little League Ball Hawk*

Daniel M. Daniel (1930–1948) *Babe Ruth: The Idol of the American Boy; The Real Babe Ruth*

Spencer Davenport (1916) *The Rushton Boys at Rally Hall, or, Great Days in School and Out*

P. H. Davis (1911) *Football, The American Collegiate Game*

Elmer Dawson (1928–1932) *Garry Grayson's Hill Street Eleven; Garry Grayson at Lennox High; Garry Grayson's Football Rivals; Garry Grayson at Stanley*

Prep; Garry Grayson Showing His Speed; Garry Grayson's Winning Kick; Garry Grayson Hitting the Line; Buck's Winning Hit; Garry Grayson's Winning Touchdown; Larry's Fadeaway; The Pickup Nine; Buck's Home Run Drive; Garry Grayson's Double Signals; Garry Grayson's Forward Pass; Larry's Speed Ball

Graham Dean (1936) *Herb Kent, West Point Cadet; Herb Kent, West Point Fullback*

Duane Decker (1947–1964) *Good Field, No Hit; Starting Pitcher; Hit and Run; The Catcher from Double-A; Fast Man on a Pivot; The Big Stretch; Wrong-Way Rookie; Switch Hitter; Mister Shortstop; Long Ball to Left Field; Third-Base Rookie; Showboat Southpaw; Rebel in Right Field; The Grand Slam Kid; Clutch Hitter* (under "Richard Wayne")

Paul Deegan (1947–1981) Dan Murphy Sports Series: *Almost a Champion; Important Decision; Dan Moves Up; The Tournaments*

Julian De Vries (1940) *The Strike-Out King*

Paul Dietzel and Everett Houghton (1965–1971) *Go, Shorty, Go; Coaching Football*

Alan Drady (1932–1935) *Red Morton, Waterboy; That Cathedral Team*

Albertus True Dudley (1903–1916) *Following the Ball; Making the Nine; In the Line; With Mask and Mitt; The Great Year; A Full-Back Afloat; The Yale Cup; The School Four; At the Home Plate; Stories of the Triangular League; The Half-Miler; Unofficial Prefect*

J. W. Duffield (1913–1914) *Bert Wilson, Marathon Winner; Bert Wilson's Fadeaway Ball, Bert Wilson on the Gridiron; Bert Wilson at the Wheel*

Montrew Dunham (1965) *Abner Doubleday: Young Baseball Pioneer*

Thomas Dygard (1977–1980) *Outside Shooter; Point Spread; Running Scared; Winning Kicker*

Jay Raymond Elderice (1915–1916) *T. Haviland Hicks, Freshman; T. Haviland Hicks, Sophomore; T. Haviland Hicks, Junior; T. Haviland Hicks, Senior*

William Everett (1868–1891) *Changing Base, or, What Edward Rice Learnt at School; Double Play; Thine Not Mine*

Johnny Evers (1913) *Baseball in the Big Leagues: A Book for Boys*

Henry Felsen (1947) *Bertie Comes Through*

Phyllis R. Fenner (1952–1965) *Crack of the Bat: Stories of Baseball; Quick Pivot: Stories of Baseball; Kick Off: Stories of Football*

Dick Fishel (1945–1951) *Terry and Bunky Play Football; Terry and Bunky Play Baseball; Terry and Bunky Play Basketball; Terry and Bunky Play Hockey; Terry and Bunky Learn to Swim*

Alice Fleming (1972) *Hosannah, The Home Run!: Poems about Sports*

Jessie Graham Flower (1915–1924) *Grace Harlowe's Plebe Year at High School, or, The Merry Doings of the Freshman Girls; Grace Harlowe's Sophomore Year in High School, or, The Record of the Girl Chums in Word and Athletics; Grace Harlowe's Junior Year at High School, or, Fast Friends in the Sororities; Grace Harlowe's Senior Year at High School, or, The Parting of the Ways.*

Louise Foley (1972–1978) *Somebody Stole Second; Tackle Twenty-Two*
Graham B. Forbes (1926) *The Boys of Columbia High on the Gridiron; Frank Allen and His Rivals; Frank Allen—Captain of the Team; Frank Allen in Camp; Frank Allen in Winter Sports; Frank Allen—Pitcher; Frank Allen Playing to Win; Frank Allen's Schooldays*
Mike Frederic (1965) *Freshman Quarterback; Frank Merriwell, Quarterback; Frank Merriwell Returns*
Michael French (1980) *The Throwing Season*
Dick Friendlich (1949–1970) *Pivot Man; Warrior Forward; Goal Line Stand; Line Smasher; Play Maker; Baron of the Bullpen; Left End Scott; Clean Up Hitter; Gridiron Crusader; Lead-Off Man; Backstop Ace; Full Court Press; All-Pro Quarterback; Relief Pitcher; Pinch Hitter; Touchdown Maker; Fullback from Nowhere; The Sweet Swing*
Samuel R. Fuller, aka Norman Brainerd (1910–1930) *Winning His Shoulder Straps; Winning the Eagle Prize; Winning the Junior Cup; Winning His Army Blue*
Hugh S. Fullerton (1910–1915) *Jimmy Kirkland and the Plot for the Pennant; Jimmy Kirkland of the Cascade College Team; Jimmy Kirkland of the Shasta Boys' Team*
Reed Fulton (1932–1938) *Lardy the Great; Rookie Coach*
William C. Gault (1951–1980) *Mr. Fullback, Day of the Rain; Bruce Benedict, Halfback; Through the Line; Little Big Foot; Backfield Challenge; The Lonely Mound; Stubborn Sam; Quarterback Gamble; Trouble at Second; Wild Willie, Wide Receiver; The Big Stick; Underground Skipper; Showboat in the Backcourt; Cut-Rate Quarterback; Thin Ice*
Steve Gelman (1961–1968) *Baseball Bonus Kid; Football Fury; Evans of the Army*
Nan Gilbert (1960) *Champions Don't Cry*
Beth Bradford Gilchrist, aka John P. Earl (1910–1938) *On the School Team; The School Team in Camp; Captain of the School Team; The School Team on the Diamond*
Fitzhugh Green (1922–1926) *Won for the Fleet; Fought for Annapolis; Hold 'em, Navy!*
Martin Harry Greenberg (1975) *Run to Starlight: Sports through Science Fiction*
Zane Grey (1909–1920) *The Short-Stop; The Redheaded Outfield and Other Baseball Stories; The Young Pitcher*
Clyde Grosscup (1953–1967) *The Winning Spirit; Pro Rookie; Pro Passer; Pro Champion; Throw the Bomb*
Donald H. Haines (1931–1945) *The Southpaw; Toss-UP; Triple Threat; Team Play; Sporting Chance; Blaine of the Backfield*
H. Irving Hancock (1910) *The High School Captain of the Team; The High School Freshman; The High School Left End; The High School Pitcher; The Grammar School Boys in Summer Athletics*
T. Truxtun Hare (1907–1919) *Making the Freshman Team; A Sophomore Half-Back; A Junior on the Line; A Senior Quarter-Back; A Graduate Coach; Phillip*

Kent; Phillip Kent in the Lower School; Phillip Kent in the Upper School; Kent of Malvern

Philip Harkins (1946–1964) *Lightning on Ice; The Big Silver Bowl; Touchdown Twins; Southpaw from San Francisco; Punt Formation; Knockout; Son of the Coach; Center Ice; Game, Carol Canning!; Breakaway Back; Fight Like a Falcon; No Head for Soccer*

Jay Heavilin (1965) *Fastball Pitcher*

Brooks Henderley (1916) *The Y.M.C.A. Boys of Cliffwood; The Y.M.C.A. Boys at Football*

Legrand Henderson (1958–1962) *How Baseball Began in Brooklyn; How Basketball Began*

Marguerite Henry (1948) *King of the Wind*

William Heuman (1950–1972) *Fighting Five; Wonder Boy; Junior Quarterback; Little League Champs; Strictly from Brooklyn; Rocky Malone; Left End Luisetti; Second String Hero; Backcourt Man; Rookie Backstop; The Wonder Five; Powerhouse Five; City High Five; The Horse That Played the Outfield; Horace Higby and the Field Goal Formula; Hillbilly Hurler; Tall Team; Scrambling Quarterback; Backup Quarterback; Horace Higby and the Scientific Pitch; City High Champions; The Goofer Pitch; Gridiron Stranger; Home Run Henri; Horace Higby and the Gentle Fullback; Fastbreak Rebel; Little League Hot Shots*

William Heyliger (1911–1945) *Bartley, Freshman Pitcher; Bucking the Line; Strike Three!; Off Side; Against Odds; Captain Fair-and-Square; The Captain of the Nine; The County Pennant; Fighting for Fairview; Bean-Ball Bill and Other Stories; The Fighting Captain, and Other Stories; Big Leaguer; The Macklin Brothers; Bill Darrow's Victory; Quarterback Hot-Head; The Gallant Crosby; Backfield Comet; Fighting Blood; Stan Kent, Freshman Fullback; Stan Kent, Varsity Man; The Loser's End; Backfield Play; Gridiron Glory; Top Lineman; "Hawley Williams": Batter Up; Quarterback Reckless; Five Yards to Go!; Johnson of Lansing; The Winning Hit; Fair Play!; Straight Ahead!; Dorset's Twister*

Al Hirshberg (1955–1975) *The Battery for Madison High; Varsity Double Play; Basketball Is My Life; Basketball's Greatest Stars; Basketball's Greatest Teams; The Al Kaline Story; From Sandlots to League President: The Story of Joe Cronin; Baseball's Greatest Catchers; Henry Aaron: Quiet Superstar; The Greatest American Leaguers; Frank Robinson: Born Leader; Frank Howard: Gentle Giant; Bobby Orr: Fire on Ice*

Syd Hoff (1969) *Baseball Mouse*

Donald Honig (1970–1980) *Fury on Skates, Johnny Lee; Way to Go, Teddy; Breaking In; Coming Back; Playing for Keeps; The Professional; Going the Distance; Running Harder; Baseball Between the Lines: Baseball in the 40's and 50's as Told by the Men Who Played It; Baseball When the Grass Was Green; Dynamite!; Last Great Season; Last Man Out; Man in the Dugout: Fifteen Big League Managers Speak Their Minds; Up from the Minor Leagues; Image of Their Greatness: An Illustrated History of Baseball from 1900 to the Present*

Appendix B

Robert Hood (1973–1976) *Let's Go to a Baseball Game; Let's Go to a Basketball Game; Let's Go to a Football Game; Let's Go to a Stock Car Race; Gas House Gang*

James Hopper (1912–1914) *The Freshman; Coming Back with the Spitball*

Nelson Hutto (1963–1967) *Breakaway Back; Goal Line Bomber; Victory Volley*

Constance H. Irwin, aka C. H. Frick (1954–1961) *Tourney Team; Five against the Odds; Patch; The Comeback Guy*

C. Paul Jackson (1947–1978) *All-Conference Tackle; Tournament Forward; Rose Bowl All-American; Rookie First Baseman; Shorty Makes First Team; Rose Bowl Line Backer; Shorty at Shortstop; Clown at Second Base; Dub, Halfback; Little Leaguer's First Uniform; Shorty Carries the Ball; Giant in the Midget League; Shorty at the State Tournament; Spice's Football; Buzzy Plays Midget League Football; Bud Plays Junior High Football; Bud Plays Junior High Basketball; The Jamesville Jets; Little League Tournament; Bud Baker, T Quarterback; World Series Rookie; Bullpen Bargain; Pro Hockey Comeback; Bud Baker, Racing Swimmer; Pro Football Rookie; Chris Plays Small Fry Football; Little Major Leaguer; Bud Plays Senior High Basketball; Pee Wee Cook of the Midget League; Fullback in the Large Fry League; Junior High Freestyle Swimmer; Minor League Shortstop; Midget League Catcher; Rookie Catcher with the Atlanta Braves; Bud Baker, High School Pitcher; Tim, the Football Nut; Big Play in the Small League; Hall of Fame Flankerback; Second Time Around Rookie; Pennant Stretch Drive; Stepladder Steve Plays Basketball; Bud Baker, College Pitcher; Pass Receiver; Rose Bowl Pro; Tim Mosely, Midget Leaguer; Halfback!; Eric and Dud's Football Bargain; Fifth Inning Fadeout; Beginner under the Backboard; "Cary Jackson": A Uniform for Harry; Haunted Halfback; "Colin Lochlons": Stretch Smith Makes a Basket; Squeeze Play; Three-and-Two Pitcher; Triple Play; Barney of the Babe Ruth League; "Jack Paulson": Fourth Down Pass; Match Point; Side Line Victory;* with O. B. Jackson: *Star Kicker; Basketball Clown; Hillbilly Pitcher; Puck Grabber; Freshman Forward; The Short Guard; High School Backstop; No Talent Letterman*

O. B. Jackson (1963–1965) *Basketball Comes to North Island; Southpaw in the Mighty Mite League*

Helen Hull Jacobs (1933–1975) *Adventure in Bluejeans; Better Physical Fitness for Girls; Beyond the Game: An Autobiography; Courage to Conquer; Famous American Women Athletes; Gallery of Champions; Modern Tennis; Tennis; The Tennis Machine; Young Sportsman's Guide to Tennis; Laurel for Judy; Center Court; Judy, Tennis Ace; Proudly She Serves!*

Lawrence Keating (1955–1966) *False Start; Kid Brother; Freshman Backstop; Junior Miler; Senior Challenge; Runner-Up; Wrong-Way Neelen; Ace Rebounder; The Comeback Year*

Heather Kellerhals-Stewart (1975) *She Shoots! She Scores!*

Bill Knott, aka Bill J. Carol (1963–1970) *Junk Pitcher; Backboard Scrambler; Circus Catch; Clutch Single; Scatback; Full-court Pirate; Hit Away!; Hard Smash* to Third; Long Pass; Inside the Ten; Lefty's Long Throw; Lefty Finds a Catcher; Touchdown Duo; Crazylegs Merrill; Lefty Plays First; Sandy Plays Third; Stop That Pass; Linebacker Blitz; Squeeze Play; Fullback Fury; High Fly to Center; Double-Play Ball; Flare Pass; Blocking Back; Single to Center

John Knowles (1959) *A Separate Peace*

R. R. Knudson (1972–1980) *Zanballer; Fox Running; Zanbanger; Zanboomer; Rhinehart Lifts; Weight Training for Young Athletes*

E. L. Konigsburg (1969) *About the B'nai Bagels*

George Kramer (1964–1968) *The Left Hander; Kid Battery*

Robert Leckie, aka Mark Porter (1960–1965) *Duel on the Cinders; Keeper Play; Overtime Upset; Set Point; Slashing Blades; Winning Pitcher; The Story of Football*

Burgess Leonard (1950–1963) *Victory Pass; Rookie Southpaw; Phantom of the Foul-Lines; One-Man Backfield; Second-Season Jinx; Stretch Bolton Comes Back; The Rookie Fights Back; Stretch Bolton's Rookies; Rebound Man; Stretch Bolton: Mr. Shortstop*

Elizabeth Levy (1975–1979) *Something Queer at the Ballpark; The Tryouts*

Robert Lipsyte (1967–1978) *The Contender; One Fat Summer; Free to Be Muhammad Ali*

Beman Lord (1958–1970) *The Trouble with Francis; Quarterback's Aim; Bats and Balls; Rough Ice; Mystery Guest at Left End; The Perfect Pitch; Shot-Put Challenge; Shrimp's Soccer Goal*

Evelyn Lunemann (1969–1972) *Fairway Danger; No Turning Back; Ten Feet Tall; Tip Off; Face-Off; Pitcher's Choice; Swimmer's Mark; Tennis Champ*

Leon McClinton (1974) *Cross-Country Runner*

Wilfred McCormick (1948–1963) *Legion Tourney; The Three-Two Pitch; Fielder's Choice; Flying Tackle; Bases Loaded; Rambling Halfback; Grand-Slam Homer; Quick Kick; First and Ten; The Man on the Bench; The Captive Coach; The Big Ninth; The Bigger Game; The Hot Corner; Five Yards to Glory; The Proud Champions; The Automatic Strike; The Last Put-Out; One O'Clock Hitter; Stranger in the Backfield; Too Many Forwards; The Bluffer; Man in Motion; The Play for One; The Double Steal; The Five Man Break; Rebel with a Glove; Too Late to Quit; Home Run Harvest; Once a Slugger; The Phantom Shortstop; Rough Stuff; The Starmaker; The Two-One-Two Attack; The Long Pitcher; The Pro Toughback; The Right-End Option; The Throwing Catcher; Wild on the Bases; The Go-Ahead Runner; Seven in Front; Touchdown for the Enemy; No Place for Heroes; Tall at the Plate; The Incomplete Pitcher; One Bounce Too Many; Rookie on First; Fullback in the Rough*

William MacKellar (1955–1979) *Kickoff; The Team That Wouldn't Quit; A Goat for Greg; Score!: A Baker's Dozen Sports Stories; Mound Menace; The Soccer Orphans*

Christy Mathewson (1910–1917) *Won in the Ninth; Catcher Craig; First Base Faulkner; Pitcher Pollock; Second Base Sloan; Battle of Base-Ball; Pitching in a Pinch, or, Baseball from the Inside*

Hamilton "Tex" Maule (1959–1973) *Footsteps; The Rookie; The Quarterback; The Shortstop; Beatty of the Yankees; The Last Out; The Linebacker: A Novel of Professional Football; The Running Back: A Novel of Professional Football; The Corner Back; The Receiver; Bart Starr: Professional Quarterback; Championship Quarterback; Game: The Official Picture History of the NFL; Game: The Official Picture History of the AFL; Jeremy Todd; Players; The Pro Season; The Pros*

Stephen Meader (1936–1968) *The Will to Win and Other Stories; Sparkplug of the Hornets; Lonesome End*

John C. Mellett, aka Jonathon Brooks (1928–1939) *Jimmy Makes the Varsity; Pigskin Soldier; Varsity Jim*

Earl Schenck Miers (1936–1969) *The Backfield Feud; Career Coach; Monkey Shines; Touchdown Trouble; The Kid Who Beat the Dodgers, and Other Sports Stories; Ball of Fire; Basketball*

Barbara Morgenroth (1978–1980) *Last Junior Year; Nicki & Wynne; Ride a Proud Horse*

Gertrude Morrison (1914–1920) *The Girls of Central High, or, Rivals for All Honors; The Girls of Central High at Basketball, or, The Great Gymnasium Mystery; The Girls of Central High on Track and Field, or, The Champions of the School League; The Girls of Central High on Lake Luna, or, The Crew That Won; The Girls of Central High in Camp, or, The Old Professor's Secret*

Lillian Morrison, ed. (1965) *Sprints and Distances: Sports in Poetry and the Poetry in Sport*

Charles Muller (1927–1928) *The Baseball Detective; Puck Chasers, Incorporated*

Mike Neigoff (1963–1976) *Free Throw; Two on First; Goal to Go; Hal, Tennis Champ; Ski Run; Playmaker; Terror on the Ice; Runner Up Nine Makes a Team*

Frank I. Odell (1910–1911) *Larry Burke, Freshman; Larry Burke, Sophomore*

Sidney Offit (1960–1964) *The Boy Who Won the World Series; Cadet Quarterback; Cadet Command; Soupbone; Cadet Attack*

Joseph Olgin (1954–1975) *Little League Champions; Backcourt Rivals; The Scoring Twins: A Story of Biddy Basketball; Sports Stories for Boys; Battery Feud; Backcourt Atom; Illustrated Football Dictionary for Young People*

Gene Olson (1956–1967) *The Tall One; The Ballhawks; Bonus Boy: The Story of a Southpaw Pitcher; Fullback Fury; Three Men on Third; Cross-Country Chaos; Bucket of Thunderbolts: A Sports Car Racing Adventure; Red, Red Roadster; Roaring Road: A Sports Car Novel*

Frank O'Rourke (1948–1954) *Flashing Spikes; The Team; Bonus Rookie; The Football Gravy Train; The Greatest Victory and Other Baseball Stories; The Heavenly World Series and Other Baseball Stories; Never Come Back; Nine Good Men; The Catcher and the Manager; High Dive*

Mark Overton (1919) *Jack Winters' Baseball Team; Jack Winters' Gridiron Chums*

Ralph D. Paine (1910–1931) *College Years; The Head Coach; Campus Days; Sons of Eli; First Down Kentucky!*

Norvin Pallas (1963) *The Baseball Mystery*

Charles E. Parker (1926) *The Whipper-Snapper*

Gilbert Patten, aka Gordon Braddock, Morgan Scott, Burt L. Standish (1900–1928) *The Rockspur Eleven; The Rockspur Nine; The Rockspur Rivals; Bill Bruce of Harvard; Cliff Stirling behind the Line; Cliff Stirling, Captain of the Nine; Cliff Stirling, Freshman at Stormbridge; Boltwood of Yale; The College Rebel; Cliff Stirling, Sophomore at Stormbridge; On College Battlefields; Call of the Varsity; Sons of Old Eli; Gordon Braddock Rex Kingdon in the North Woods; Rex Kingdon of Ridgewood High; Rex Kingdon behind the Bat; Rex Kingdon on Storm Island; Rex Kingdon at Walcott Hall; Morgan Scott Ben Stone at Oakdale; Boys of Oakdale Academy; Rival Pitchers of Oakdale; Great Oakdale Mystery; Oakdale Boys in Camp; New Boys at Oakdale;* "Burt L. Standish": Frank Merriwell series and others

Lawrence Perry (1916–1924) *The Big Game; For the Game's Sake; The Fullback; Touchdowns*

Clem Philbrook (1954–1973) *The Magic Bat; Skimeister; Ollie's Team and the Baseball Computer; Ollie's Team and the Football Computer; Ollie's Team and the Basketball Computer; Ollie, the Backward Forward; Ollie's Team Plays Biddy Baseball; Ollie's Team and the Alley Cats; Ollie's Team and the Two-Hundred Pound Problem; Ollie's Team and the Million Dollar Mistake; Slope Dope; Ollie, the Foul Shooter*

Maurice Phillips (1963) *Lightning on Ice*

Arthur Stanwood Pier (1903–1931) *The Triumph; Boys of St. Timothy's; The Jester of St. Timothy's; Harding of St. Timothy's; The New Boy; The Crashaw Brothers; Grannis of the Fifth; Dormitory Days; David Ives; Friends and Rivals; The Coach; The Captain; The Rigor of the Game; The Cheer Leader; The Champion*

Chaim Potok (1967) *The Chosen*

Marion Renick (1940–1977) *Champion Caddy; Skating Today; Swimming Fever; A Touchdown for Doc; The Dooleys Play Ball; Nickey's Football Team; Jimmy's Own Basketball; Pete's Home Run; The Heart for Baseball; Bats and Gloves of Glory; Young Mr. Football; The Tail of the Terrible Tiger; Boy at Bat; The Big Basketball Prize; Football Boys; Ricky in the World of Sport; Take a Long Jump; Five Points for Hockey; Sam Discovers Soccer; Famous Forward Pass Pair;* with James L. Renick: *David Cheers the Team; Tommy Carries the Ball; Steady*

Noel Sainsbury (1934–1942) *Cracker Stanton; The Fighting Five; Gridiron Grit;* "Charles Lawton": *Ros Hackeny, Halfback; Clarksville's Battery; The Winning Forward Pass; Home Run Hennessy; Touchdown to Victory*

Alice Sankey (1963) *Basketballs for Breakfast*

Harriet May Savitz (1970) *Fly, Wheels, Fly*

Walter Sawyer (1906–1912) *Captain Jack Lorimer; Jack Lorimer's Champions; Jack Lorimer's Holidays; Jack Lorimer's Substitute; Jack Lorimer, Freshman*

Jackson V. Scholz (1927–1971) *Split Seconds; Soldiers at Bat; Pigskin Warriors; Goal to Go; Batter Up; Gridiron Challenge; Fielder from Nowhere; Johnny King, Quarterback; Keystone Kelly; Fullback for Sale; Deep Short; One-Man Team; End Zone; Base Burglar; Fighting Chance; Man in a Cage; Bench Boss; Little*

League Town; The Perfect Game; The Football Rebels; Center-Field Jinx; Halfback on His Own; Dugout Tycoon; Fairway Challenge; Rookie Quarterback; Sparkplug at Short; Backfield Buckaroo; The Big Mitt; Fullback Fever; Hot-Corner Hank; Backfield Blues

Leonard Shortall (1965) Ben on the Ski Trail

Harold M. Sherman (1927–1972) Fight 'em, Big Three; Mayfield's Fighting Five; One Minute to Play; Get 'em, Mayfield; Touchdown!; Bases Full!; Block That Kick!; Safe!; Flashing Steel; Hit and Run!; Hit by Pitcher; Over the Line; Batter Up!; Flying Heels and Other Hockey Stories; Hold That Line!; Number 44 and Other Football Stories; Shoot That Ball! And Other Basketball Stories; Goal to Go!; It's a Pass!; Slashing Sticks and Other Hockey Stories; Strike Him Out!; Crashing Through!; Double Play! And Other Baseball Stories; Down the Ice and Other Winter Sports Stories; Interference and Other Football Stories; The Tennis Terror and Other Tennis Stories; Under the Basket and Other Basketball Stories; Captain of the Eleven

Alan Sillitoe (1959) The Loneliness of the Long Distance Runner

Earl Reed Silvers (1916–1932) Dick Arnold of Raritan College; Dick Arnold Plays the Game; Dick Arnold of the Varsity at Hillsdale High; Ned Beals, Freshman; Jackson of Hillsdale High; Ned Beals Works His Way; Barry, the Undaunted; Barry and Budd; Barry Goes to College; The Hillsdale High Champions; The Spirit of Menlo; The Red-Headed Halfback; Team First; The Scarlet of Avalon; The Glory of Glenwood; Code of Honor

Alfred Slote (1970–1978) Stranger on the Ball Club; Jake; The Biggest Victory; My Father, the Coach; Hang Tough; Tony and Me; Matt Gargan's Boy; The Hotshot; Love and Tennis

Doris Buchanan Smith (1976) Up and Over

Robert Smith (1947–1978) Football Twins; Little League Catcher; Babe Ruth's America; Baseball: A Historical Narrative of the Game, the Men Who Played It, and Its Place in America; Baseball in America; Baseball in the Afternoon: Tales from a Bygone Era; Baseball's Hall of Fame; Grantland Rice Award Prize Sports Stories; Great Teams of Pro Football; Heroes of Baseball; Hit Hard! Throw Hard!: The Secrets of Power Baseball; Illustrated History of Baseball; Illustrated History of Pro Football; Pioneers of Baseball; Pro Football: The History of the Game and the Great Players; Secrets of Big League Play; World Series: The Games and the Players

Albert G. Spalding (1911) Baseball, America's National Game

Charles Spink (1910) Baseball, The National Game

Amos Alonzo Stagg (1927) Touchdown!

W. O. Stoddard (1885–1909) Winter Fun; The Village Champion; Zeb, a New England Boy

David Stone (1923–1925) Yank Brown, Forward; Yank Brown, Halfback; Yank Brown, Miler; Yank Brown, Pitcher; Yank Brown, Honor Man

Raymond Stone (1912) Tommy Tiptop and His Baseball Nine; Tommy Tiptop and His Football Eleven; Tommy Tiptop and His Winter Sports

Edward Stratemeyer, aka Captain Ralph Bonehill, Lester Chadwick, Frank V. Webster, Arthur M. Winfield, and Clarence Young (1894–1925) *Dave Porter at Oak Hall; Dave Porter's Return to School; The Baseball Boys of Lakeport; The Football Boys of Lakeport; Dave Porter and His Classmates; Dave Porter and His Rivals;* "Captain Ralph Bonehill": *The Winning Run; The Rival Cyclists; The Young Oarsmen of Lakeview;* "Lester Chadwick": *A Quarterback's Pluck; The Rival Pitchers; Batting to Win; The Winning Touchdown; For the Honor of Randall; The Eight-Oar Victory; Baseball Joe of the Silver Stars; Baseball Joe on the School Nine; Baseball Joe at Yale; Baseball Joe in the Central League; Baseball Joe in the Big League; Baseball Joe on the Giants; Baseball Joe in the World Series; Baseball Joe around the World; Baseball Joe, Home Run King; Baseball Joe, Saving the League; Baseball Joe, Captain of the Team; Baseball Joe, Champion of the League; Baseball Joe, Club Owner; Baseball Joe, Pitching Wizard;* "Frank V. Webster": *The High School Rivals; Harry Watson's High School Days;* "Arthur M. Winfield": *The Rover Boys at School; The Putnam Hall Cadets; The Putnam Hall Rivals; The Putnam Hall Champions; The Rover Boys at Colby Hall; The Rover Boys at College;* "Clarence Young": *Jack Ranger's Schooldays; Jack Ranger's School Victories*

Noel Streatfeild (1937–1938) *Ballet Shoes; Tennis Shoes*

Paschal N. Strong, aka Kennedy Lyons (1930–1937) *West Point Wins; Three Plebes at West Point;* "Kennedy Lyons": *West Pointers on the Gridiron*

Richard Summers (1970) *Ball-Shy Pitcher*

James Terzian (1968–1973) *Pete Cass: Scrambler; The New York Giants*

Everett T. Tomlinson (1897–1914) *Ward Hill at Weston; Ward Hill—The Senior; Ward Hill at College; The Winner; Winning His "W"; Captain Don Richards; The Pennant; Carl Hall of Tait*

Walter Kellogg Towers (1915) *Letters from Brother Bill, Varsity Sub, to Tad, Captain of the Beechville High School Eleven*

Mary Towne (1976) *First Serve*

John R. Tunis (1928–1973) *The Tennis Racket; Iron Duke; The Duke Decides; The Kid from Tompkinsville; Champion's Choice; World Series; All-American; Keystone Kids; Rookie of the Year; Yea! Wildcats!; The Kid Comes Back; Highpockets; Young Razzle; The Other Side of the Fence; Go, Team, Go!; Buddy and the Old Pro; Schoolboy Johnson; The American Way in Sport; Democracy and Sport; Sports for the Fun of It; Sports, Heroics and Hysterics; A City for Lincoln; His Enemy, His Friend; Grand National*

Anthony Tuttle (1969–1978) *Catchers; Meet the Catchers; Bob McAdoo; Drive for the Green; Steve Cauthen, Boy Jockey*

James Ullman (1941–1975) *Banner in the Sky; Man of Everest: The Autobiography of Tenzing; Age of Mountaineering; High Conquest: The Story of Mountaineering; Kingdom of Adventure*

Guernsey Van Riper Jr. (1949–1975) *Lou Gehrig, Boy of the Sandlots; Knute Rockne, Young Athlete; Babe Ruth, Baseball Boy; Jim Thorpe, Indian Athlete;*

Yea, Coach!: Three Great Coaches; Golfing Greats: Two Top Pros; The Mighty Macs: Three Great Baseball Managers; World Series Highlights: Four Famous Contests; Behind the Plate: Three Great Catchers

Charles Spain Verral (1953–1978) *Captain of the Ice; Champion of the Court; The Wonderful World Series; The King of the Diamond; The Winning Quarterback; Mighty Men of Baseball; Babe Ruth: Sultan of Swat; Casey Stengel: Baseball's Great Manager*

Amelia Elizabeth Walden (1951–1977) *A Girl Called Hank; Queen of the Courts; Victory for Jill; Three Loves Has Sandy; My Sister Mike, Basketball Girl of the Year; Play Ball, McGill; Go, Philips, Go!; Escape on Skis; Heartbreak Tennis*

Frank Waldman, aka Joe Webster (1950–1956) *Giant Quarterback; Bonus Pitcher; Delayed Steal; Basketball Scandal; Glory Boy; The Challenger; Lucky Bat Boy;* "Joe Webster": *Dodger Doubleheader; The Rookie from Junction Flats*

Charles Wardlaw (1920–1924) *Basket Ball and Indoor Baseball for Women; Basket Ball: A Handbook for Coaches and Players; Baseball Fundamentals*

Frank Warner (1915–1921) *Bobby Blake at Rockledge School; Bobby Blake and His School Chums; Bobby Blake on the School Nine; Bobby Blake on the School Eleven*

Manly Wade Wellman (1960–1971) *Third String Center; Fast Break Five*

Robert W. Wells (1967–1973) *Five-Yard Fuller of the N.Y. Gnats; The Saga of Shorty Gone; Mean on Sunday: The Autobiography of Ray Nitschke; Five Yard Fuller and the Unlikely Knights; Five Yard Fuller's Mighty Model T;* "*Mad Anthony" Wayne*

H. C. Witwer (1918–1924) *From Baseball to Boches; Alex the Great; Kid Scanlon; No Base Like Home; The Leather Pushers; Fighting Blood; Fighting Back; Bill Grim's Progress*

Isador Young (1952–1969) *A Hit and a Miss; The Two-Minute Dribble; Carson at Second; Quarterback Carson; Carson's Fast Break*

Appendix C

Chris Crowe's Top 100 Young Adult Sports Books of All Time

Adler, C. S. *Winning*. Clarion, 1999.
Barbour, Ralph Henry. *The Crimson Sweater*. 1906.
Bee, Clair. *Freshman Quarterback*. Grosset & Dunlap, 1952.
Bennett, James. *The Squared Circle*. Scholastic, 1995.
Blais, Madeline. *In These Girls, Hope Is a Muscle: The True Story of Hoop Dreams and One Very Special Team*. Warner, 1995.
Blessing, Richard. *A Passing Season*. Little, Brown, 1982.
Bloor, Edward. *Tangerine*. Scholastic Inc., 1997.
Brancato, Robin. *Winning*. Bantam, 1984.
Brooks, Bruce. *The Moves Make the Man*. HarperCollins, 1984.
———. *What Hearts*. HarperCollins, 1990.
Bissinger, H. G. *Friday Night Lights: A Town, a Team, and a Dream*. HarperCollins, 1990.
Cadnum, Michael. *Heat*. Viking, 1998.
Cannon, A. E. *Shadow Brothers*. Delacorte, 1990.
Carson, John F. *The Coach Nobody Liked*. Laurel Leaf, 1960.
Cayleff, Susan E. *Babe Didrikson: The Greatest All-Sport Athlete of All Time*. Conari, 2000.
Cheripko, Jan. *Imitate the Tiger*. Boyd Mills, 1996.
Cochran, Thomas. *Roughnecks*. Harcourt Brace, 1997.
Cohen, Steven A., ed. *The Games We Played: A Celebration of Childhood and Imagination*. Simon & Schuster, 2001.
Connelly, Neil. *St. Michael's Scales*. Arthur A. Levine/Scholastic, 2002.
Crutcher, Chris. *Running Loose*. Greenwillow, 1983.
———. *Staying Fat for Sarah Byrnes*. Greenwillow, 1993.
———. *Stotan!* Greenwillow, 1986.
———. *Ironman*. Greenwillow, 1995.
———. *Athletic Shorts*. Greenwillow, 1991.

Davis, Terry. *Vision Quest*. Viking, 1979.
Deuker, Carl. *Heart of a Champion*. Little, Brown, 1993.
———. *Painting the Black*. Houghton Mifflin, 1997.
———. *Night Hoops*. Houghton Mifflin, 2000.
———. *On the Devil's Court*. Little, Brown, 1988.
Douglas, Gilbert. *Hard to Tackle*. Laurel Leaf, 1956.
Draper, Sharon M. *Tears of a Tiger*. Atheneum, 1994.
Duder, Tessa. *Alex in Rome*. Houghton Mifflin, 1992.
———. *In Lane Three, Alex Archer*. Houghton Mifflin, 1989.
Doherty, Berlie. *The Snake Stone*. Orchard, 1996.
Due, Linnea. *High and Outside*. Harper & Row, 1980.
Dygard, Thomas. *The Rookie Arrives*. Morrow, 1988.
Fogelin, Adrian. *Crossing Jordan*. Peachtree Press, 2000.
Freedman, Russell. *Babe Didrikson Zaharias: The Making of a Champion*. Houghton Mifflin, 1999.
Gallo, Donald R., ed. *Ultimate Sports: Short Stories by Outstanding Writers for Young Adults*. Delacorte, 1995.
Gottesman, Jane. *Game Face: What Does a Female Athlete Look Like?* Random House, 2001.
Green, Michelle Y. *A Strong Right Arm: The Story of Mamie "Peanut" Johnson*. Dial, 2002.
Guy, David. *Football Dreams*. Seaview, 1980.
Heyliger, William. *High Benton*. Appleton, 1919.
Hughes, Dean. *Hooper Haller*. Deseret, 1981.
———. *End of the Race*. Atheneum, 1993.
Jacobs, Helen Hull. *The Tennis Machine*. Scribner's, 1972.
Jenkins, A. M. *Damage*. HarperCollins, 2001.
Johnson, Scott. *Safe at Second*. Philomel, 1999.
Klass, David. *California Blue*. Scholastic, 1994.
———. *Danger Zone*. Scholastic, 1996.
———. *Wrestling with Honor*. Lodestar/Dutton, 1988.
Kluger, Steve. *Last Days of Summer*. Bard, 1998.
Knudson, R. R. *Fox Running*. Harper, 1975.
———. *Zanballer*. Delacorte, 1972.
Knudson, R. R., and May Swenson, eds. *American Sports Poems*. Orchard Books, 1995.
Lannin, Joanne. *A History of Basketball for Girls and Women: From Bloomers to Big Leagues*. Lerner Sports, 2000.
Lee, Marie G. *Finding My Voice*. Bantam Doubleday Dell, 1992.
———. *Necessary Roughness*. HarperCollins, 1996.
Lehrman, Robert. *Juggling*. Harper, 1982.
Lipsyte, Robert. *The Contender*. HarperCollins, 1967.
———. *Jim Thorpe: 20th Century Jock*. HarperCollins, 1993.
Lynch, Chris. *Iceman*. HarperCollins, 1994.

———. *Shadow Boxer*. HarperCollins, 1993.
Macy, Sue. *A Whole New Ball Game: The True Story of The All-American Girls Professional Baseball League*. Henry Holt, 1993.
———. *Winning Ways: A Photohistory of American Women in Sports*. Holt, 1996.
———., ed. *Girls Got Game: Sports Stories and Poems*. Henry Holt, 2001.
Macy, Sue, and Jane Gottesman, eds. *Play Like a Girl: A Celebration of Women in Sports*. Henry Holt, 1999.
McKissack, Patricia, and Frederick McKissak Jr. *Black Diamond: The Story of the Negro Baseball Leagues*. Scholastic, 1994.
Miklowitz, Gloria. *Anything to Win*. Delacorte, 1989.
Myers, Walter Dean. *The Greatest: Muhammad Ali*. Scholastic, 2001.
———. *Hoops*. Dell, 1983.
———. *Slam!* Scholastic, 1996.
Naughton, Jim. *My Brother Stealing Second*. Harper & Row, 1989.
Osborn, Kevin. *Scholastic Encyclopedia of Sports in the United States*. Scholastic, 1997.
Powell, Randy. *Dean Duffy*. Farrar Straus Giroux, 1995.
———. *My Underrated Year*. 1991.
———. *The Whistling Toilets*. Farrar Straus Giroux, 1996.
Revoyr, Nina. *The Necessary Hunger*. Simon & Schuster, 1997.
Ritter, John H. *Choosing Up Sides*. Philomel, 1998.
———. *Over the Wall*. Philomel, 2000.
Robinson, Jackie. *I Never Had It Made: An Autobiography*. Ecco, 1997.
Rottman, S. L. *Head above Water*. Peachtree Press, 1999.
Scholz, Jackson. *The Perfect Game*. Morrow, 1959.
Slote, Alfred. *Finding Buck McHenry*. HarperCollins, 1991.
Soto, Gary. *Baseball in April*. Harcourt Brace Jovanovich, 1990.
Thayer, Ernest Lawrence. *Casey at the Bat: A Ballad of the Republic Sung in the Year 1888*. Handprint, 2000.
Tunis, John. *Iron Duke*. Harcourt Brace, 1938.
———. *The Kid from Tompkinsville*. Harcourt Brace, 1940.
———. *All-American*. Harcourt Brace, 1942.
———. *Rookie of the Year*. Harcourt Brace, 1944.
Voigt, Cynthia. *The Runner*. Mass Market, 1985.
———. *Tell Me If Lovers Are Losers*. Atheneum, 1982.
Wallace, Rich. *Shots on Goal*. Knopf, 1997.
———. *Wrestling Sturbridge*. Knopf, 1996.
Weaver, Will. *Farm Team*. HarperCollins, 1995.
———. *Hard Ball*. HarperCollins, 1998.
———. *Striking Out*. HarperCollins, 1993.
Wells, Rosemary. *When No One Was Looking*. Dial, 1980.
Wolff, Virginia Euwer. *Bat 6*. Scholastic Press, 1998.
Zusak, Markus. *Fighting Ruben Wolfe*. Arthur A. Levine, 2001.

Appendix D
Sports Literature and Related Topics on the Internet

AUTHORS' WEBSITES

Laurie Halse Anderson: www.writerlady.com
Clair Bee: www.chiphilton.com
James W. Bennett: www.jameswbennett.com
A. E. Cannon: www.aecannon.com
Matt Christopher: www.mattchristopher.com
Chris Crutcher: www.aboutcrutcher.com
Terry Davis: www.terrydavis.net
Carl Deuker: members.authorsguild.net/carldeuker
Tessa Duder: www2.vuw.ac.nz/nzbookcouncil/writers/duder.htm
Michelle Y. Green: www.childrensbookguild.org/auth_ill/green.htm
Dan Gutman: www.dangutman.com
Maureen Holohan: www.bplayers.com/pages/author/theauthor.htm
Dean Hughes: www.deanhughes.net
Gordon Korman: gordonkorman.com
Elizabeth Levy: www.elizabethlevy.com
Sue Macy: www.suemacy.com
Roy MacGregor: www.screechowls.com/roy.html
Gary Paulsen: www.garypaulsen.com
Randy Powell: www.randypowell.com
John H. Ritter: www.johnhritter.com
Graham Salisbury: www.grahamsalisbury.com
Jeff Savage: www.jeffsavage.com
Gary Soto: www.garysoto.com
Will Weaver: www.intraart.com/willweaver
Jacqueline Woodson: www.jacquelinewoodson.com

Appendix D

BIBLIOGRAPHIES, REFERENCE SOURCES, AND ARCHIVES

All-American Girls Professional Baseball League, 1943–1954: www.aagpbl.org
Baseball Almanac: www.baseball-almanac.com
The Baseball Archive: www.baseball1.com
Baseball Cards, 1887–1914: memory.loc.gov/ammem/bbhtml/bbhome.html
Baseball Prose, Poems & Songs: www.baseball-almanac.com/poetry/po_donn.shtml
Berkeley Public Library: Athletic Fiction: www.infopeople.org/bpl/teen/sports.html
Boys' Life Magazine, Archives 1911–1959: www.trussel.com/prehist/boyslife/boyslife.htm
Crossing Boundaries: An International Anthology of Women's Experiences in Sport: www.exrx.net/Store/HK/CrossingBoundaries.html
Crossing Boundaries: Women, Sport, and Literature: raw.rutgers.edu/womenandsports/Boundaries/index.htm
"Dime Novels and Penny Dreadfuls": www-sul.stanford.edu/depts/dp/pennies/home.html
Girls in Sports: www.seemore.mi.org/booklists/SportsGirls.txt
Girltech.com Sports: www.girltech.com/sports/SP_menu.html
Guide to Baseball Fiction: Children's Books: www.uta.edu/english/tim/baseball/juv
Harry Potter and Quidditch: harrypotter.warnerbros.com/game/?fromtout=games_static
Jackie Robinson and Other Baseball Highlights, 1860s–1960s: memory.loc.gov/ammem/jrhtml/jrhome.html
New York Public Library On Lion for Kids: Sports: www2.nypl.org/home/branch/kids/sports/index.cfm
New York Public Library Sports for Kids: www2.nypl.org/home/branch/kidstext/sports/index.cfm
Olympic Games Sites on the Internet: www.tntech.edu/history/olympics.html
The Olympic Games: www.olympic.org
The Olympics: A Guide to Reference Sources: www.loc.gov/rr/main/olympics
Sport History on the Web: www2.tltc.ttu.edu/Harper/3338Sports/Weblinks/links.htm
The Sporting News Archive: www.sportingnews.com/archives/
Sports Bibliography for Young Adults: falcon.jmu.edu/~ramseyil/sportsbib.htm
Sports Books for Teens: www.teencybercenter.org/lists/sport.htm
Sports Literature & Internet Sites for Young Adults: falcon.jmu.edu/~ramseyil/sports.htm

Sports Lesson Plans: www.experienceorigins.com/lesson.htm
Sports Stories for Teens: www.berkeley.lib.sc.us/yabib0.html#sports
Suggested Sports Titles: www.chipublib.org/008subject/003cya/teened/readlist.html#sports
Tucker Center for Research on Girls and Women in Sports: education.umn.edu/tuckercenter
Women and Sports: www.public.iastate.edu/~womenstu/sports.html
Women in Sports: journalism.nyu.edu/pubzone/wis/
Women's Studies Resources: Sports: bailiwick.lib.uiowa.edu/wstudies/sports.html

FULL-TEXT DOCUMENTS ON THE WEB

Athletic Sports for Boys: A Repository of Graceful Recreation for Youth (1866): www.hti.umich.edu/cgi/t/text/text-idx?c=moa;idno=AFL3769

"Casey at the Bat" (1888), Ernest Lawrence Thayer: www.sporting-news.com/archives/baseball/94640.html

The Cash Boy (1906), Horatio Alger: etext.lib.virginia.edu/etcbin/toccernew2?id=AlgCash.sgm&images=images/modeng&data=/texts/english/modeng/parsed&tag=public&part=all

Frank Merriwell's Limit (1900), Burt L. Standish: www-sul.stanford.edu/depts/dp/pennies/texts/standish1_toc.html

Fred Fearnot's Day, or The Great Reunion at Avon (1914), Hal Standish: www-sul.stanford.edu/depts/dp/pennies/texts/standish3_toc.html

The Girls of Central High, or The Play that Took the Prize (1914), Gertrude W. Morrison: digital.library.upenn.edu/women/morrison/stage/stage.html

Healthful Sports for Boys (1910), Alfred Rochefort: ibiblio.org/gutenberg/etext04/hfsfb10.txt

Jane Allen, Junior (1921), Edith Bancroft: ibiblio.org/gutenberg/etext04/jnljr10.txt

The New Boy at Hilltop (1910), Ralph Henry Barbour: ibiblio.org/gutenberg/etext04/nbhlt10.txt

The Redheaded Outfield and Other Baseball Stories (1920), Zane Grey: ibiblio.org/gutenberg/etext96/rhout10.txt

Tom Brown's School Days (1857), Thomas Hughes: ibiblio.org/gutenberg/etext98/tbssd10.txt

JOURNALS AND ARTICLES

Aethlon: The Journal of the Sports Literature Association: www.etsu.edu/english/aethlon.htm

American Book Review, March/April 2000: "The Sporting Life": www.litline.org/ABR/issues/Volume21/Issue3/abr213.html
English Journal: "Sports Literature for Young Adults": www.ncte.org/pdfs/subscribers-only/ej/0906-july01/EJ0906Young.pdf
"The History of the NCAA": www.ncaa.org/about/ncaacenturyseries.html
The International Journal of the History of Sport: www.frankcass.com/jnls/ihs.htm
Scholarly Sports Sites: Serials: www.ucalgary.ca/library/ssportsite/serials.html
"Since Title IX: Female Athletes in Young Adult Fiction": www.viterbo.edu/personalpages/faculty/GSmith/HerStory.htm
"Title IX at 30: Athletics Receive C+": www.womenssportsfoundation.org/binary-data/WSF_ARTICLE/pdf_file/902.pdf

SPORTS HALLS OF FAME

Basketball Hall of Fame: www.hoophall.com
College Football Hall of Fame: www.collegefootball.org
Hockey Hall of Fame: www.hhof.com/index.htm
National Baseball Hall of Fame: www.baseballhalloffame.org
National Wrestling Hall of Fame: www.wrestlinghalloffame.org
The Negro Leagues Baseball Museum: www.nlbm.com
Pro Football Hall of Fame: www.profootballhof.com

SPORTS NEWS AND COMMENTARY

ABC Sports: espn.go.com/abcsports
Baseball Spot: www.baseballspot.org
CBS Sportsline: cbs.sportsline.com
ESPN: espn.go.com
Fox Sports: www.foxsports.com
Girls Soccer World Online: www.girlsoccerworld.com
"Only a Game," NPR Radio Program: www.onlyagame.org
Real Sports: www.real-sports.com/index.html
Runner's World: www.runnersworld.com
Soccer America Magazine: www.socceramerica.com
The Sporting News: www.sportingnews.com
Sports Illustrated: sportsillustrated.cnn.com
Sports Illustrated Women: sportsillustrated.cnn.com/siwomen
Sports Illustrated forKids: www.sikids.com
SwimSport Web Magazine: www.swimsport.com

Tennis Magazine: www.tennis.com
Track and Field News: www.trackandfieldnews.com
USA Today Sports: www.usatoday.com/sports/front.htm
Volleyball Magazine: www.volleyballmag.com
World Sports News: www.sportsnews.com
Wrestling International Magazine: www.win-magazine.com
Yahoo Sports: sports.yahoo.com

SPORTS ORGANIZATIONS

Amateur Athletic Foundation of Los Angeles: www.aafla.com
Association for the Advancement of Applied Sports Psychology: www.aaasponline.org/index2.html
Association for Women in Sports Media: www.awsmonline.org
British Society of Sports History: www2.umist.ac.uk/sport/bssh.html
International Association of Athletics Federations: www.iaaf.org
League of Fans: Sports History and Sociology Associations: www.leagueoffans.org/historyandsociology.html
National Collegiate Athletic Association: www.ncaa.org
National Federation of State High School Associations: www.nfhs.org
National Sports Library of The National Sports Foundation: www.natlsportsfoundation.com/Library.html
Negro Leagues Baseball Players Association: www.nlbpa.com/history.html
North American Society for Sports History: www.nassh.org
North American Society for the Sociology of Sport: www.nasss.org
Scholarly Sports Sites: Associations: www.ucalgary.ca/library/ssportsite/assoc.html
Society for American Baseball Research: www.sabr.org
Sports Literature Association Discussion Group: www2.h-net.msu.edu/~arete
Women's Sports Foundation: www.womenssportsfoundation.org/cgi-bin/iowa/index.html

Index

"400-Meter Freestyle," 51

Aaseng, Nathan, 57
Abrahamson, Richard F., 47
Adler, C. S., 35
Adoff, Arnold, 52
Aethlon, 1, 64
Alex in Rome, 70
Alger, Horatio, 11
All-American, 18–19
American Sports Poems, 52
Angel Park, 20
Archibald, Joe, 34, 80
archives. *See* bibliographies
Arete, 1. *See also Aethlon*
Armstrong, Jack, 17
articles. *See* journals
Athletic Shorts, 31
authors' websites, 159
autobiography, 48–49, 54–55
award-winning books, 3–4

Baines, Lawrence, 6–7
Bambara, Toni Cade, 32
Bancroft, Edith, 59
Bandy, Susan, 59
Barbour, Ralph Henry, 15
Barron, Ronald, 39
"Base-Ball," 50–51

baseball, 16, 30, 44, 51; first in sports fiction, 14; in poetry, 51
Baseball in April, 87
Baseball Joe, 16
basketball, 30
Bat 6, 70–71
"Batting after Sophie," 92
Beadle and Adams, 11, 15
Becoming Joe DiMaggio, 52
Bee, Clair, 17, 34, 40
bibliographies, 160–61
bibliotherapy, 7
A Big Ticket: Sports and Commercialism, 57
biography, 49, 54–55, 73, 74–75
Bishop, Curtis K., 34
Bissinger, H. G., 2, 4, 55
Blais, Madeline, 2, 4, 56
Blaustein, Noah, 52
The Book of Sports, 54
books, best for young adults, 3
Boys' Life, 30, 31
The Boys' Life Book of Sports, 31
The Boy's Own Book, 53–54
boys' school story, 11, 14
Bronc Burnett. *See* Burnett, Bronc
Brooks, Bruce, 3, 6, 18–19, 21, 35, 43, 82
Brooks, Noah, 14

Buchwald, Emily, 52
Burnett, Bronc, 17

Cadnum, Michael, 43, 70
Cannon, A. E., 88
Carlsen, G. Robert, 19
Carson, Sharon G., 64
Carter, Betty, 47
Carter, Linda Purdy, 6–7
Carver, Robin, 54
"Casey at the Bat," 15, 51
celebrity: autobiography, 48, 55; biography, 48, 55
Celine, 84
Chadwick, Lester, 16
Changing Base, 14
Cheripko, Jan, 42
Chester, I Love You, 84
Chinese Handcuffs, 88
Chip Hilton. *See* Hilton, Chip
The Chocolate War, 81
Christopher, Matt, 17, 34, 35
Cicada, 30
Clarke, William, 53
Cline, Nancy Lieberman. *See* Lieberman-Cline, Nancy
Coach and Athletic Director, 25
coaches, 16–17, 79; 1950s and 1960s style, 83; as antagonists, 79, 86; as mentors, 16, 79, 80, 86–89, 91–92; feedback from, 90–91; female, 89; importance of, 79; in lone girl stories, 89–90; in young women's stories, 89–92; roles in YA novels, 79, 92
Cochran, Thomas, 42
Cole, Brock, 84
collective biography, 49
Colton, Larry, 56
Colton, Matthew M., 16–17
coming of age, 9, 21, 28, 36, 38, 39, 40, 71
commentary. *See* sports news and commentary

Cormier, Robert, 81
Counting Coup: The True Story of Basketball and Honor on the Little Big Horn, 4, 56
Cox, William R., 36
The Crazy Horse Electric Game, 85, 88
"Cream Puff," 91
Crepeau, Dick, 79
Crutcher, Chris, xi–xii, 3, 4, 6, 32, 21, 40–42, 43, 82, 88

Danziger, Lucy, 66
Darden, Anne, 69
Deford, Frank, 5, 9
dementor, 81, 82, 86
Deuker, Carl, 3, 4, 32, 43
didacticism in sports stories, 13–14, 19, 30, 39
Didrickson, Babe, 74
dime novels, 2, 12–13, 20, 39; sports in, 13
Donelson, Kenneth, 3, 28–29, 83
Duder, Tessa, 3, 6, 43, 69
Due, Linnea A., 33, 69, 91
Dygard, Thomas J., 4, 20, 21, 32, 37

Edwards, Margaret A., 18
encyclopedias, 49, 57
Evans, Walter, 14
Everett, William, 14
"Ex-Basketball Player," 51

Farm Team, 39
Faulkner, William, 31, 65
feminism, 64–65, 67
Fimrite, Ron, 86
Finding My Voice, 70
Flower, Jessie Graham, 59
football, 30; first in sports fiction, 14
Football Dreams, 38–39, 81–82, 85, 87
Football Fury, 34
Forman, Jack, 29–30
formula fiction, 13, 15, 80

Index

Frank Merriwell. *See* Merriwell, Frank
Frank, Monica, 90–91
Friday Night Lights, 55

Gallo, Donald R., 4, 30, 32–33
game novels, 33–36; changes in, 35–36; defined, 33
The Games They Played: Sports in History, 56
Gelman, Steve, 34
gender, 66, 90
Gibson, Althea, 74
Gill, Sam D., 6–7
girls. *See* young women
Girls Got Game, 33
The Girls of Central High, 60
Glenn, Mel, 52
Go, Team, Go!, 19
Griffin, Patricia, 63–64
Gutman, Bill, 31
Gutman, Dan, 4
Guy, David, 38, 81

halls of fame. *See* sports halls of fame
Harry Potter. *See* Potter, Harry
Hazard, Paul, 65
Heat, 43, 70, 91
Hemingway, Ernest, 31, 32, 65
heroes, 40–41
Heuman, William, 34
Heyliger, William, 15
Higgs, Robert J., 1
High and Outside, 69
high school teams, 55–56, 75
Hilton, Chip, xii, 17, 40; contrasted with modern heroes, 40–41
Hirshey, David, 73
history, 49, 55, 56, 57, 75
A History of Basketball for Girls and Women, 56
Home Court Is Where You Find It, 36–37

Horatio Alger, 11, 13
Horn Book Magazine, 29
Horvath, Brooke, 64
Housman, A. E., 51
how-to, 49; for boys, 122–24; for girls, 140–41
Hu, Evelyn, 57
Hughes, Dean, 20, 35, 37
Hunter, Maxine Grace, 60–61

Iceman, 8
idealism, 36, 80
Imitate the Tiger, 42
In Lane Three, Alex Archer, 69–70, 91
In These Girls, Hope Is a Muscle, 56
Infield Hit, 20
informational books. *See* nonfiction
Internet, full-text documents, 161
Iron Duke, 18

Jack Armstrong. *See* Armstrong, Jack
Jackson, C. Paul, 17, 34
Jacobs, Helen Hull, 34, 60
Janeczko, Paul, 50, 52
journals, 161–62
Joyner-Kersee, Jackie, 63
Jump Ball: A Basketball Season in Poems, 52

Kane, Mary Jo, 62, 68
Kersee, Jackie Joyner. *See* Joyner-Kersee, Jackie
Knudson, R. R., 3, 50, 52, 67, 68, 69, 85, 89
Koertge, Ron, 52
Kumin, Maxine, 51
künstlerroman, 38

Lannin, Joanne, 56
Lardner, Ring, 31, 32
Lee, Marie G., 70
A Level Playing Field: Sports and Race, 57

Lieberman-Cline, Nancy, 62
Lipsyte, Robert, 7, 85
The Locker Room Mirror: How Sports Reflect Society, 57
London, Jack, 31
lone girl stories, 31, 68–69; coaches in, 89–90
losing, 18
Lukens, Rebecca J., 17
Lynch, Chris, 4, 6, 8, 9, 21, 32, 39, 43
Lyttle, Richard B., 56

Macy, Sue, 4, 33, 92
magazines, 11–13, 30, 52
Maniac Magee, 88–89
Markels, Robin Bells, 64
Mazer, Norma Fox, 32
McCormick, Wilfred, 17
McInerney, Jay, 32
McKay, Robert, 35
Merriwell, Frank, 15, 17, 30, 41, 80; model sports hero, 16, 28
Messenger, Christian, 1, 11, 13
metaphor, 9; sports as, 9, 39, 40
Michener, James, 86
middle grade books, 20, 38, 50, 53
Miskin, Kristana, xiii
Modern Library, 25
modern sports stories, 20–21, 27
morality, 28–29
more-than-a-game novels, 36–38; changes in, 38; defined, 36
Morrison, Gertrude, 59
Morrison, Lillian, 52
Motion: American Sports Poems, 52
The Moves Make the Man, 3, 82
My Father, the Coach: And Other Sports Stories, 31
Myers, Walter Dean, 4, 6, 8, 9, 43

The Necessary Hunger, 71–73
Newbery, John, 51
Newbery Medal, 3, 51

news. *See* sports news and commentary
Nilsen, Alleen Pace, 83
nonfiction, 47–48; defined, 47; for young women, 74–75
Nonfiction for Young Adults: From Delight to Wisdom, 47
novels in verse, 52–53

Olsen, Lyle I., 1
Optic, Oliver, 11
organizations. *See* sports organizations
Oriard, Michael, 1, 12, 13, 15, 25, 26, 27, 28, 60, 61, 65, 67
Our Baseball Club and How It Won the Championship, 14
Outside Shooter, 20
Owen, Frank, 30

Patten, Gilbert, 11, 12–13, 15, 17, 19
Phantom Blitz, 34, 80
Plimpton, George, 44
poetry, 50–51
Potter, Harry, 44
Powell, Randy, 4, 43, 44
publishers' attitudes, 14, 44, 54, 62, 65, 73, 75
pulp fiction, 15

Quick Picks for Reluctant Readers, 7
Quidditch, 44

The Random House Book of Sports Stories, 32
realism, 19, 36, 39, 41, 60–61, 63, 67–68
reference sources. *See* bibliographies
reluctant readers, 6–7
Revoyr, Nina, 6, 71, 72
Ritter, John H., 9, 21, 40
Ritter, Lawrence S., 57

The Rookie Arrives, 37
Roster, Ruth, 52
Roughnecks, 42
Rowling, J. K. 44
Rudolph, Wilma, 74
The Running Back, 35
Running Loose, 82–83, 88

Salisbury, Graham, 32
Sandoz, Joli, 59, 62, 63, 64
School Library Journal, 25, 62
Scrappers, 20–21
September 11, 2001, 5
serial magazines, 12
series books, 17, 20–21, 53; boys', 99–100, 108–9, 116, 120–21; girls', 128–29, 133–34
sexism, 65–66
Shadow Brothers, 88
Shakespeare Bats Cleanup, 52
Sherrill, Anne, 67
short stories, 30–33
Shots on Goal, 42
Slote, Alfred, 35
small ball theory, 44
Smith, Charles R., 52
soccer, 11, 20, 33, 42, 49, 58, 68, 75
Soccer Duel, 35
social issues, 18, 50, 57
softball, 31, 33, 44, 68, 69, 70–71, 88, 92
Soto, Gary, 32, 87
Spinelli, Jerry, 88, 90
The Sporting Life: Poems about Sports and Games, 52
sportlerroman, xii, 21, 30, 38–45; defined, 38; for young women, 68, 69; function of sport in, 39–40, 41
sports halls of fame, 162
Sports Illustrated, 2
Sports in America, 86
sports in American society, 3, 5, 13, 39, 79, 80–81
sports literature, 1–2; "Chris Crowe's Top 100 Young Adult Sports Books," 155–57; defined, 27; not about sports, vii; origins of, 11–14; poetry, 51; reception of, 25–26, 64; short stories, 14
Sports Literature Association, 1, 2
sports news and commentary, 162–63
sports organizations, 163
sports story formula, 26, 32–33, 36, 73, 80
Sports World: An American Dreamland, 85
St. Nicholas, 11
Standish, Burt L. *See* Patten, Gilbert
statistics. *See* trivia
Steinberg, Renee, 62, 66
Steindorf, Sara, 89
The Story of Baseball, 57
Stotan!, 3, 87
Strasser, Todd, 32
Stratemeyer, Edward, 11, 59
Street & Smith, 11
Striking Out, 39
Sullivan, Ed, 47
Swenson, May, 52

team biography, 49, 55, 75
Team Picture, 37
Teenage Sports Stories, 30
The Tennis Machine, 34
terrorist attacks. *See* September 11, 2001
Testa, Maria, 52
Thayer, Ernest L., 15, 51
There's a Girl in My Hammerlock, 90
Throwing Smoke, 35
Thurber, James, 32
Tip Top Weekly, 11
Title IX, 20, 61–62, 67, 68, 73–74; increases in female athletes since, 62
"To An Athlete Dying Young," 51

Tom Brown's School Days, 11–12
"The Top One Hundred Sports Books of All Time," 2; YA books in, 2
trivia, 50, 57, 127–28
Tunis, John R., 2, 3, 18, 19, 21, 36; on heroes, 18; on losing, 18, 36; on realism, 36; on respecting readers, 19–20

Ultimate Sports, 32
Umphlett, Wiley Lee, 1, 12, 13–14
Unsworth, Robert, 64
Updike, John, 32, 51, 65

Van Dyken, Amy, 63
VanDerveer, Tara, 64–65
Vanlandingham, Michael, 1
Venderwerken, David, 1

Walden, Amelia Elizabeth, 60
Wallace, Rich, 4, 21, 42, 43
Way to Go! Sports Poems, 52
Weaver, Will, 39
Wells, Rosemary, 69
Wertz, Spencer K., 1
Whale Talk, 43
When No One Was Looking, 69
A Whole Other Ball Game, 63
Winners and Losers: An Anthology of Great Sports Fiction, 31
Winning, 35
Wolff, Virginia Euwer, 32, 33, 70
women's sports, 74
Women's Sports and Fitness, 66
Woodsie, 35
Woodson, Jacqueline, 33

Yorgason, Blaine M., 84
Yorgason, Brenton G., 84
young adult sports fiction, 2; 1900s–1960s moral stances in, 28–29; adults in, 16; age of readers, xvi, 20; changes in, 20–21, 26, 29, 31–32, 41; defined, 27–28; differences from adult sports literature, 28; distribution of sports in, 20, 33, 44, 68; not about sports, vii, xi, 8–9, 26, 39, 40, 41–42; origins of, 11–13, 15; popularity of, 3–4, 6; quality of, 20, 26; reception of, 2–3, 5, 17, 26; short stories, 33–33
young adult sports nonfiction, 48–50; age of readers, 53; categories of, 48–50; current trends in, 54–55
poetry, 50, 52–53; popularity of, 48; quality of, 48, 50, 54–55, 58, 74;
young women, 59; attitudes toward, 60; biographies for, 73–74, 75; eras of sports literature for, 60–61; lack of sports stories, 64–67; need for sports stories, 33, 62–64; participation in sports, 62; sports literature compared to boys', 64–65, 68, 74, 75; sports nonfiction for, 75–75; sports represented in literature, 68–69; sports stories about, 31, 33, 59

Zanballer, 67, 69, 85, 89
Zanbanger, 67, 69
Zanboomer, 69

About the Author

Chris Crowe, a former high school teacher and coach, is a professor of English at Brigham Young University and past president of the Assembly on Literature for Adolescents of the National Council of Teachers of English. He is the author of *Mississippi Trial, 1955* (2002), *Getting Away with Murder: The True Story of the Emmett Till Case* (2003), and other books.